PALESTINE

(WEST BANK AND GAZA)

T0292974

INVESTMENT AND BUSINESS PROFILE

BASIC INFORMATION AND CONTACTS FOR SUCCESSFUL INVESTMENT AND BUSINESS ACTIVITY

International Business Publications, USA
Washington DC, USA - Palestine

PALESTINE
INVESTMENT AND BUSINESS PROFILE
BASIC INFORMATION AND CONTACTS FOR SUCCESSFUL INVESTMENT AND BUSINESS ACTIVITY

UPDATED ANNUALLY

Cover Design: International Business Publications, USA

We express our sincere appreciation to all government agencies and international organizations which provided information and other materials for this profile

2017 Updated Reprint International Business Publications, USA
ISBN 978-15145-1148-0

This profile provides basic information for starting or/and conducting business in the country. The extraordinary volume of materials covering the topic, prevents us from placing all these materials in this profile. For more detailed information on issues related to any specific investment and business activity in the country, please contact Global Investment Center, USA
Please acquire the list of our business intelligence and marketing profiles and other business publications. We constantly update and expand our business intelligence and marketing materials. Please contact the center for the updated list of profiles on over 200 countries.

in the USA:
For additional analytical, business and investment opportunities information,
please contact Global Investment & Business Center, USA
at (703) 370-8082. Fax: (703) 370-8083. E-mail: ibpusa3@gmail.com
Global Business and Investment Info Databank - www.ibpus.com

Printed in the USA

For additional analytical, business and investment opportunities information,
please contact Global Investment & Business Center, USA
at (703) 370-8082. Fax: (703) 370-8083. E-mail: ibpusa3@gmail.com
Global Business and Investment Info Databank - www.ibpus.com

PALESTINE
(WEST BANK AND GAZA)
INVESTMENT AND BUSINESS PROFILE
BASIC INFORMATION AND CONTACTS FOR SUCCESSFUL INVESTMENT AND BUSINESS ACTIVITY

TABLE OF CONTENTS

For additional analytical, business and investment opportunities information, please contact Global Investment & Business Center, USA at (703) 370-8082. Fax: (703) 370-8083. E-mail: ibpusa3@gmail.com Global Business and Investment Info Databank - www.ibpus.com

**For additional analytical, business and investment opportunities information,
please contact Global Investment & Business Center, USA
at (703) 370-8082. Fax: (703) 370-8083. E-mail: ibpusa3@gmail.com
Global Business and Investment Info Databank - www.ibpus.com**

**For additional analytical, business and investment opportunities information,
please contact Global Investment & Business Center, USA
at (703) 370-8082. Fax: (703) 370-8083. E-mail: ibpusa3@gmail.com
Global Business and Investment Info Databank - www.ibpus.com**

For additional analytical, business and investment opportunities information,
please contact Global Investment & Business Center, USA
at (703) 370-8082. Fax: (703) 370-8083. E-mail: ibpusa3@gmail.com
Global Business and Investment Info Databank - www.ibpus.com

For additional analytical, business and investment opportunities information,
please contact Global Investment & Business Center, USA
at (703) 370-8082. Fax: (703) 370-8083. E-mail: ibpusa3@gmail.com
Global Business and Investment Info Databank - www.ibpus.com

PALESTINE (WEST BANK AND GAZA) - STRATEGIC PROFILES

BASIC PROFILE

Capital	• Jerusalem (proclaimed) • Ramallah (administrative)
Largest city	Jerusalem (proclaimed) Gaza (de facto)
Official languages	Arabic
Government	De jure parliamentary democracy operating de facto as a semi-presidential system
- President	Mahmoud Abbas[b]
- Speaker of Parliament	Salim Zanoun
Legislature	National Council
	Sovereignty disputed with Israel
- Declaration of Independence	15 November 1988
- UNGA observer state resolution	29 November 2012
- Statehood	not in effect
	Area
	6,220 km^2
- Total	• West Bank: 5,860 km^2 • • Dead Sea: 220 km^2 • Gaza Strip: 360 km^2
	2,400 sq mi
	Population
- 2010 (July) estimate	4,260,636[a] (124th)
GDP (PPP)	2008[a] estimate
- Total	$11.95 billion[a] (–)
- Per capita	$2,900[a] (–)
Gini (2009)	35.5 medium
HDI (2007)	▼0.731[a] high · 106th
Currency	Israeli shekel (NIS) (ILS)
Time zone	(UTC+2)
- Summer (DST)	(UTC+3)
Drives on the	right
Calling code	+970
ISO 3166 code	PS
Internet TLD	.ps

The **State of Palestine** is a state that was proclaimed on 15 November 1988 by the Palestine Liberation Organization's (PLO's) National Council (PNC) in exile in Algiers which unilaterally adopted the Palestinian Declaration of Independence. It claims the Palestinian territories (defined according to the 1967 borders) and has designated Jerusalem as its capital. The areas constituting the State of Palestine have been occupied by Israel since 1967.

The 1974 Arab League summit designated the PLO as the "sole legitimate representative of the Palestinian people" and reaffirmed "their right to establish an independent state of urgency." The PLO held observer status at the United Nations as a "non-state entity" from 22 November 1974, which entitled it to speak in the UN General Assembly but not to vote. After the Declaration of Independence, the UN General Assembly officially "acknowledged" the proclamation and voted to use the designation "Palestine" instead of "Palestine Liberation Organization" when referring to the Palestinian permanent observer. In spite of this decision, the PLO did not participate at the UN in its capacity of the State of Palestine's government. On 29 November 2012 the UN General Assembly passed resolution 67/19, upgrading Palestine from an "observer entity" to a "non-member observer state" within the United Nations system, and implicitly recognizing PLO's sovereignty.

In 1993, in the Oslo Accords, Israel acknowledged the PLO negotiating team as "representing the Palestinian people", in return for the PLO recognizing Israel's right to exist in peace, acceptance of UN Security Council resolutions 242 and 338, and its rejection of "violence and terrorism". As a result, in 1994 the PLO established the Palestinian National Authority(PNA or PA) territorial administration, that exercises some governmental functions in parts of the West Bank and the Gaza Strip. In 2007, the Hamas takeover of Gaza Strip politically and territorially divided the Palestinians, with Abbas's Fatah left largely ruling the West Bank and recognized internationally as the official Palestinian Authority, while Hamas has secured its control over the Gaza Strip. In April 2011, the Palestinian parties signed an agreement of reconciliation, but its implementation has stalled since.

On November 29, 2012, in a 138-9 vote (with 41 abstentions and 5 absences), General Assembly resolution 67/19 passed, upgrading Palestine to "non-member observer state" status in the United Nations.

The new status equates Palestine's with that of the Holy See; similarly, Switzerland was a non-member observer state for more than 50 years (until 2002). The UN has permitted Palestine to title its representative office to the UN as 'The Permanent Observer Mission of the **State of** Palestine to the United Nations', and Palestine has instructed its diplomats to officially represent 'The State of Palestine', and no longer the 'Palestine National Authority.' On 17 December 2012, UN Chief of Protocol Yeocheol Yoon declared that 'the designation of "State of Palestine" shall be used by the Secretariat in all official United Nations documents', thus recognising the title 'State of Palestine' as the nation's official name for all UN purposes. As of April 2013, 132 (68.4%) of the 193 member states of the United Nations have recognised the State of Palestine. Many of the countries that do not recognise the State of Palestine nevertheless recognise the PLO as the "representative of the Palestinian people". The PLO's executive committee is empowered by the PNC to perform the functions of government of the State of Palestine

STRATEGIC INFORMATION

The region did not have a separate existence until 1948–9, when it was defined by the Armistice Agreement between Israel and Jordan. The name "West Bank" was apparently first used by Jordanians at the time of their annexation of the region, and has become the most common name used in English and related languages. Prior to this usage, the region was referred to as Judea and Samaria, its long-standing name. For example, U.N. Resolution 181, The 1947 Partition Plan explicitly refers to part of the area as Judea and Samaria.

The territories now known as the West Bank were part of the Mandate of Palestine granted to Great Britain by the League of Nations after WW1. The current border of the West Bank was not a dividing line of any sort during the Mandate period. When the United Nations General Assembly voted in 1947 to partition Palestine into a Jewish State, an Arab State, and an internationally-administered enclave of Jerusalem, almost all of the West Bank was assigned to the Arab State. In the ensuing 1948 Arab-Israel war, the territory was captured by the neighboring kingdom of Jordan. It was annexed by Jordan in 1950 but this annexation was recognized only by the United Kingdom. (Pakistan is often, but apparently falsely, assumed to have recognized it also.)

The 1949 Armistice Agreements established the "Green Line" separating the territories held by Israel and Jordan. During the 1950s, there was a significant influx of Palestinian refugees and violence together with Israeli reprisal raids across the Green Line. In the Six-Day War of 1967, Israel captured this territory, and in

November, 1967, UN Security Council Resolution 242 was unanimously adopted. All parties eventually accepted it and agree to its applicability to the West Bank.

In 1988, Jordan ceded its claims to the West Bank to the Palestine Liberation Organization, as "the sole legitimate representative of the Palestinian people."

The 1993 Oslo Accords declared the final status of the West Bank to be subject to a forthcoming settlement between Israel and the Palestinian leadership. Following these interim accords, Israel withdrew its military rule from some parts of West Bank, which was then split into:

- Palestinian-controlled, Palestinian-administered land (Area A)
- Israeli-controlled, but Palestinian-administered land (Area B)
- Israeli-controlled, Israeli-administered land (Area C)

Areas B and C constitute the majority of the territory, comprising the rural areas and the Jordan River valley region, while urban areas – where the majority of the Palestinian population resides – are mostly designated Area A.

Israelis refer to the region either as a unit: "The West Bank" (Hebrew: "ha-Gada ha-Ma'aravit" or as two units: Judea (Hebrew: "Yehuda" and Samaria (Hebrew: "Shomron" "), after the two biblical kingdoms (the southern Kingdom of Judah and the northern Kingdom of Israel — the capital of which was, for a time, in the town of Samaria). The border between Judea and Samaria is a belt of territory immediately north of Jerusalem sometimes called the "land of Benjamin".

The future status of the West Bank, together with the Gaza Strip on the Mediterranean shore, has been the subject of negotiation between the Palestinians and Israelis, although the current Road Map for Peace, proposed by the "Quartet" comprising the United States, Russia, the European Union, and the United Nations, envisions an independent Palestinian state in these territories living side by side with Israel (see also proposals for a Palestinian state).

The Palestinian people believe that the West Bank ought to be a part of their sovereign nation, and that the presence of Israeli military control is a violation of their right to self-determination. The United Nations calls the West Bank and Gaza Strip *Israeli-occupied* (see Israeli-occupied territories). The United States generally agrees with this definition. Many Israelis and their supporters prefer the term *disputed territories*, claiming it comes closer to a neutral point of view; this viewpoint is not accepted by most other countries, which consider "occupied" to be the neutral description of status.

Israel argues that its presence is justified because:

1. Israel's eastern border has never been defined by anyone;
2. The *disputed territories* have not been part of any state (Jordanian annexation was never officially recognized) since the time of the Ottoman Empire;
3. According to the Camp David Accords (1978) with Egypt, the 1994 agreement with Jordan and the Oslo Accords with the PLO, the final status of the territories would be fixed only when there was a permanent agreement between Israel and the Palestinians.

Palestinian public opinion is almost unanimous in opposing Israeli military and settler presence on the West Bank as a violation of their right to statehood and sovereignty.

Israeli opinion is split into a number of views:

- Complete or partial withdrawal from the West Bank in hopes of peaceful coexistence in separate states (sometimes called the "land for peace" position); (According to a 2003 poll 73% of Israelis support a peace agreement based on that principle).

For additional analytical, business and investment opportunities information,
please contact Global Investment & Business Center, USA
at (703) 370-8082. Fax: (703) 370-8083. E-mail: ibpusa3@gmail.com
Global Business and Investment Info Databank - www.ibpus.com

- Maintenance of a military presence in the West Bank to reduce Palestinian terrorism by deterrence or by armed intervention, while relinquishing some degree of political control;
- Annexation of the West Bank while considering the Palestinian population as (for instance) citizens of Jordan with Israeli residence permit as per the Elon Peace Plan;
- Annexation of the West Bank and assimilation of the Palestinian population to fully fledged Israeli citizens;
- Annexation of the West Bank.
- transfer of the East Jerusalem Palestinian population (a 2002 poll at the height of the Al Aqsa intifada found 46% of Israelis favoring Palestinian transfer of Jerusalem residents. http://www.tau.ac.il/jcss/sa/v5n1p4Ari.html]; in 2005 two polls using a different methodology put the number at approximately 30%)

PALESTINIAN NATIONAL AUTHORITY

The **Palestinian National Authority** (**PNA** or **PA** *As-Sulta Al-Wataniyya Al-Filastīniyya*) is an interim administrative organization that governs parts of the West Bank and the Gaza Strip.

The Palestinian National Authority was established in 1994, pursuant to the Oslo Accords between the Palestinian Liberation Organisation (PLO) and the government of Israel, as a 5-year transitional body during which final status negotiations between the two parties were to take place. According to the Accords, the Palestinian Authority was designated to have control over both security-related and civilian issues in Palestinian urban areas (referred to as "Area A"), and only civilian control over Palestinian rural areas ("Area B"). The remainder of the territories, including Israeli settlements, the Jordan Valley region, and bypass roads between Palestinian communities, were to remain under exclusive Israeli control ("Area C"). East Jerusalem was excluded from the Accords.

OVERVIEW

The Palestinian Authority is a subsidiary agency of the Palestinian Liberation Organisation. Also, it is the Palestinian Liberation Organisation, not the Palestinian National Authority, which enjoys international recognition as the organization representing the Palestinian people. The Palestinian diaspora, living outside the West Bank and Gaza, which constitutes the majority of the Palestinian people, do not vote in elections for Palestinian National Authority offices. Under the name "Palestine", Palestinian Liberation Organisation has an observer status in the United Nations (UN) since 1974. After the 1988 Palestinian Declaration of Independence, the PLO's representation at the United Nations was renamed Palestine. It is the PLO, not the PNA, which has participated in General Assembly debates, without voting, since 1998, and which was in 1994 recognized by Israel as the representative of the Palestinian people following the signing of the Oslo Accords.

The PNA previously received considerable financial assistance from the European Union and the United States (approximately USD $1,000,000,000 combined in 2005), but both suspended all direct aid on April 7, 2006 (as threatened in January 2006 and following Canada's March 29, 2006 decision to cut all aid) as a result of the Hamas victory in parliamentary elections.

The Gaza International Airport was built by the PNA in the city of Rafah, but operated for only a brief period before being razed by Israel following the outbreak of Al-Aqsa Intifada in 2000. A sea port was also being constructed in Gaza but was never completed (see below).

The PA maintains an official uniformed armed service which various sources estimate to include anywhere from 40,000 to 80,000 recruits employing some armored cars, and a limited number carry automatic weapons. Officially termed a "police force", it is accused by some of violating the Oslo Accords which limit the force to 30,000 recruits.

Many Palestinians are dependent on access to the Israeli job market. During the 1990s, Israel began to replace Palestinians with foreign workers. The process was found to be economical and also addressed security concerns. This hurt the Palestinian economy, in particular in the Gaza strip, where 45.7% of the population is under the poverty line according to the CIA World Factbook.

ADMINISTRATIVE DIVISIONS

After the signing of the Oslo Accords, the West bank and the Gaza Strip were divided into areas (A, B, and C) and governorates. Area A refers to the area under PA security and civilian control. Area B refers to the area under Palestinian civilian and Israeli security control. Area C refers to the area under full Israeli control such as settlements.

Since the Battle of Gaza (2007) most of the Gaza Strip is in control of the Hamas with the PA stating it is officially no longer in control of the Gaza Strip.
Map showing governorates and areas of formal Palestinian control (Areas A and B in dark green)
The PNA divides the Palestinian territories into 16 governorates

- Jenin Governorate
- Tubas Governorate
- Nablus Governorate
- Tulkarm Governorate
- Qalqilya Governorate
- Ramallah and al-Bireh Governorate
- Jericho Governorate
- Jerusalem Governorate
- Bethlehem Governorate
- Hebron Governorate
- North Gaza Governorate
- Gaza Governorate
- Deir el-Balah Governorate
- Khan Yunis Governorate
- Rafah Governorate

OFFICIALS

Main office holders			
Office	Name	Party	Since
President	Mahmoud Abbas	Fatah	January 15, 2005
Prime Minister	Salam Fayyad	Third Way	June 15, 2007
Foreign Minister	Salam Fayyad	Third Way	June 15, 2007

Past Prime Ministers:

- Mahmoud Abbas: March 19, 2003 - October 7, 2003
- Ahmad Qurei: October 7, 2003 - December 15, 2005
- Nabil Shaath: December 15, 2005 - December 24, 2005
- Ahmad Qurei: December 24, 2005 - February 19, 2006
- Ismail Haniya: February 19, 2006 - June 14, 2007

Past Presidents:

- Yasser Arafat: July 5, 1994 - November 11, 2004
- Rauhi Fattouh (acting): November 11, 2004 - January 15, 2005

Past Foreign Ministers

- Nasser al-Kidwa:
- Nabil Shaath: April 3, 2003-
- Mahmoud al-Zahar: March 20, 2006 - June 14, 2007

For additional analytical, business and investment opportunities information,
please contact Global Investment & Business Center, USA
at (703) 370-8082. Fax: (703) 370-8083. E-mail: ibpusa3@gmail.com
Global Business and Investment Info Databank - www.ibpus.com

HISTORY

For the history of the territories currently controlled by the PNA prior to its establishment, see History of Palestine and History of the Palestinian territories.

The Oslo Accords were signed on 13 September 1993 between the Palestine Liberation Organization and Israel. The Accords led to the creation of the Palestinian Authority. This was an interim organization created to administer a limited form of Palestinian self-governance in the Palestinian territories for a period of five years during which final-status negotiations would take place. The Palestinian Authority became responsible for civil administration in some rural areas, as well as security in the major cities of the West Bank and the Gaza Strip. Although the five-year interim period expired in 1999, the final status agreement has yet to be concluded despite attempts such as the Camp David 2000 Summit, the Taba summit, and the unofficial Geneva Accords.

After the inability of the Palestinians to reach any position in the Israel-Palestinian peace process, and with the continuing Second Intifada, in 2005 Israeli forces unilaterally withdrew its military and civilians from the Gaza Strip, ceding full effective internal control of the Strip to the Palestinian Authority but retained control of its borders including air and sea (except for the Egyptian border).

Palestinian legislative elections took place on 25 January 2006. Hamas was victorious and Ismail Haniyeh was nominated as Prime Minister on 16 February 2006 and sworn in on 29 March 2006. However, when a Hamas-controlled government was formed, Israel, the United States, Canada, and the European Union froze all funds to the Palestinian Authority, after Hamas refused to recognize Israel, renounce violence, and agree to past agreements. These countries view Hamas as a terrorist organization.

In an attempt to resolve the financial and diplomatic impasse, the Hamas-led government together with Chairman Abbas agreed to form a unity government. Haniyeh resigned on 15 February 2007 as part of the agreement. The unity government was finally formed on 18 March 2007 under Prime Minister Ismail Haniyeh and consisted of members from Hamas, Fatah and other parties and independents.

After the takeover in Gaza by Hamas on 14 June 2007, Palestinian Authority Chairman Mahmoud Abbas dismissed the government and on 15 June 2007 appointed Salam Fayad Prime Minister to form a new government. Though the new government's authority is claimed to extend to all Palestinian territories, in effect it is limited to the Palestinian Authority controlled areas of the West Bank. The Fayad government has won widespread international support. Egypt, Jordan, and Saudi Arabia said in late June 2007 that the West Bank-based Cabinet formed by Fayad was the sole legitimate Palestinian government, and Egypt moved its embassy from Gaza to the West Bank. Hamas, which has effective control of the Gaza Strip, faces international diplomatic and economic isolation.

CURRENT EVENTS

Since the beginning of the Second Intifada, the Palestinian Authority (PA) has been undermined both in the Palestinian occupied territories (Gaza strip and West Bank) and abroad. Ariel Sharon and the George W. Bush administration refused to negotiate with Yasser Arafat, leader of the Palestine Liberation Organization (PLO) and former president of the PA, whom they asserted formed "part of the problem" (concerning the Israeli-Palestinian conflict) and not of its solution this despite Arafat's signature of the 1993 Oslo Accords. In January 2006, Hamas won the legislative elections, and thus replaced Arafat's Fatah as leading party of the Palestinian people. The PNA is therefore now led by president Mahmoud Abbas (Fatah), elected in January 2005, and by prime minister Ismail Haniyah (Hamas). However, on February 15, 2007 Ismail Haniyah resigned his post clearing the way for a government of national unity.

Israel has accused the Palestinian Authority of ignoring and covertly sponsoring the violence against Israelis. The prolonged support and participation of his (Yaser Arafat's?) own private militia, the Fatah, in suicide bombings, reinforces that claim. This view has been officially accepted by the United States in summer 2002, which decided then to halt most sorts of negotiations with the current Palestinian authority, pending a fundamental organizational change. The US Council on Foreign Relations think tank has declared the Palestinian Authority under Arafat a haven for terrorism

During the Intifada, Israel has often targeted Palestinian Authority personnel and resources. In particular, many of the people arrested, assassinated or killed in action because of their alleged terrorist activities, were employees of the Palestinian Authority's security forces or militias. In Operation Defensive Shield Israel has captured documents that allegedly prove that the Palestinian Authority officially sponsors "terrorist activities", which are carried out by its personnel as "shadow jobs". For instance, Israel arrested and convicted Marwan Barghouti, a prominent leader of Fatah, for his role as leader of the Al-Aqsa Martyrs' Brigades. Barghouti maintains his innocence, and rejects the impartiality of the Israeli courts.

Israel has also targeted Palestinian Authority infrastructure; in particular it has closed and destroyed parts of the Palestinian sea and air ports, that were used, it claimed, to transport terrorists and their equipment. Israel's incursions during the Intifada also led to damage to some of the Palestinian computer infrastructure, though it is not clear to what extent it was deliberate.
These moves were criticized by the Palestinians, who claim that the Palestinian Authority is nearing collapse, and is no longer able to carry out its internal and external obligations. This is because these repeated degradations of PA resources and infrastructure have led to complaints by the PA and some of its EU funders that Israel is deliberately hobbling the PA to restrict its powers of law enforcement in order to present an image of terrorism and lawlessness in the Palestinian Territories. On July 7, 2004, the Quartet of Middle East mediators informed Ahmed Qurei, Prime Minister of the PA from 2003 to 2006, that they were "sick and tired" of the Palestinians failure to carry out promised reforms: "If security reforms are not done, there will be no (more) international support and no funding from the international community"

On July 18, 2004, United States President George W. Bush stated that the establishment of a Palestinian state by the end of 2005 was unlikely due to instability and violence in the Palestinian Authority.
> In order for there to be a Palestinian state, it is essential for its leaders to be open to reform and be dedicated to their people.
> The problem of the Palestinians is a territorial one – they have no state and they have no leaders. Palestinians that want change need to demand that a security force be established. The real problem is that there is no leadership that is able to say 'help us establish a state and we will fight terror and answer the needs of the Palestinians'.

Following Arafat's death on November 11, 2004, Rawhi Fattuh, leader of the Palestinian Legislative Council became Acting President of the Palestinian Authority as provided for in Article 54(2) of the Authority's Basic Law.

> If the office of the President of the National Authority becomes vacant due to any of the above cases, the Speaker of the Palestinian Legislative Council shall assume the powers and duties of the Presidency of the National Authority, temporarily for a period not exceeding (60) sixty days, during which free and direct elections to choose a new president shall take place in accordance with the Palestinian Elections Law.

On June 14, 2007, the Palestine president Mahmoud Abbas, under the impressions of the Battle of Gaza (2007), has dismissed the Hamas led government and declared a state of emergency. Since the Hamas attacks against Fatah security forces in Gaza Strip in June 2007, most of the Gaza Strip is under the control of Hamas, whereas the West Bank remains under the control of Fatah and the Palestinian president.

POLITICS AND INTERNAL STRUCTURE

The Palestinian Authority (PA) has historically been associated with the PLO, with whom Israel negotiated the Oslo Accords. The Chairman of the PLO, Yasser Arafat, was elected as President of PA in a landslide victory in 1996. Subsequent elections were postponed, ostensibly due to the eruption of the Al-Aqsa Intifada and the Israeli military clampdown that accompanied it. However, internal Palestinian strife was also a reason for the disorganization in government. After Arafat's death in 2004, new elections occurred on both presidential and local levels. Although almost 80% of the employees of the PA were local Palestinians, higher posts were occupied mostly by PLO officials who returned from exile once the PA was established in 1994. To many local Palestinians, these "returnees" were a source of bureaucracy and corruption.

Arafat's administration was criticized for its lack of democracy, wide-spread corruption among officials, and the division of power among families and numerous governmental agencies with overlapping functions. He established over ten distinct security organizations through various mechanisms in an alleged *divide et impera* scheme, which is claimed to have guaranteed an atmosphere of power-struggle in the Authority which enabled him to preserve overall control. Both Israel and the US declared they lost trust in Arafat as a partner and refused to negotiate with him, regarding him as linked to terrorism. Arafat denied this, and was visited by other leaders around the world up until his death. However, this began a push for change in the Palestinian leadership. In 2003, Arafat succumbed to domestic and international pressure and appointed

Mahmoud Abbas (Abu Mazen) as prime minister of the PA. Abbas resigned four months later because of lack of support from Israel, the US, and Arafat himself. He was later chosen as his Fatah party's candidate for president of the PA in 2004 after the death of Arafat. He won the presidency on January 9, 2005 with 62% of the vote.

According to the Palestinian "Basic Law" which was signed by Arafat in 2002 after a long delay, the current structure of the PA is based on three separate branches of power: executive, legislative, and judiciary. The Judiciary Branch has yet to be properly formalized. The president of the PA is directly elected by the people, and the holder of this position is also considered to be the commander-in chief of the armed forces. In an amendment to the Basic Law approved in 2003 (and which may or may not become part of the Palestinian constitution once independence is established), the president appoints a "prime minister" who is also chief of the national security services. The prime minister chooses a cabinet of ministers and runs the government, reporting directly to the president. Former prime minister Ahmed Qureia formed his government on February 24, 2005 to wide international praise because, for the first time, most ministries were headed by experts in their field as opposed to political appointees.

The Palestinian Legislative Council (PLC) is an elected body of 88 representatives and acts as a parliament. The PLC must approve all government cabinet positions proposed by the prime minister, and must also confirm the prime minister himself upon nomination by the president. As opposed to other Arab countries, the PLC has historically demonstrated considerable power, and has frequently caused changes in government appointments through threats of no-confidence votes. Many critical votes are won in the government's favor without an outright majority. Since the death of Arafat, the PLC has reinvigorated its activity, and commonly summons senior executive officials to testify before it. Parliamentary elections were conducted in January 2006 after the recent passage of an overhauled election law that increased the number of seats from 88 to 132.

POLITICAL PARTIES AND ELECTIONS

From the establishment of the Palestinian Authority in 1993 until the death of Yasser Arafat in late 2004, only one election had taken place. All other elections were deferred for various reasons.
A single election for president and the legislature took place in 1996. The next presidential and legislative elections were scheduled for 2001, but were delayed following the outbreak of the Al-Aqsa Intifada. Following Arafat's death, elections for the President of the Authority were announced for January 9, 2005. The PLO leader Mahmoud Abbas won 62.3% of the vote, while Dr. Mustafa Barghouti, a physician and independent candidate, won 19.8%.
Main article: Palestinian presidential election, 2005

Summary of the 9 January 2005 Palestinian presidential election results

Candidates - Nominating parties	Votes	%
Mahmoud Abbas - Fatah or Liberation Movement of Palestine (Harakat al-Tahrâr al-Filistini)	501,448	62.52
Mustafa Barghouti- Independent	156,227	19.48
Taysir Khald- Democratic Front for the Liberation of Palestine (Al-Jabhah al-Dimuqratiyah Li-Tahrir Filastin)	26,848	3.35
Abdel Halim al-Ashqar- Independent	22,171	2.76
Bassam al-Salhi - Palestinian People's Party (Hizb al-Sha'b al-Filastini)	21,429	2.67
Sayyid Barakah - Independent	10,406	1.30
Abdel Karim Shubeir - Independent	5,717	0.71
Invalid Ballots	30,672	3.82
Blank Ballots	27,159	3.39
Total (turnout %)	802,077	100.0
Source: Central Elections Commission		

On May 10, 2004 the Palestinian Cabinet announced that municipal elections would take place for the first time. Elections were announced for August 2004 in Jericho, followed by certain municipalities in the Gaza Strip. In July 2004 these elections were postponed. Issues with voter registration are said to have contributed to the delay. Municipal elections finally took place for council officials in Jericho and 25 other towns and villages in the West Bank on December 23, 2004. On January 27, 2005, the first round of the municipal elections took place in the Gaza Strip for officials in 10 local councils. Further rounds in the West Bank took place in May 2005.

Elections for a new Palestinian Legislative Council (PLC) were scheduled for July 2005 by Acting Palestinian Authority President Rawhi Fattuh in January 2005. These elections were postponed by Mahmoud Abbas after major changes to the Election Law were enacted by the PLC which required more time for the Palestinian Central Elections Committee to process and prepare. Among these changes were the expansion of the number of parliament seats from 88 to 132, with half of the seats to be competed for in 16 localities, and the other half to be elected in proportion to party votes from a nationwide pool of candidates.

Summary of the 25 January 2006 Palestinian Legislative Council election results

Alliances and parties	Votes (Proportional)	% (Proportional)	Seats (Proportional/District seats)
Change and Reform Hamas, harakat al-muqāwamah al-islāmiyyah (Islamic Resistance Movement)	440,409	44.45	74 (29/45)
Fatah, harakat al-tahrīr al-filastīnī (Liberation Movement of Palestine)	410,554	41.43	45 (28/17)
Martyr Abu Ali Mustafa (Popular Front for the Liberation of Palestine) (al-jabhah al-sha`biyyah li-tahrīr filastīn)	42,101	4.25	3 (3/0)
The Alternative (al-Badeel) Democratic Front for the Liberation of Palestine (al-jabhah al-dīmūqrātiyyah li-tahrīr filastīn) Palestinian People's Party (hizb al-sha`b al-filastīnī) Palestine Democratic Union (al-ittihād al-dīmūqrātī al-filastīnī) Independents	28,973	2.92	2 (2/0)
Independent Palestine Palestinian National Initiative (al-mubādara al-wataniya al-filastīniyya) Independents	26,909	2.72	2 (2/0)
Third Way	23,862	2.41	2 (2/0)
Freedom and Social Justice Palestinian Popular Struggle Front (jabhat al-nidal al-sha'biyya al-filastiniyya)	7,127	0.72	0 (0/0)
Freedom and Independence Palestinian Arab Front	4,398	0.44	0 (0/0)
Martyr Abu Abbas Palestine Liberation Front	3,011	0.30	0 (0/0)
National Coalition for Justice	1,806	0.18	0 (0/0)

and Democracy (Wa'ad)			
Palestinian Justice	1,723	0.17	0 (0/0)
Independents	-	-	4 (0/4)
Total (turnout: 74.6%)	990,873	100.0%	132 (66/66)
Source: Central Election Commission, Preliminary results,Final tally amendments, 2006-01-29, Final results			

The following organizations, listed in alphabetic order, have taken part in recent elections inside the Palestinian National Authority:

- Democratic Front for the Liberation of Palestine (*Al-Jabhah al-Dimuqratiyah Li-Tahrir Filastin*)
- Fatah or Liberation Movement of Palestine (*Harakat al-Tahrâr al-Filistini*)
- Hamas or Islamic Resistance Movement (*Harakat al-Muqawamah al-Islamiyah*)
- Palestine Democratic Union (*al-Ittihad al-Dimuqrati al-Filastini*, FiDA)
- Palestinian National Initiative (*al-Mubadara al-Wataniya al-Filistiniyya*)
- Palestinian People's Party (*Hizb al-Sha'b al-Filastini*)
- Popular Front for the Liberation of Palestine (*Al-Jabhah al-sha'abiyah Li-Tahrir Filastin*)

October 2006 polls have shown that Fatah and Hamas have equal strength.
On June 14, 2007, after the Battle of Gaza (2007), Palestine president Mahmoud Abbas has dismissed the Hamas led government, leaving the government under his control for 30 days, after which the temporary government has to be approved by the Palestinian Legislative Council.

ECONOMY

Following the 2006 legislative elections, won by Hamas, Israel has ceased transferring the $55 million tax-receipts to the PA; since the PA has no access point (ports, airports, etc.) to receive taxes, it is Israel that is charged with this duty. These funds accounted for a third of the PA's budget, two thirds of its proper budget, and ensure the wages of 160 000 Palestinian civil servants (among them 60 000 security and police officers), on which a third of the Palestinian population is dependent.

Israel has also decided to increase controls on check-point, which has been since the beginning of the Second Intifada a main cause of the 2001-2002 economic recession, which the World Bank has compared to the 1929 economic crisis. Furthermore, the US and the EU have stopped direct aid to the PA, while the US imposed a financial blockade on PA's banks, impeding some of the Arab League's funds (e.g. Saudi Arabia and Qatar) from being transferred to the PA. On May 6 and 7, 2006, hundreds of Palestinians demonstrated in Gaza and the West Bank demanding payment of their wages. Tension between Hamas and Fatah has been slowly risen with the "economic squeeze" on the PA. The UN institution underlines that unemployment, which was estimated to 23% in 2005, would increase to 39% in 2006, while poverty, estimated at 44%, would increase to 67% in 2006.

FOREIGN AID AND BUDGET DEFICIT

Due to the specific conditions of the disputed territories, the Palestinian Authority (PA) has received unprecedented financial support from the international community. According to the World Bank, USD $929 million were given by the international community to the PNA in 2001, $891 million in 2003 and $1.1 billion in 2005 (representing 53% of the budget in 2005). The main objectives are support to the budget, development aid and public health. In 2003, the US funded $224 million, the EU $187 million, the Arab League $124 million, Norway $53 million, the World Bank $50 million, the United Kingdom $43 million, Italy $40 million, and the last $170 million by others. According to the World Bank, the budget deficit was about of $800 million in 2005, with nearly half of it financed by donors. "The PA's fiscal situation has become increasingly unsustainable mainly as a result of uncontrolled government consumption, in particular a rapidly increasing public sector wage bill, expanding social transfer schemes and rising net lending," said the World Bank report. Government corruption is widely seen as the cause of much of the PA financial difficulties.

ECONOMIC SANCTIONS FOLLOWING JANUARY 2006 LEGISLATIVE ELECTIONS

Following the January 2006 legislative elections, won by Hamas, the Quartet threatened to cut funds to the Palestinian Authority. On February 2, 2006, according to the AFP, the PNA accused Israel of "practicing collective punishment after it snubbed US calls to unblock funds owed to the Palestinians." Prime minister Ahmed Qorei "said he was hopeful of finding alternative funding to meet the budget shortfall of around 50 million dollars, needed to pay the wages of public sector workers, and which should have been handed over by Israel on the first of the month."

The US Department criticized Israel for refusing to quickly unblock the funds. The funds were later unblocked. However, the *New York Times* alleged on February 14, 2006 that a "destabilization plan" of the United States and Israel, aimed against Hamas, winner of the January 2006 legislative elections, centered "largely on money" and cutting all funds to the PA once Hamas takes power, in order to delegitimize it in the eyes of the Palestinians. According to the news article, "The Palestinian Authority has a monthly cash deficit of some $60 million to $70 million after it receives between $50 million and $55 million a month from Israel in taxes and customs duties collected by Israeli officials at the borders but owed to the Palestinians." Beginning March 2006, "the Palestinian Authority will face a cash deficit of at least $110 million a month, or more than $1 billion a year, which it needs to pay full salaries to its 140,000 employees, who are the breadwinners for at least one-third of the Palestinian population. The employment figure includes some 58,000 members of the security forces, most of which are affiliated with the defeated Fatah movement." Since January 25 elections, "the Palestinian stock market has already fallen about 20 percent", while the "Authority has exhausted its borrowing capacity with local banks."

EUROPEAN UNION ASSISTANCE

In February 2004, it was reported that the European Union (EU) anti-fraud office (OLAF) was studying documents suggesting that Yasser Arafat and the Palestinian Authority had diverted tens of millions of dollars in EU funds to organizations involved in terrorist attacks, such as the Al-Aqsa Martyrs Brigades. However, in August 2004, a provisional assessment stated that "To date, there is no evidence that funds from the non-targeted EU Direct Budget Assistance to the Palestinian Authority have been used to finance illegal activities, including terrorism."
A separate EU "Working Group" also issued a report in April 2004, adopted by a 7-6 vote, which covers the period from the end of 2000 to the end of 2002, stating that EU aid has not been siphoned off to Palestinian militants carrying out attacks on Israelis: "There is no conclusive evidence, to date, that the EU non-targeted direct budgetary support was used to finance illegal activities, including the financing of terrorism".

Furthermore, the EU has changed the way it funded the Palestinians and now uses targeted aid for specific purposes. From April 2003, money is only handed over if various conditions are met, such as the presentation of invoices for bills the Palestinians need to pay. The EU remains the biggest donor to the Palestinian Authority.

PAYMENTS TO PALESTINIAN PRISONERS IN ISRAELI PRISONS

On July 22, 2004, Salam Fayyad, PNA Minister of Finance, in an article in the Palestinian weekly, *The Jerusalem Times*, detailed the following payments to Palestinians imprisoned by the Israeli authorities:

1. Prisoner allowances increased between June 2002 and June 2004 to $9.6m monthly, an increase of 246 percent compared with January 1995-June 2002.
2. Between June 2002 and June 2004, 77 million shekels were delivered to prisoners, compared to 121 million between January 1995 and June 2002, which is an increase of 16 million shekels yearly. The increase of annual spending between the two periods registers 450 percent, which is much higher than the percentage of increase of the number of prisoners.
3. Between 2002 and 2004, the PNA paid 22 million shekels to cover other expenses — lawyers' fees, fines, and allocations for released prisoners. This includes lawyers' fees paid directly by the PNA and fees paid through the Prisoners Club.

STATE OF PALESTINE

The **"State of Palestine"** is the name given to a proposed Palestinian state that would govern the occupied Palestinian territories, but does not currently have sovereignty there. It was declared in Algiers on November

15, 1988, by the Palestinian National Council, the legislative body of the Palestine Liberation Organization (PLO). The aim of the Council is for the state to comprise both the West Bank and the Gaza Strip with Jerusalem as its capital. The declaration was approved by the Palestinian National Council in Algiers on November 15, 1988 by a vote of 253 in favour 46 against and 10 abstentions.

The declaration invoked the Treaty of Lausanne (1923) and UN General Assembly Resolution 181 in support of its claim to a "State of Palestine on our Palestinian territory with its capital Jerusalem". The proclaimed "State of Palestine" was recognized immediately by the Arab League. The State of Palestine is not recognized by the United Nations. Though not recognising the State of Palestine, the European Union, as well as most of its member states, maintain diplomatic ties with the Palestinian Authority, established under the Oslo Accords. Leila Shahid, envoy of the PLO to France since 1984, was named representative of the Palestinian Authority for Europe in November 2005

The declaration is generally interpreted as recognizing Israel within its pre-1967 boundaries, or was at least a major step on the path to recognition. Just as in Israel's declaration of establishment, it partly bases its claims on UN GA 181. By reference to "resolutions of Arab Summits" and "UN resolutions since 1947" (like SC 242) it implicitly and perhaps ambiguously restricted its immediate claims to the Palestinian territories and Jerusalem. It was accompanied by a political statement that explicitly mentioned SC 242 and other UN resolutions and called only for withdrawal from "Arab Jerusalem" and the other "Arab territories occupied." Yasser Arafat's statements in Geneva a month later were accepted by the United States as sufficient to remove the ambiguities it saw in the declaration and to fulfill the longheld conditions for open dialogue with the United States.

The PLO envisages the establishment of a State of Palestine to include all or part of the West Bank, the Gaza Strip, and East Jerusalem (the Palestinian territories), living in peace with Israel under a democratically elected and sovereign government. To this end, it took part in negotiations with Israel resulting in the 1993 Declaration of Principles, which along with subsequent agreements between the two parties provided for the establishment of a Palestinian interim self-governing authority with partial control over defined areas in the Palestinian territories. This authority, known as the Palestinian Authority or Palestinian National Authority (PNA), however, does not claim sovereignty over any territory and therefore is not the government of the "State of Palestine" proclaimed in 1988 More than 100 states recognize the State of Palestine, and 20 more grant some form of diplomatic status to a Palestinian delegation, falling short of full diplomatic recognition.The following are listed in alphabetical order by region.

Africa
Algeria
Benin
Burkina Faso
Cameroon
Chad
Comoros
Djibouti
Ethiopia
Gabon
Gambia
Ghana
Guinea
Guinea-Bissau
Libya
Mali
Mauritania
Morocco
Mozambique
Niger
Nigeria
Senegal
Sierra Leone
Somalia
Sudan

Asia
Afghanistan
Bangladesh
Brunei
India
Indonesia
Malaysia
Maldives
Pakistan
Philippines
Tajikistan
Turkmenistan
Vietnam

Europe
Albania
Azerbaijan
Cyprus
Montenegro
Poland
Russia
Turkey
Ukraine

Middle East
Bahrain
Egypt

For additional analytical, business and investment opportunities information, please contact Global Investment & Business Center, USA at (703) 370-8082. Fax: (703) 370-8083. E-mail: ibpusa3@gmail.com Global Business and Investment Info Databank - www.ibpus.com

Togo
Tunisia
Uganda
Americas
Argentina

Iran
Iraq
Jordan
Kuwait
Lebanon
Oman
Qatar
Saudi Arabia
Syria
United Arab Emirates
Yemen

COUNTRIES GRANTING DIPLOMATIC STATUS TO NON-STATE REPRESENTATIVES

The delegations and embassies listed below on the left, are recognized as the representatives of the Palestinian people by the nations listed to their right:

- General Delegation of Palestine: Ireland
- Palestinian General Delegation: Greece
- Palestinian Special Delegation: Mexico

UNITED NATIONS REPRESENTATION

The Palestine Liberation Organization gained observer status at the United Nations General Assembly in 1974 (General Assembly resolution 3237). Acknowledging the proclamation of the State of Palestine, the UN redesignated this observer status as belonging to Palestine in 1988 (General Assembly resolution 43/177.) In July 1998, the General Assembly adopted a new resolution (52/250) conferring upon Palestine additional rights and privileges, including the right to participate in the general debate held at the start of each session of the General Assembly, the right of reply, the right to co-sponsor resolutions and the right to raise points of order on Palestinian and Middle East issues. By this resolution, "seating for Palestine shall be arranged immediately after non-member States and before the other observers." This resolution was adopted by a vote of 124 in favor, 4 against (Israel, USA, Marshall Islands, Micronesia) and 10 abstentions.

CITIES AND SETTLEMENTS IN THE WEST BANK

The most densely populated part of the region is a mountainous spine, running north-south, where the cities of Jerusalem, Nablus, Ramallah, Bethlehem, and Hebron are located. Jenin, in the extreme north of the West Bank is on the southern edge of the Jezreel Valley, Qalqilyah and Tulkarm are in the low foothills adjacent to the Israeli coastal plain, and Jericho is situated near the Jordan River, just north of the Dead Sea.

EAST JERUSALEM

East Jerusalem is not recognized by Israel as a separate entity, and is the location where Palestinians hope to establish their future capital. All existing definitions of East Jerusalem include the Jerusalem Old City and some of the holiest sites in the Jewish, Muslim and Christian religions, including the Western Wall, the Temple Mount/Noble Sanctuary (containing the Dome of the Rock and the Al-Aqsa Mosque), and the Church of the Holy Sepulchre.

MA'ALE ADUMMIM

Ma'ale Adummim (Hebrew: מעלה אדומים) is an Israeli city in the Judea region of the West Bank, east of Jerusalem. Founded in 1976, it is now sometimes considered to be a suburb of Jerusalem, mainly because most of its population works in Jerusalem. Ma'ale Adummim is one of the largest Jewish communities in the West Bank. As of 2005, the estimated population of Ma'ale Adummim is 32,000. Ma'ale Adummim is seen by Palestinians as a threat to the territorial continuity of any future Palestinian state, given its strategic situation between the northern and southern areas of the West Bank.

RAMALLAH

Ramallah is generally considered the most affluent and cultural as well as the most liberal, of all Palestinian cities. Ramallah (not to be confused with the Israeli city of Ramla) is a major Palestinian cultural and economic center, and is the location of Yasser Arafat's burial spot. The city is located close to the biblical Bet El, the location where Jacob had his divine revelation dream in Genesis, and the location where the Israelites built a temple to worship in the book of Kings. Although mentions of Ramallah can be found throughout historical texts, modern Ramallah was founded in the mid 1500s by the Hadadeens, a tribe of brothers who were descended from Yemenite Christian Arabs. Ramallah is also famous for the Mukata'a which now serves as the governmental headquarters of the Palestinian Authority in Ramallah. The Mukata'a also recently became known as "Arafat's Compound". The Israeli settlement of Bet El is located, just east, adjacent to Ramallah.

TULKARM

Tulkarm or Tulkarem (Arabic ūlkarm) is a Palestinian city in the West Bank. The city's origins can be traced back to at least the third century C.E. under the name "Berat Soreqa", and in later centuries as "Tur Karma", which means "mount of vineyards" in Aramaic, as the city is known for the fertility of the land and the vines around it. Avnei Hefetz, Sal'it and Einav are the three Israeli settlements in the Tulkarm district.

BETHLEHEM

Bethlehem, which is south of Jerusalem, has great significance for Christianity as it is believed to be the birthplace of Jesus of Nazareth and the Church of the Nativity. The traditional site of Rachel's Tomb, which is important in Judaism, lies at the city's outskirts. Bethlehem is also home to one of largest Christian communities in the Middle East. The Bethlehem agglomeration includes the small towns of Beit Jala and Beit Sahour, the latter also having biblical significance. The equally remote Greek Orthodox monastery of Mar Saba lies hidden along a silent, empty wadi 15 miles east of Bethlehem.

JENIN

Jenin was known in ancient times as the Biblical village of En-gannim (Biblical Hebrew Ēn-Gannīm, "gardens spring"), a city of the Levites of the Tribe of Issachar. The modern Arabic name Jenin ultimately derives from this ancient name. The State of Israel built a nearby Israeli settlement, Ganim, also named after the ancient village. This settlement was evacuated in August 2005 as part of Israel's unilateral disengagement plan.

Background:	The Israel-PLO Declaration of Principles on Interim Self-Government Arrangements (the DOP), signed in Washington on 13 September 1993, provided for a transitional period not exceeding five years of Palestinian interim self-government in the Gaza Strip and the West Bank. Under the DOP, Israel agreed to transfer certain powers and responsibilities to the Palestinian Authority, which includes the Palestinian Legislative Council elected in January 1996, as part of the interim self-governing arrangements in the West Bank and Gaza Strip. A transfer of powers and responsibilities for the Gaza Strip and Jericho took place pursuant to the Israel-PLO 4 May 1994 Cairo Agreement on the Gaza Strip and the Jericho Area and in additional areas of the West Bank pursuant to the Israel-PLO 28 September 1995 Interim Agreement, the Israel-PLO 15 January 1997 Protocol Concerning Redeployment in Hebron, the Israel-PLO 23 October 1998 Wye River Memorandum, and the 4 September 1999 Sharm el-Sheikh Agreement. The DOP provides that Israel will retain responsibility during the transitional period for external and internal security and for public order of settlements and Israeli citizens. Direct negotiations to determine the permanent status of Gaza and West Bank that began in September 1999 after a three-year hiatus, were derailed by a second intifadah that broke out in September 2000. The resulting widespread violence in the West Bank and Gaza Strip, Israel's military response, and instability within the Palestinian Authority continue to undermine progress toward a permanent agreement. Following the death of longtime Palestinian leader Yasir ARAFAT in November 2004, the election of his successor Mahmud ABBAS in January 2005 could bring a turning point in the conflict.

GEOGRAPHY

Israeli Settlements in the Gaza Strip, December 1993

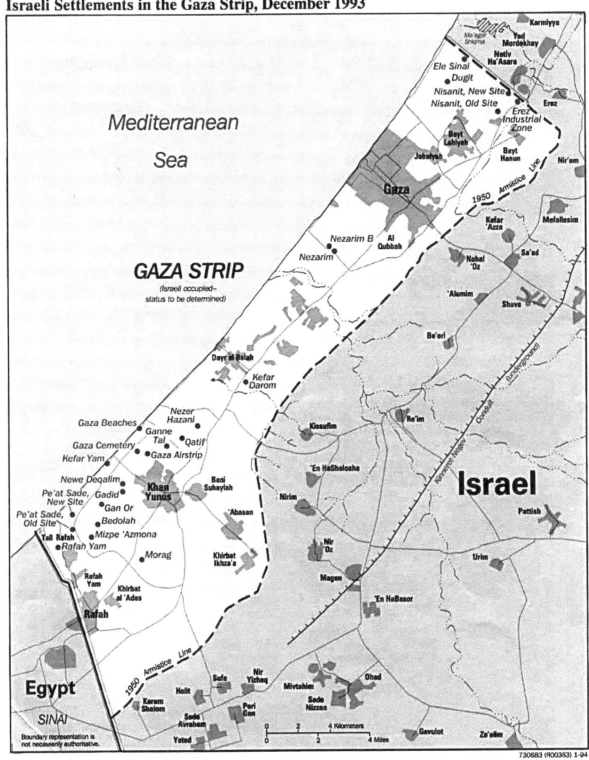

For additional analytical, business and investment opportunities information,
please contact Global Investment & Business Center, USA
at (703) 370-8082. Fax: (703) 370-8083. E-mail: ibpusa3@gmail.com
Global Business and Investment Info Databank - www.ibpus.com

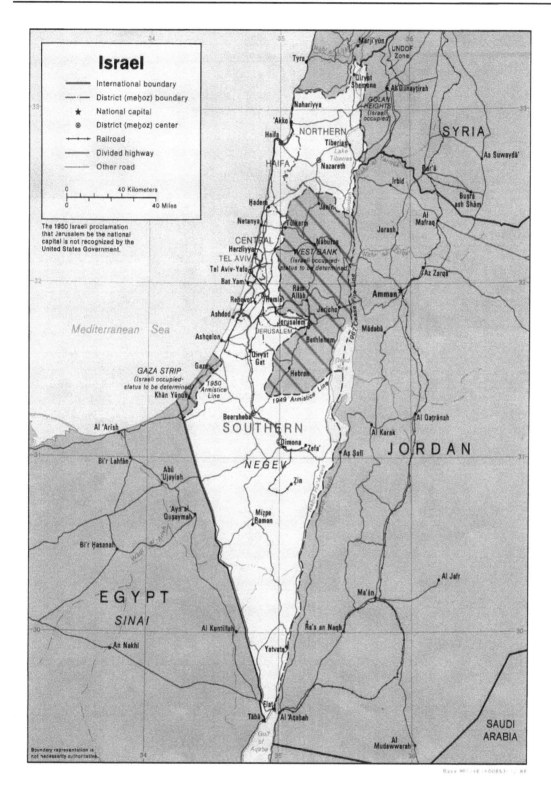

Location:	Middle East, west of Jordan

Geographic coordinates:	32 00 N, 35 15 E
Map references:	Middle East
Area:	total: 5,860 sq km land: 5,640 sq km water: 220 sq km note: includes West Bank, Latrun Salient, and the northwest quarter of the Dead Sea, but excludes Mt. Scopus; East Jerusalem and Jerusalem No Man's Land are also included only as a means of depicting the entire area occupied by Israel in 1967
Area - comparative:	slightly smaller than Delaware
Land boundaries:	total: 404 km border countries: Israel 307 km, Jordan 97 km
Coastline:	0 km (landlocked)
Maritime claims:	none (landlocked)
Climate:	temperate; temperature and precipitation vary with altitude, warm to hot summers, cool to mild winters
Terrain:	mostly rugged dissected upland, some vegetation in west, but barren in east
Elevation extremes:	lowest point: Dead Sea -408 m highest point: Tall Asur 1,022 m
Natural resources:	arable land
Land use:	arable land: 16.9% permanent crops: 18.97% other: 64.13%
Irrigated land:	NA sq km
Natural hazards:	droughts
Environment - current issues:	adequacy of fresh water supply; sewage treatment
Geography - note:	landlocked; highlands are main recharge area for Israel's coastal aquifers; there are 244 West Bank settlements and 29 East Jerusalem settlements in addition to at least 20 occupied outposts

PEOPLE

Population:	2,385,615 note: in addition, there are about 187,000 Israeli settlers in the West Bank and fewer than 177,000 in East Jerusalem
Age structure:	0-14 years: 43.4% (male 530,197/female 504,794) 15-64 years: 53.2% (male 649,610/female 619,335) 65 years and over: 3.4% (male 34,803/female 46,876)
Median age:	total: 18.14 years male: 17.99 years female: 18.3 years
Population growth rate:	3.13%
Birth rate:	32.37 births/1,000 population
Death rate:	3.99 deaths/1,000 population
Net migration rate:	2.88 migrant(s)/1,000 population
Sex ratio:	at birth: 1.06 male(s)/female under 15 years: 1.05 male(s)/female 15-64 years: 1.05 male(s)/female 65 years and over: 0.74 male(s)/female total population: 1.04 male(s)/female
Infant mortality rate:	total: 19.62 deaths/1,000 live births male: 21.66 deaths/1,000 live births female: 17.45 deaths/1,000 live births

For additional analytical, business and investment opportunities information,
please contact Global Investment & Business Center, USA
at (703) 370-8082. Fax: (703) 370-8083. E-mail: ibpusa3@gmail.com
Global Business and Investment Info Databank - www.ibpus.com

Life expectancy at birth:	total population: 73.08 years male: 71.33 years female: 74.95 years
Total fertility rate:	4.4 children born/woman
Nationality:	noun: NA adjective: NA
Ethnic groups:	Palestinian Arab and other 83%, Jewish 17%
Religions:	Muslim 75% (predominantly Sunni), Jewish 17%, Christian and other 8%
Languages:	Arabic, Hebrew (spoken by Israeli settlers and many Palestinians), English (widely understood)
Literacy:	definition: NA total population: NA% male: NA% female: NA%

GOVERNMENT

Country name:	conventional long form: none conventional short form: West Bank

ECONOMY

Economy - overview:	The West Bank - the larger of the two areas under the Palestine Authority - has experienced a general decline in economic growth and a degradation in economic conditions made worse since the second intifadah began in September 2000. The downturn has been largely the result of the Israeli closure policies - the imposition of border closures in response to security incidents in Israel - which disrupted labor and commodity market relationships. In 2001, and even more severely in 2002, Israeli military measures in Palestine Authority areas resulted in the destruction of much capital plant, the disruption of administrative structure, and widespread business closures. Including the Gaza Strip, the UN estimates that more than 100,000 Palestinians out of the 125,000 who used to work in Israeli settlements, or in joint industrial zones, have lost their jobs. International aid of $2 billion to the West Bank and Gaza strip in 2004 prevented the complete collapse of the economy and allowed some reforms in the government's financial operations. Meanwhile, unemployment has continued at more than half the labor force. ARAFAT's death in 2004 leaves open more political options that could affect the economy.
GDP:	purchasing power parity - $1.8 billion
GDP - real growth rate:	6%
GDP - per capita:	purchasing power parity - $800
GDP - composition by sector:	agriculture: 9% industry: 28% services: 63% note: includes Gaza Strip
Population below poverty line:	59%
Household income or consumption by percentage share:	lowest 10%: NA highest 10%: NA
Inflation rate (consumer prices):	2.2% (includes Gaza Strip)
Labor force:	364,000
Labor force - by occupation:	agriculture 15%, industry 25%, services 60%
Unemployment rate:	27.2% (includes Gaza Strip)

For additional analytical, business and investment opportunities information, please contact Global Investment & Business Center, USA at (703) 370-8082. Fax: (703) 370-8083. E-mail: ibpusa3@gmail.com Global Business and Investment Info Databank - www.ibpus.com

Budget:	revenues: $676.6 million expenditures: $1.155 billion, including capital expenditures of NA; note - these budget data include Gaza Strip
Agriculture - products:	olives, citrus, vegetables; beef, dairy products
Industries:	generally small family businesses that produce cement, textiles, soap, olive-wood carvings, and mother-of-pearl souvenirs; the Israelis have established some small-scale, modern industries in the settlements and industrial centers
Industrial production growth rate:	NA
Electricity - production:	NA kWh; note - most electricity imported from Israel; East Jerusalem Electric Company buys and distributes electricity to Palestinians in East Jerusalem and its concession in the West Bank; the Israel Electric Company directly supplies electricity to most Jewish residents and military facilities; some Palestinian municipalities, such as Nablus and Janin, generate their own electricity from small power plants
Electricity - consumption:	NA kWh
Electricity - imports:	NA kWh
Exports:	$205 million f.o.b., includes Gaza Strip
Exports - commodities:	olives, fruit, vegetables, limestone
Exports - partners:	Israel, Jordan, Gaza Strip
Imports:	$1.5 billion c.i.f., includes Gaza Strip
Imports - commodities:	food, consumer goods, construction materials
Imports - partners:	Israel, Jordan, Gaza Strip
Debt - external:	$108 million (includes Gaza Strip)
Economic aid - recipient:	$2 billion (includes Gaza Strip)
Currency:	new Israeli shekel (ILS); Jordanian dinar (JOD)
Currency code:	ILS; JOD
Exchange rates:	new Israeli shekels per US dollar - 4.4877 (2005), 4.482 (2004), 4.5541 (2003), 4.7378 (2002), 4.2057 (2001)
Fiscal year:	calendar year (since 1 January 1992)

COMMUNICATIONS

Telephones - main lines in use:	301,600 (total for West Bank and Gaza Strip)
Telephones - mobile cellular:	480,000 (cellular subscribers in both West Bank and Gaza Strip)
Telephone system:	general assessment: NA domestic: NA international: NA note: Israeli company BEZEK and the Palestinian company PALTEL are responsible for communication services in the West Bank
Radio broadcast stations:	AM 1, FM 0, shortwave 0 note: the Palestinian Broadcasting Corporation broadcasts from an AM station in Ramallah on 675 kHz; numerous local, private stations are reported to be in operation
Television broadcast stations:	NA
Internet country code:	.ps
Internet users:	145,000 (includes Gaza Strip)

TRANSPORTATION

Airports:	3
Airports - with paved runways:	total: 3 2,438 to 3,047 m: 1 1,524 to 2,437 m: 1 under 914 m: 1

TRANSNATIONAL ISSUES

Disputes - international:	West Bank and Gaza Strip are Israeli-occupied with current status subject to the Israeli-Palestinian Interim Agreement - permanent status to be determined through further negotiation; Israel continues construction of a "seam line" separation barrier along parts of the Green Line and within the West Bank; Israel announced its intention to pull out settlers and withdraw from four settlements in the northern West Bank in 2005; since 1948, about 350 peacekeepers from the UN Truce Supervision Organization (UNTSO), headquartered in Jerusalem, monitor ceasefires, supervise armistice agreements, prevent isolated incidents from escalating, and assist other UN personnel in the region
Refugees and internally displaced persons:	refugees (country of origin): 665,246 (Palestinian Refugees (U

For additional analytical, business and investment opportunities information,
please contact Global Investment & Business Center, USA
at (703) 370-8082. Fax: (703) 370-8083. E-mail: ibpusa3@gmail.com
Global Business and Investment Info Databank - www.ibpus.com

IMPORTANT INFORMATION FOR UNDERSTANDING PALESTINE (WEST BANK AND GASA)

Palestine is not only a Holy Place for the three monotheistic religions, but also a country in which to find culture, history and relaxation. It is a country of culture where tourists can experience Palestinian folklore and heritage by visiting many museums and folk centers. They can also stay with families to experience the life style of the Palestinians and enjoy their well known hospitality.

Palestine's long and interesting history comes alive when you visit the many archaeological sites. For example, there is ancient Jericho the oldest town in the whole world. There is Jerusalem, Hebron, Nablus and Gaza with their significant archaeological sites which tell of a history that goes back thousands of years, not forgetting Bethlehem and its biblical significance as the birthplace of Jesus Christ.

Finally, it is a country in which to relax. Visitors enjoy the lovely weather throughout the spring and summer seasons in most of the cities in the West Bank and Gaza and the warmth of Jericho in winter. Besides, there are comfortable hotels and many tourist facilities such as shops, festivals, pubs, restaurants and cafes.

Since the beginning of this century, the Palestinians have been fighting for their land, independence, and liberty. In 1917, Palestine was governed by the British. It was in that year that the "Balfour Declaration" was drafted as a result of continuing Zionist pressure supporting a Jewish state in the area. Over thirty years later, in 1948, Israel was finally declared a state. The State of Israel was founded on approximately four-fifths of Palestine, taking more land than the United Nations' 1947 Partition Plan had proposed.

During and after the 1948 War, a transfer policy was carried out and four out of every five Palestinians in the area inside Israel became refugees. Approximately 714,000 of the 800,000 Palestinians in this area lost their land, homes, and property. At least 418 villages were depopulated and demolished (PASSIA, 1997).

One major consequence of the 1948 War was that a whole segment of the rural highland of central Palestine (which became known as the West Bank) became isolated from its cultivable land, coastal markets, and metropolitan centers as the State of Israel was founded on the fertile coastal plains. The population became landlocked. Those areas of Palestine that were not incorporated into the State of Israel were incorporated into the neighboring countries. Jordan took over control of the West Bank and Egypt administered the Gaza Strip.

Beginning on June 5, 1967, the Six Days War allowed the Israeli army to occupy the West Bank (including East Jerusalem), the Gaza Strip, the Sinai, and the Golan Heights. A new wave of more than 350,000 Palestinian refugees were forced to leave the area, and many of the Palestinian villages close to Jerusalem were destroyed.

In 1967, Israel expanded the borders of East Jerusalem from 6.5 to over 70 km² to include vacant lands from many West Bank villages, while excluding populated areas. Later, in 1980, Israel formally annexed the extended East Jerusalem as part of Israel, and placed the Palestinian part of the city, including the Old City, under the legal jurisdiction of Israel and the Israeli Municipality of Jerusalem. There are now more than 250 Israeli colonies and sites built in the West Bank, including Palestinian East Jerusalem. Despite international pressure against the Israeli colonizing campaigns, which are in direct violation of international laws, Israel is continuing with its colony expansion policy.

Tension between the Israeli occupation army and the Palestinians in the West Bank and the Gaza Strip grew and finally erupted in December of 1987. The "Intifada" was an unplanned popular uprising, which came from inside Palestinian society, and acted to change the political situation. In 1988, the Palestine Liberation Organization (PLO) declared the establishment of a Palestinian State in the West Bank, including East Jerusalem, and Gaza Strip. At the same time, the PLO officially accepted the concept of a two-state solution to the Palestinian problem and the right of Israel to exist.

The major turning point in the Arab/Israeli conflict occurred on 29 October 1991 with the start of the Madrid Peace Conference. For the first time, the Palestinian Territories were invited to a meeting addressing the

Middle East conflict. Although it was not on an equal basis, it was a start. This conference provided the legitimacy and the framework for future rounds of peace negotiations and agreements. The direct outcome of the Madrid Conference was the birth of two separate negotiating tracks: the bilateral and multilateral talks. Soon after, separate bilateral negotiations were initiated between Israel from one side and the Palestinians, Lebanon, Jordan, and Syria on the other. Multilateral talks on key regional issues have been frequently held as well. Negotiations between Israel and the Palestinians on the interim period started in Washington, D.C. The composition of the Palestinian negotiating team was restricted at this time to members who were residents of the West Bank and Gaza Strip.

The lack of progress in the bilateral negotiations led to secret meetings arranged and hosted by the Norwegians. These meetings led to the adoption of a two-stage solution. The first stage was an interim period of five years during which Palestinians would be permitted limited autonomy in the West Bank and Gaza Strip. The critical issues of water allocation control over resources, East Jerusalem refugees, and the Israeli settlements were to be negotiated during the permanent status negotiations, which were scheduled to start on May 1, 1996. The behind-the-scenes negotiations, which took place in Oslo, Norway, achieved a major breakthrough in the Palestinian-Israeli relations, and brought the PLO and Israel to sign the "Declaration of Principles" (DOP) in September, 1993.

The DOP contained mutually agreed upon general principles for the interim period. It requested Israel to turn its authority over civil issues in the West Bank to the Palestinian Authority. During the interim period, Israel would continue to control security of borders and Israeli colonists in the West Bank and Gaza Strip. In order to elaborate on the practical application of the DOP, the "Agreement on the Gaza Strip and the Jericho Area", was signed on May 1994. That agreement, which later became known as Oslo I, resulted in the withdrawal of the Israeli forces from approximately 78% of the Gaza Strip and 6,130 hectares in the Jericho area. The 22% of the Gaza Strip which remained under Israeli control included "yellow areas," Israeli colonies, and an Israeli security zone.

The Israeli-Palestinian Interim Agreement on the West Bank and the Gaza Strip was initiated in Washington, D.C. on September 28, 1995, and is commonly known as "Oslo II." Oslo II set out a policy for election of the Palestinian Council and defined its authority, established Palestinian self-government in the West Bank, and set a schedule for redeployment of the Israeli army from populated Palestinian areas. The agreement also focused on security arrangements between Israel and the Palestinian Authority. As of today, Israel has not fulfilled a large segment of the Oslo II Agreement.

The Interim agreements have divided the lands of the West Bank into three classifications: areas A, B, and C. The Israeli military withdrew from lands classified as area A, and complete autonomy over administrative and security issues was assumed by the Palestinian Authority. Area A, according to the Oslo II agreement, covered the main cities of the West Bank, except for Hebron which had a special agreement. The city of Hebron was divided into areas of different control called H1 and H2. Area H1 is defined as area A and area H2, which houses 400 colonists, remains under Israeli control.

In areas B, the Palestinians have full control over civil affairs while Israel continues to have overriding responsibility for security. These areas comprise most of the Palestinian towns and villages. Areas C, covering almost 74.3% of the West Bank, are under Israeli control. Areas C covers the area, which falls outside areas A and B. In this area, the Palestinian Authority provides civil services; however, Israel retains full control over land, security, people, and natural resources. The majority of Palestinian agricultural land lies in these areas.

In the summer of 1996, there was a change of government in Israel and Benjamin Netanyahu, the Likud party leader, rose to power. His agenda concerning the occupied territories diverged from that of his predecessors and the peace process plunged into a series of crises. Not only that but there was also an upsurge in the colonizing activities to the extent that Israeli officials publicly called upon the colonists to grab as many hilltops as they can. That land grab policy resulted in the establishment of over 40 outposts during the three years that Likud held power.

Furthermore, Netanyahu was reluctant to honor the agreements signed by the previous government putting the peace talks into a stalemate. Consequently, on October 23, 1998 the Wye River Memorandum was signed to "facilitate implementation" the Interim agreement between the Palestinians and Israel. The memorandum stipulated further redeployments that would give the Palestinians control over about 40% of the West Bank (Table 1). The redeployments were to be conducted in three stages and it was projected that after completion of the third stage, area A would be approximately 18.2% of the West Bank, area B would be 21.8%, and the remaining areas would continue to be area C (Wye River Memorandum, 1998). The first stage was put into effect on November 20, 1998, two weeks after the agreed timeline and the following two stages were stalled. On December 15, 1998, the Israeli government announced its decision to stop further redeployment, and froze the implementation of the Wye agreement indefinitely.

Table 1: The redeployments as mentioned in the Wye River Memorandum.

	Total Area A	Total Area B	Total Area C
Stage I	10.1%	18.9%	71.0%
Stage II (not implemented)	10.1%	23.9%	66.0%
Stage II (not implemented)	18.2%	21.8%	60.0%

Source: adapted from *The Wye River Memorandum*, October 23, 1998.

Since the Wye River Memo encountered obstacles in implementation, it needed a new agreement in order to see it through. So on the 4th of September 1999, the Sharm El-Sheikh Memorandum was signed. In general, this memo reiterated each party's commitment to uphold its previous obligations yet with a bit of detailing on certain issues. The Permanent Status talks were to resume in an accelerated manner and a deadline was set (September 2000) for their conclusion. The memo also contained clauses detailing the release of prisoners, the operation of the Gaza Port, the Safe Passage Route, and modifications in the stages of redeployment. The first and second stages were implemented (albeit after delays) while the third stage, which was scheduled for the 20th of January 2000, has not been implemented (Table 2)

Table 2: The redeployments as mentioned in the Sharm El-Sheikh Memorandum.

	Total Area A	Total Area B	Total Area C
Stage I	10.1%	25.9%	64.0%
Stage II (implemented in delay)	12.1%	26.9%	61.0%
Stage II (not implemented)	18.2%	21.8%	60.0%

Source: adapted from *The Sharm El-SheikhMemorandum*, September 4, 1999.

The final status negotiations, which were supposed to commence in May 1996 and end by 1999, were officially started in early September 1999. In the meantime, the Israeli government has not stopped its unilateral practices in the West Bank and Gaza strip by which it created de facto realities on the ground. These de facto realities are clearly prejudicing the outcome of negotiations on the final status of the Occupied Territories to Israel's favor. Such activities are in total violation of United Nations' resolutions, particularly 298 and 242, as well as standing Palestinian-Israeli agreements.

GEOGRAPHY OF PALESTINE

Historical Palestine is located in Western Asia, between latitudes 29,30 and 33,15 north and longitudes 24,10 and 35,40 east of Greenwich. Palestine is bordered on the west by the Mediterranean, with a coastline that is 230 kilometers (km) long; on the east by Syria, with whom it shares a border of 70 km, and Jordan, with whom it shares a border of 360 km; on the north by Lebanon (and Syria), sharing with them a border of 79 km; and on the south by the Sinai and the Gulf of Aqaba. The border from Taba, on the Gulf of Aqaba, to Rafah, on the Mediterranean, is approximately 240 km long. The Palestinian coast on the Gulf of Aqaba is 10.5 km long.

The border between Historical Palestine, on the one hand, and Lebanon and Syria, on the other, was determined in accordance with the Anglo-French Agreement concluded on 23 December 1920. That between Palestine and Trans-Jordan (as it was known at that time) was determined by the British High Commissioner for Palestine and Trans-Jordan on 1 September 1922. The border between Palestine and Egypt was determined by the agreement concluded on 1 October 1906 between the Khideve of Egypt and the Ottoman Government.

Palestine has an oblong shape, measuring from north to south some 430 km. Its width varies from 51 to 70 km in the north and from 72 to 95 km in the middle. In the south, however, it becomes wider, extending to some 117 km. It then narrows again into a triangular shape, the tip of which touches on the Red Sea. .

The total surface area of Palestine is approximately 27,000 km2 (10,429 square miles), out of which 704 km2 (272 square miles) is water surface, constituting Lake Hula, Lake Tiberias and one half of the Dead Sea.

PALESTINIAN TOPOGRAPHY

1. The coastal area;
2. The mountainous area, including intervening plains;
3. *Al-Ghor* (The Rift Valley), including the Araba Valley;
4. The area of *Be'r es-Sabe'* (Beersheba) and the Desert.

THE COASTAL AREA

The Palestinian coast extends from Ras Al-Naqura in the north to Rafah in the south. It forms almost a straight line, except for the Bay of Acre. This coastal plain covers an area of 3244 km2, varying in width from 8 to 16 km near Acre. It narrows at the foot of Mount Carmel to almost 180 meters. South of Mount Carmel, it widens again, varying from 10 to 11 km and extends unevenly thereafter, reaching 21 km in the vicinity of Jaffa. It extends further east in the vicinity of Gaza, reaching 32 km and overlapping with the area of Be'r es-Sabe'.

THE MOUNTAINOUS AREA

This area covers 8612 km2. It runs in the middle of the country north to south, forming its backbone and covering two-thirds of its width. On the west, it starts from the edge of the coastal plain with a range of chalk and limestone hills separated from the high mountains by wide shallow valleys. The Palestinian Mountains form a southward extension of the Lebanese Mountains. They form a large plateau, ending to the north of Be'r es-Sabe'. It is divided into two parts: the northern part is know as the Galilee Mountains, which slope southwards to the Marj Ibn Amer (the Vale of Esdralon), which separates it from the southern part. The latter is the Central Plateau, extending to the southern part of the country, which is divided into two parts: the Nablus Mountains and the Jerusalem Mountains. Both parts form one natural mass, with no dividing lines in between. The mountains slope gently to the west, but sharply to the east, particularly the area overlooking the Dead Sea. Much of the Galilee Mountains are formed of basalt stone, whereas the other parts are, like the southern mountains, formed of limestone, with varying degrees of disintegration.

AL-GHOR (THE RIFT VALLEY)

This area lies in the eastern part of the country, on the border with Jordan and Syria. The Jordan River and its lakes run through this area from north to south. The Al-Ghor forms part of the Great Depression that starts from the Toros Mountains in Asia Minor and continues south through Syria, the Dead Sea, the Valley of Araba and the Gulf of Aqaba, ending up in Lake Victoria in central Africa. This depression was formed by a sudden fissure in the earth's crust. The northern part of the Al-Ghor is called the Plain of Al-Hula. It is only 8 km wide, with an area of 262 km2. The part, which lies between Lake Tiberias in the north and the Dead Sea in the south, is known as the Jordan Valley, with an area of 681 km2.

For additional analytical, business and investment opportunities information,
please contact Global Investment & Business Center, USA
at (703) 370-8082. Fax: (703) 370-8083. E-mail: ibpusa3@gmail.com
Global Business and Investment Info Databank - www.ibpus.com

THE JORDAN RIVER, THE LAKES AND THE DEAD SEA

The Jordan River, also known as Al-Shari'a, springs from the eastern and western foothills of Jabal esh-Shaykh (Mount Hermon), which lies in the southern border area between Syria and Lebanon. It has 4 headsprings: Banias, Tell El-Qadhi, El-Hasbani and El-Bregheith. Lake Hula is 5 km long and less than 3 km wide. It was drained in 1958. The Jordan flows south from Lake Hula, descending in its course from 210 to 636 feet below sea level at the northern end of Lake Tiberias. The pear-shaped lake is 21 km long and 12 km wide (at its widest point), covering an area of 162 km2. It is situated at 212 meters below sea level. After exiting Lake Tiberias, the Jordan River continues its course southwards, emptying in the Dead Sea. The distance from Lake Tiberias to the Dead Sea, measured as the crow flies, is only 104 km, but because of its ever-winding course the river measures 194 km. The Jordan is not, in general, a navigable river because of its currents, winding course and shallow waters. The Dead Sea (also known as Lake Lot) is situated at the lowest point of the Al-Ghor. This oblong body of water is 76 km long and 17 km wide (at its widest point), covering an area of 1,050 km2. It is bordered by mountains varying in height from 427 to 457 meters. The surface of the Dead Sea is 392 meters below sea level, which makes it the lowest point on earth. It is called the Dead Sea because there is no life in it and its water is intensely saline.

THE AREA OF *BE'R ES-SABE'* AND THE DESERT

This is the triangle-shaped southern part of Palestine, the apex of which lies at the Al-Murashash on the Gulf of Aqaba. It covers all the area between Gaza and Hebron districts, the Sinai and Jordan south of the Dead Sea. This district covers an area of 12,577 km2, i.e., almost half of the total area of Palestine. More than 10,500 km, of this area is desert, extending south of the line connecting Al-Auja, Aslouj and Kurnub. It consists of a series of hills extending east-west, interspersed by stony plains unevenly spread. The lower slopes of these hills are covered with rock and pebbles. Some scattered areas are covered with wind-driven sands.

For additional analytical, business and investment opportunities information,
please contact Global Investment & Business Center, USA
at (703) 370-8082. Fax: (703) 370-8083. E-mail: ibpusa3@gmail.com
Global Business and Investment Info Databank - www.ibpus.com

THE PALESTINIAN LEGAL SYSTEM - BASIC INFORMATION

Palestinian law is the law administered by the Palestinian National Authority within the territory pursuant to the Oslo Accords. It has an unusually unsettled status, as of 2014, due to the complex legal history of the area, the overlapping jurisdictions, and the lawlessness and high crime rate in those areas. Palestinian law includes many of the legal regimes and precepts used in Palestinian ruled territory and administered by the Palestinian Authority (West Bank areas A and B) and Hamas (Gaza Strip), which is not an independent nation-state.

The Palestinian legal system is in the process of being modernized. For this process to be valid and all-encompassing, it will naturally take some time. Once the draft laws have been drawn up, each piece of legislation will call for ratification with the Palestinian Legislative Council (PLC) and promulgation.

Currently, the legal environment in the West Bank and Gaza Strip represents a conglomeration of a variety of laws imposed upon the areas by historical governments. The current series of laws being established will add new layers, modernize, unify the existing laws, and establish new laws where necessary.

Considerable international assistance in the form of technical expertise and financial aid is being provided in order to both speed up the process, and ensure the new laws are just and effective in the long-term. The process of defining a new legal system for a nation in its infancy is even at the best of times, a rightly drawn out process.

The scope of this article is to explain the legal history, context and development of law, the current fields of study of law in Palestinian ruled territory, as well as the state of lawlessness in those territories. It is also to discuss the domestic and international positions on which set of laws are controlling in Palestinian ruled territory today.

The Palestinian judicial system is unique because Palestine has been occupied and influenced by different powers and rulers over the last century, which shaped today's legal and judiciary systems. Ottoman, British, Jordanian, Egyptian and Israeli law are all still enforceable in parallel with Palestinian law. Palestinian law was enacted after the creation of the Palestinian National Authority as the result of the 1993 Oslo Accord between the Palestinian Liberation Organization (PLO) and Israel. To understand the components of the current judiciary system in Palestine, we need to review, in brief, the background of the legal system in Palestine throughout history. As part of the Ottoman State from 1516 to 1917, Palestine was subject to Ottoman law. The Ottoman legal system was a compilation of Islamic and French law. The British occupation over Palestine from 1917 to 1948 maintained the Ottoman laws but added a new set of laws based on the common law system. At the end of the British Mandate for Palestine in 1948, the legal system of Palestine became a mixture of Islamic law, French law and the common law systems.

In 1948, Israel occupied Palestine and this resulted in the Balfour Promise, which granted Palestine as an alternative state for the Jewish people in the world. At that time and as result of the occupation, Palestine was divided into three parts: the Israeli state, the West Bank and the Gaza Strip. The West Bank was annexed to Jordan, while the Gaza Strip fell under the administration of Egypt. Jordan extended its laws, a mixture of Ottoman and British laws, to the West Bank. Egypt kept the original legal system in the Gaza Strip, as it was under the British Mandate, with insignificant modifications. When Israel occupied the West Bank, including East Jerusalem, and the Gaza Strip in 1967, it maintained the previous laws with some changes made in the form of military orders.

For additional analytical, business and investment opportunities information, please contact Global Investment & Business Center, USA at (703) 370-8082. Fax: (703) 370-8083. E-mail: ibpusa3@gmail.com Global Business and Investment Info Databank - www.ibpus.com

Before the adoption of the Judicial Authority Act, West Bank courts operated according to pre-1967 Jordanian laws, while Gaza Strip courts operated according to the British Mandate laws enacted in Palestine before 1948. The Judicial Authority Act placed all courts under a single administrative body called the High Judicial Council. This council is comprised of the President, the two most senior judges selected by the High Court Assembly, the presiding judges of the Courts of Appeal in Jerusalem, Gaza and Ramallah, the attorney general and the deputy minister of justice. The tasks and the functions of the council are judicial inspection, grievances, appealing decisions, disciplinary inquiry of judges and administrative duties.

The Law of the Formation of Regular Courts provides that the courts in Palestine consist of the High Court of Justice, the Courts of Appeal, the Court of First Instance and the Court of Conciliation. The High Court of Justice convenes under the president and at least two judges. In the absence of a president, the most senior vice-president, followed by the most senior judge on the panel, presides over the court.

The High Court of Justice exercises its jurisdiction over disputes related to elections, requests aimed at the cancellation of final administrative regulations, decisions and decrees concerning persons or assets of public judicial persons including professional syndicates and appeals for the release of persons who are illegally detained. Disputes are related to public employees concerning appointments, promotions, pay raises, salaries, transfers, retirements, disciplinary measures, layoffs, dismissals and all matters related to personnel affairs. Refusal or negligence occurs when an administrative authority does not make a decision that is required by the provisions of the laws or bylaws.

All administrative disputes are not considered court cases, but are merely injunctions or summons that exist outside of the jurisdiction of any court. Such disputes are adjudicated in the interest of justice and pursuant to the law. Appeals and disputes brought before the High Court of Justice by persons or authorities must be related to: jurisdictional or procedural errors, violations of laws or bylaws, mistakes in enforcement, mistakes in drafting or an arbitrary or abusive use of legal authority. Article 94 of the 2002 Basic Law provides for the establishment of the Constitutional Court. However, this court has not yet been created, and the High Court of Justice is serving the functions of the Constitutional Court in the interim.

The Court of Cassation, also known as the court of the law, reviews cases related to criminal and civil matters. The Court of Cassation consists of the president of the High Court of Justice and four additional judges. In the absence of the president, the most senior vice-president presides over the court.

The Court of Cassation has jurisdiction over appeals brought before it from the Courts of Appeal in felony cases, civil cases, personal status matters for non-Muslims, appeals brought before it from Courts of First Instance in their appellate capacity, matters related to changing the terms of reference of a case and any matter brought before it pursuant to the law.

The Courts of First Instance consist of a president and an adequate number of judges. The Courts of First Instance have jurisdiction over all felonies and misdemeanors. If one act constitutes several crimes, or if several crimes are committed with one object and are so connected as to be indivisible and one of those crimes comes under the jurisdiction of a Court of First Instance, then this court shall review all of them.

If a Court of First Instance finds that the incident as described is a misdemeanor, it may rule that it lacks jurisdiction over the controversy and refer it to the Conciliation Court. If the Conciliation Court finds that the crime presented before it comes under the jurisdiction of the Court of First

Instance, it may conversely rule that it lacks jurisdiction and refer the case to the Public Prosecution to take action as it deems fit.

Within the circuit of jurisdiction of each Court of First Instance, one or more Conciliation Courts have been established as necessary. The Conciliation Courts exercise their jurisdiction pursuant to the law. A Conciliation Court convenes before the most senior judge, who shall exercise administrative control. The Conciliation Courts have jurisdiction over all contraventions and misdemeanors coming under the scope of their jurisdiction.

the legal system in 'Palestine' consists of layer upon layer of law that almost all remain in effect."[2] The major issue is the:

question of whether the emerging state of Palestine will be capable of overseeing a system of rule of law. This debate is important not only in the political arena but in the legal arena as well, since a viable state must have a legal system that is functional and reliable. Despite the historically deteriorated condition of the Gazan and West Bank legal systems under occupation, the Palestinians recently have sought to seize the opportunity to determine the fate of their own legal heritage. To determine how this may be possible, we must look at what laws currently exist in the Palestinian territories. The law applied in different parts of the West Bank and Gaza strip is a combination of the various laws imposed on said areas throughout this century. Instead of each new law superseding the previous law, almost all of these laws remain in effect in the territories. Therefore, one would have to research multiple legal systems and codes to determine the law in one area. This is quite a confusing situation. The Palestinian legal system can be compared to a tossed salad, with layers of different laws and systems all mixed up into a confused mess. This situation in the Palestinian Territories is perhaps unprecedented in modern history.

__[2]

The laws that applied come from many jurisdictions through history: "Customary Law ... Ottoman Law ... British Law ... Jordanian Law ... Egyptian Law ... Israeli" law and even the informal strictures of the intifadah, and finally, the Palestinian National Authority's Basic law.[2]

BASIC LAW

The *Basic law*, established in 2002, is the proposed constitution of a future Palestinian state.[3] According to one report, "Palestinians had been requesting that the law be signed into effect since 1997, in order to formally guarantee a modicum of basic rights."[3] It was enacted by the PLC (the Legislature of PNA) and signed by Yasser Arafat.[3][4] It was amended on March 19, 2003 "to allow the creation of the Prime Minister Position in the Palestinian National Authority...."The Basic Law is based loosely on Shari'a:

According to Article 4:

1. Islam is the official religion in Palestine. Respect and sanctity of all other heavenly religions shall be maintained.
2. The principles of Islamic Shari'a shall be the main source of legislation.
3. Arabic shall be the official language.

The Basic Law is introduced with "In The Name of God, The Merciful, The Compassionate,"[5] as are most documents in Islamic countries.

ARTICLES OF THE BASIC LAW

With 121 articles, it is more akin to a state constitution in comprehensiveness, detail and length.

The "bill of rights" Articles of the Basic Law, as amended March 19, 2003, cover the following topics:

1. "Palestine is part of the large[r] Arab World ...." [5]
2. "The People is the source of power" and the 3 branches of government enshrines "the principle of separation of powers" [5]
3. States that "Jerusalem is the Capital of Palestine." [5]
4. Islamic law is the basis, and Arabic is the official language, of Palestine
5. Creates "a democratic parliamentary system based on political and party pluralism" and a popularly elected President
6. Recognizes the "principle of the rule of law" [5]
7. Regulates citizenship
8. Defines the official flag
9. Protects against "discrimination because of race, sex, color, religion, political views, or disability" [5]
10. Protection of human rights
11. Protection of freedom and procedural due process
12. Rights to "be informed of the reasons for his arrest or detention",[5] to contact an attorney, and a speedy trial (see Miranda rights)
13. No duress, torture or forced confessions
14. Rights to be "innocent until proven guilty",[5] to a defense, and to a lawyer for defense
15. Crime and punishment defined by law
16. Right to bodily integrity
17. Prohibition of searches except by lawful order
18. Freedom of private religious practice ("Freedom of belief, worship, and performance of religious rituals are guaranteed, provided that they do not violate public order or public morals." [5])
19. Freedom of expression
20. Freedom of movement
21. Creation of a free market economy and prohibition against taking without fair compensation
22. Insurance for health, disability, retirement, "welfare of families of martyrs'", and prisoners of war [5]
23. Right to housing
24. Right to an education

STATUTES AND LEGISLATION

There is some confusion amongst jurists, scholars and laymen about exactly what legal regime exists, and which laws apply, in Palestinian ruled territory.

Mahdi Abdul Hadi, a legal scholar, believes that all prior and current law continues to apply in the Palestinian territories, including "the British Mandate laws, the Jordanian laws that used to govern the West Bank before 1967 and the Egyptian law that governed Gaza Strip before 1967, in addition to the Israeli military orders."[2][6] According to Abdul Hadi, the first step was the organization of "Palestinian civil society", that is, a traditional law, "then came the Madrid Conference and the Oslo Accords which drafted laws to govern the Palestinian political life for the interim period."[6] Following that, "the general elections in 1996 ... brought about the Palestinian Legislative Council as the legislative body of the Palestinian people in the Palestinian lands."[6]

Ottoman law has governed Palestine since 1517, and the Ottoman Land Code of 1858 is still in force, one of the causes of international controversy over land seizures.[2][7] The Ottoman statutory "codification mirrored Islamic law but also incorporated elements of European law, especially the law of France."[2]

JUDICIAL AND CUSTOMARY LAW

Islamic customary law applies in Palestinian ruled territory:

Alongside every formal legal system in Palestinian history, there existed a system of customary law known as "Urf", which means "that which is known" in Arabic. This was a system of rules outside the court system, which handles disputes based on traditional oral customs.

___ [2]

For additional analytical, business and investment opportunities information, please contact Global Investment & Business Center, USA at (703) 370-8082. Fax: (703) 370-8083. E-mail: ibpusa3@gmail.com Global Business and Investment Info Databank - www.ibpus.com

The term urf, meaning "to know", refers to the customs and practices of a given society. Although this was not formally included in Islamic law,[8] the Sharia recognizes customs that prevailed at the time of Muhammad but were not abrogated by the Qur'an or the tradition (this is called "Divine silence"). Practices later innovated are also justified, since Islamic tradition says what the people, in general, consider good is also considered as such by God. Urf is the Islamic equivalent of "common law".[9]

In the application of urf, custom that is accepted into law should be commonly prevalent in the region, not merely in an isolated locality; jurists also tend, with caution, to give precedence to custom over doctoral opinions of highly esteemed scholars.[9]

CRIMINAL LAW

For the most part, crimes and violent acts are considered crimes of violence and fall under the purview of the criminal justice system. The Palestinian Authority operates under its own criminal law, such as its Penal Code. In addition, "the Palestinian Authority also imposes the death penalty pursuant to the PLO Revolutionary Penal Code, of 1979." The PNA utilizes both military and special, state security courts for most death penalty cases.[10]

CIVIL LAW

Civil law used the customary law in Palestine: "*Urf* covered disputes such as contracts, family disputes, personal injury, and land matters."[2]

PARTICIPATORY JUSTICE

Through the use of *urf*, Palestinians use alternative dispute resolution, specifically forms of participatory justice: "This system stressed conciliation, mediation, and family honour."[2]

PALESTINIAN LAND LAW

Palestinian land laws covers the ownership of land under the Palestinian Authority (PA). These laws prohibit Palestinians from selling Palestinian-owned lands to "any man or judicial body corporation of Israeli citizenship, living in Israel or acting on its behalf."[1][2][3] These land laws were originally enacted during the Jordanian occupation of the West Bank (1948–1967). Land sales to Israelis are considered treason by the Palestinians because they threaten the founding of a future state and to "halt the spread of moral, political and security corruption".[4] Palestinians who sell land to Israelis can be sentenced to death, although death penalties are seldom carried out; a death sentence has to be approved by the Palestinian Authority President

Israel captured the West Bank from Jordan and Gaza from Egypt during the Six-Day War of 1967. Under international law, Jordanian laws as they existed on 4 June 1967 (the eve of the occupation) are applicable to the West Bank, including East Jerusalem,[8] and Israel as an Occupying Power is obliged to respect these laws.

Shortly after the war, Israel began establishing settlements in these territories based on the legal opinion of Plia Albeck, in contradiction with legal advice of others, including from Theodor Meron, the Israeli Foreign Ministry's advisor.[9] In 2005, Israel dismantled its settlements in Gaza, but Israeli settlements in East Jerusalem, along with their security zones, still account for about 60% of the area.[10] In the West Bank, settlements have continued to slowly grow and as of April 2009, included about 400,000 settlers.[6] All Israeli settlements in the occupied territories (including those in East Jerusalem) have been declared illegal under international law, but Israel disputes this finding.[6]

Palestinians argue that the growth of Israeli settlements compromises their ability to establish a viable state of their own in the territories, in accordance with the proposed two-state solution.[11] In April 2009, a Chief

Islamic Judge of the Palestinian Authority reminded of an existing fatwa that bans Palestinians from selling property to Jews, which is considered high treason and punishable by death.[3]

LAND SALE TO NON-PALESTINIANS

The Negotiations Affairs Department of the State of Palestine (PLO-NAD) declared in 2008, that all transactions with Israelis and other foreigners transferring confiscated land in the Occupied Territories violate international law and are null and void.[8] It stated that under the Hague Regulations an occupant may only administer public property as a usufructuary and does not gain sovereignty or title over any part of occupied territory. Israel thus has no right to sell Palestinian state land, nor does it have a right to lease state land for long periods or for the purpose of settlements.[8] According to the PLO-NAD, the Palestinian government of the future Palestinian state will not be under any obligation to honour Israeli transactions in occupied Palestinian property that took place during Israel's occupation.[8]

PROPERTY TRANSACTIONS UNDER PALESTINIAN LAW

In a 2009 case, in which a Palestinian was convicted of selling land to foreigners, it appears that some additional laws were used to obtain the conviction. The *Jerusalem Post* states that the defendant was convicted under a law prohibiting sale of Palestinian land to "the enemy" (possibly a reference to the old Jordanian law), as well as a Palestinian "military law" which, according to the Jerusalem Post, "states that it is forbidden to sell land to Jews", and two earlier laws dating from the 1950s which forbade trade with the state of Israel.[12]

While Palestinian Authority courts can impose death sentences, they cannot be carried out without the approval of the PA President. The current President, Mahmoud Abbas, has consistently refused to approve executions.[13] In September 2010, a Palestinian court reaffirmed that the sale of Palestinian land to Israelis is punishable by death. The Palestine General Prosecution said that the ruling represented "a consolidation of the previous legal principle," and that the "ruling aimed to protect the Palestinian national project to establish an independent Palestinian state."[4]

Sources differ on the number of Palestinians officially executed for the offence, with the *Jerusalem Post* stating that none have been executed[12] while a BBC report indicates that there have been two executions.[6] However, a number of extrajudicial killings have also taken place since the death penalty was first announced. In May 1997 for example, three Palestinians convicted under the statute were later found murdered. Human Rights Watch argued that the circumstances of the murders "strongly suggested official tolerance if not involvement" by the PA, citing as evidence "inflammatory statements" by PA Justice Minister Frei Abu Medein "which seemed to give a green light to violence against suspected land dealers." Medein is quoted as saying: "... expect the unexpected for these matters because nobody from this moment will accept any traitor who sells his land to Israel."[citation needed]

In 1998, Amnesty International reported that torture of those accused of selling land to Israelis appeared to be systematic, and unlawful killings were also reported against those accused.[14]

An additional consequence has reportedly been increased intimidation of Palestinian Christians, as many ordinary Palestinians have misinterpreted the law to mean prohibition on sale of property not only to Jews but also to any other non-Muslim. This misperception has been fuelled by a number of fatwas issued by Palestinian Muslim clerics in support of the PA's death penalty which fail to distinguish between Jews and Christians, but which simply condemn sale of property to "infidels" (i.e. non-Muslims).[15]

In March 2007, the Palestinian Authority and Jordan arrested two Palestinians accused of selling a house in Hebron to Israelis. According to Hebron's Jewish Committee, "The arrest exposes once again the anti-Semitic nature of the PA. We call upon the government to accept the racial hatred prevalent in the PA." Knesset member Uri Ariel demanded that the government act to secure the release of the arrested Palestinians, while Orit Struk of the committee said the arrest proves that the house legally belongs to the Jewish community.[16]

In 2012, Mohammad Abu Shahala, a former PA intelligence officer, was reportedly sentenced to death for selling land to Jews. The Jewish community of Hebron petitioned the UN, the US, and the Israeli government to step in on Abu Shahala's behalf

STRATEGIC AND LEGAL INFORMATION FOR CONDUCTING BUSINESS

IMPORTANT INFORMATION FOR CONDUCTING BUSINESS

GENERAL INFORMATION

Area
Palestine lies on the western edge of the Asian continent and the eastern extremity of the Mediterranean Sea. It is comprised of two land areas; the West Bank and Gaza Strip (WBGS-Palestinian National Authority). The geographic location has historically given Palestine religious, cultural and economic importance as it joins the three continents of the ancient world. This is a land at the crossroads of history and the heart of a global network of land, air and sea routes.

Palestinian Territories: 6,170 Km2

-West Bank 5,800 Km2; 130 Km long and 40-65 Km in width

-Gaza 370 Km2; 45 Km long and 5-12 Km in width

Population
Today's Palestinians are direct descendants of the Arab people and share their culture, language and history.

Recent history has been far from generous with the Palestinian people. Due to imperialism and the continued colonization that the Palestinians have had to endure in the past 50 years, the majority of the Palestinian people live in the Diaspora. Palestinians number approximately 8 million of which 3.5 million are war-displaced refugees living in neighboring countries and approximately 3 million are residing in the West Bank and Gaza. Over a million Palestinian live in their native towns and villages in present day Israel.

Population growth rate in the Palestinian Territories is 4%.

Religion
Palestine is the Holy Land for three monotheistic religions: Islam, Christianity, and Judaism. Bethlehem and Palestinians celebrated the year 2000 commemorating the occasion of the birth of Jesus Christ. Palestine is also the place where Prophet Mohammed ascended to heaven. Islam has dominated the culture of Palestine for the past 1400 years. The city of Bethlehem has long been a destination for Christian pilgrims from all points of the globe, whereas Jerusalem is still the world's biggest religious attraction for Moslem, Christian and Jewish pilgrims.

GOVERNMENT SYSTEM

The Palestinian National Authority (PNA) was established on the basis of the Declaration of Principles signed between the Palestine Liberation Organization (PLO) and Israel on Sept. 13,1993 and governs Palestinian affairs in self-rule areas. It consists of the elected President (Yasser Arafat), the appointed cabinet (Ministerial Board currently composed of 25 PNA Ministers) and the Palestinian Legislative Council (PLC- 88 emembers). The final status issues will be negotiated to conclude a final settlement with Israel.

Languages
Arabic is the official language of the Palestinian Territories. However, Palestinians are multilingual people, with English being widely spoken and used in business. Several other languages such as Hebrew, French, German, Italian and Spanish are also widely spoken.

For additional analytical, business and investment opportunities information,
please contact Global Investment & Business Center, USA
at (703) 370-8082. Fax: (703) 370-8083. E-mail: ibpusa3@gmail.com
Global Business and Investment Info Databank - www.ibpus.com

Weights and Measurements
Palestine uses the Metric System for
Weight: milligram, gram, kilogram, and ton
Length: millimeter, centimeter (cm), meter (m), and kilometer (km)
Area: 1 square cm, 1 square m, a donom, and 1 square km
Volume: liter 1000 ccm, cubic m
Watt-hour
Voltage 220 Volt

Capital and Principal Main Cities
The City of Jerusalem is the capital of Palestine. Principal main cities include: Gaza, Ramallah, Nablus, Hebron, Jenin, Rafah, Khan Younis, Tulkarem, Qalqilia. Bethlehem and Jericho.

Currency
The Palestinian National Authority has no national currency. Palestinian banks accept deposits and withdrawals of foreign currencies. Major currencies that are used in Palestine include the Jordanian Dinar and the Israeli Shekel. Moreover, the US Dollar is quickly becoming the most popular currency for both deposits and credits in the Banks.

As of the month of November 2002
CURRENCY PURCHASE PRICE SELL PRICE
USD/SHEKEL (NIS) 4.7300 4.7700
USD/Jordan Dinar (JD) 0.7085 0.7125
JD/NIS 6.6293 6.7325

Climate
Mediterranean – hot, dry summers and short, wet, cool winters. Mountainous areas usually have cool summer nights. Because of regional differences, temperature and rainfall vary depending on the topographic area. Areas include the coastal plain, Jordan valley, eastern slopes, central highlands, and semi-coastal zone. Rain usually falls in the period between November and March with occasional snowstorms in the mountainous areas.

Working Hours/Week
Business is usually conducted assuming a six-day work week, with Friday being the official day off. Special arrangements may be made for other days such as Sunday. Hours of Work are from 08:00 until 16:00 accumulating to 48 hours per week.

Direct Dial Country Code
Palestine has its own country code +970- which is currently operating with some Arab countries such as Egypt and Jordan. However, the Israeli Country Code 972- key is used the most- wherever available.

City Codes:
Gaza, Rafah, Khan Younis: +972-7- seven-digit telephone number
Jerusalem, Jericho, Ramallah, Bethlehem, and Hebron:+972-2- seven-digit telephone number
Tulkarem, Qalqilia, and Nablus: +972-9- seven-digit telephone number
Jenin: +972-6- seven-digit telephone number

Holidays
Salaried employees are entitled to a paid annual holiday of two to three weeks, depending on the length of service and contractual agreements. In addition, companies and PNA employees are entitled to the following holidays:

National Holidays Independence Day 15 November	Islamic Holidays Eid Al-Fiter - 3days	Christian Holidays Epiphany

For additional analytical, business and investment opportunities information, please contact Global Investment & Business Center, USA at (703) 370-8082. Fax: (703) 370-8083. E-mail: ibpusa3@gmail.com Global Business and Investment Info Databank - www.ibpus.com

Land Day 30 March Labor day 1 May New Year 1 January	Eid Al-Adha – 3days Muslim New Year –1day Prophet Mohammed's Birthday Isra' and Mi'raj Day	Annunciation Palm Sunday Good Friday Easter Sunday Ascension Day Whitsunday Christmas

Time Differential from GMT is +2

Travel requirements and visa Regulations
In order for potential investors in the Palestinian territories to obtain residency permit, they are required to:

- Fill out an application obtained from the Investment Department at the Ministry of Economy and Trade.
- The Ministry will then obtain a three month visa for the applicant.
- The visa can be extended for another four months.
- A special working permit for employees can be obtained from the Ministry of Labor.

In order to obtain work residency, a potential investor has to:

- Fill out an application for investment obtained from the Investment Department at the Ministry of Economy and Trade.
- Provide a feasibility study on the investment project.
- Provide a copy of the certificate of company registration (in the case of a company).
- Provide a passport copy.
- Provide four personal photographs.
- After three weeks of evaluation, the Ministry of Economy and Trade will respond to the applicant. In the case of acceptance, the investor will be given an investment certificate that will grant a one-year visa.

ECONOMIC PROFILE

POLITICAL CONTEXT

Economic growth and development patterns in the West Bank and Gaza Strip (the Palestinian Territories) have to a great extent been dictated by the larger Israeli economy. The direct Israeli control over the Palestinian economy, and enforcement of the customs and monetary union with Israel over almost 27 years of occupation, has resulted in substantial changes in the economic and trade structures. The Palestinian economy became very dependent on the Israeli economy and isolated from the rest of the World. Israel has become the sole trading partner and a large portion of the Palestinian labor force relies on jobs in the Israeli market.

ISRAELI OCCUPATION

During the 1970's and early 1980's, the Palestinian economy grew steadily. During the mid 1980's, it entered into chronic stagnation, which lasted until the early 1990's. Throughout the occupation period, the Israeli policies and market forces brought about distortions to the macroeconomic and sectoral structures, labor, land, and capital markets, and restrained the expansion of private productive sectors. Domestic production patterns in the Palestinian territories were shaped largely by the needs of the Israeli market and trade priorities, while both tariff and non-tariff barriers limited interaction with the Jordanian and other Arab markets. This created a situation whereby Palestinian earnings in Israel became the single most important source of household income, most of which was then re-channeled into consumption of Israeli imports.

AFTER OSLO

When the Palestinian National Authority (PNA) began to exercise its functions in May 1994, the economy was weighed down by imbalance and fragmentation in all markets, coupled with institutional underdevelopment and under-provisioning of public goods and services. The new situation engendered by the peace process promised a fresh beginning for the economy and a departure from the economic legacy of occupation. The new economic relationship between the Palestinian National Authority and Israel was drawn up in the Protocol on Economic Relations, signed in Paris in April 1994, along with subsequent agreements between the two parties. The development path for the Palestinian Authority, henceforth, was to be based on equitable economic cooperation between the two nations, with special importance given to greater openness in mutual trade flows and expansion of trade with Jordan, Egypt, and other new markets. It was hoped that the macroeconomic policy instruments assigned by the PNA during the interim period would allow it to pursue a policy targeting growth in agriculture and industry and geared towards creating domestic employment, expanding exports, and curtailing imports.

Unfortunately, the underlying promises of peace remain largely unfulfilled. Before the peace accords, movement of people and goods between Israel and the Palestinian Territories and within the now PNA-controlled areas was relatively unconstrained. Following 1993, a strict system of restrictions, in the form of security checkpoints, border closures, and permit procedures, was put in place that effectively reduced the large flow of income from Israel into the Palestinian Authority. The average number of Palestinians employed in Israel fell from 116,000 workers in 1992 to an unprecedented low of 25,100 workers in 1996, but climbed to 44,500 in 1998. This resulted in an unemployment crisis and an increase in the incidence of poverty in the Palestinian territories. The Palestinian National Authority has only begun taking the first steps on the development path that will move it from having been almost fully dependent on a much larger Israeli economy towards becoming an autonomous self-determined economy.

This transitional stage has been fraught with difficulties, many of a political nature. However, the establishment of an independent Palestinian Authority has enabled the WBGS to build trade links with a number of external markets under favorable terms. In addition this has facilitated the set up of a functioning civil service, and the removal of many bottlenecks which previously hampered the development of Palestine's productive base. These developments, along with others such as donor funded infrastructure development and strong growth in the financial sector, set the stage for a speedy economic recovery once a political settlement is finally in place.

TODAY

Since the end of September 2000, the areas of the WBG under PNA jurisdiction have been subject to a combination of border closures and internal movement restrictions. It can be argued that these closures constitute the most severe and sustained set of restrictions imposed by Israel since 1967. The negative impact on the Palestinian private sector has been severe, and damage has intensified in the last two months, due to the massive incursions of PNA territories.

The immediate and direct impact have been job losses and/or reductions of income to all sections of the private sector due to failure to reach places of employment or obtain business inputs and /or sell their goods and services. On average, the direct economic losses were estimated at 51% of GDP produced in the period October-November 2000 (UNSCO, January 2001 and PCBS, December 2000).

Assuming that the net value of goods and services produced in the Palestinian economy is distributed evenly over the work year, the internal direct losses in income-earning opportunities are estimated at US$ 9 million per day.

In the first nine months of 2000 there was an estimated average of 130,000 Palestinians employed in Israeli-controlled area on a daily basis. The average worker was earning a daily wage of about US$ 27, or around US$ 3 million in total. Using January - September 2000 period as the reference period, the average monthly wage income loss is estimated at US$ 60 million, which is translated into total cumulative wage loss of around US$ 600 million since October 2000. Therefore, aggregate direct losses inflicted on the Palestinian economy may be estimated at US$ 2.7 billion, equivalent to over 50% of the estimated GDP for 2000.

For additional analytical, business and investment opportunities information, please contact Global Investment & Business Center, USA at (703) 370-8082. Fax: (703) 370-8083. E-mail: ibpusa3@gmail.com Global Business and Investment Info Databank - www.ibpus.com

Estimates on direct physical damage to private and public assets, (buildings, infrastructure etc.) vary. Some reports indicate that upwards of 3,000 structures from partial to total damage during the October 2000 - July 2001 period. The value of such damage has been estimated in tens of millions of dollars. While the MOF and PCBS give a total estimate of around US$ 272 million for direct physical damage, other reports place the figure much lower .

Clearly, the most damaging impact of this current period is the reduction in private sector investment in employment creation. A recent World Bank survey of private businessmen and investors indicated that uncertainty (high risk perception) deepening under the current circumstances. The World Bank estimates that total private investments would drop in 2000 in the range of 15-20% compared to 1999 (West Bank and Gaza Update, February 2001). An unpublished study by MAS estimated that drop to be around 24%.

ECONOMIC INDICATORS

2.1 Economic Trends
The Palestinian Economy, building on a 4.1 per cent real GDP growth rate in 1998, continued to generate employment opportunities at a robust pace in 1999. There were an estimated 47,100 new jobs created between first-half 1998 and first-half-1999 which contributed to further reductions in unemployment and an increase in the real average monthly wage. Moreover, while Palestinian labor flows to Israel remained important in overall employment, 6 out of 10 new jobs were located in the Palestinian economy where almost three-quarters of new employment was absorbed in the private sector. There were also positive trends in planned business construction and credit creation by the banking system and relative stability in consumer prices.

2.2 Government Role in the Economy
The Palestine National Authority (PNA) has a considerable responsibility towards encouraging Palestine's economic development with other members of the international community. As a product of high level diplomacy and joint economic cooperation with the international community, Palestine now enjoys several international trade agreements with the world:

- An economic protocol signed with Israel made it possible for Palestinians to benefit from border crossings at land, sea, and airports, promoting free trade with Israel and access for Palestinian goods to outside markets.
- The USA extends preferential status on Palestinian products entering its land, in all quantities and of all types of goods. Likewise, all imports from the US are duty free. This type of agreement is the first of its kind between the US government and an Arab country.
- Canada and the Palestinian Authority signed a joint framework for economic cooperation and trade in order to expand and encourage trade relations, and facilitate enhanced market access on a reciprocal basis
- An agreement with the EU grants free trade on all Palestinian goods into the European markets and promotes joint projects between the Palestinian and the European private business sector
- An agreement with the EFTA countries (Switzerland, Liechtenstein, Iceland, and Norway) allows for free trade on all imports and exports
- The PNA is party to bilateral commercial agreements with both Jordan and Egypt, granting preferential treatment to some Palestinian products.
- Unilateral custom-free entry of Palestinian products is allowed into Saudi Arabia, Qatar, United Arab Emirates, Bahrain, Tunisia, and Morocco.
- All imports from other countries enjoy an average tariff rate of 7-10%(MFN)
- Exports from Palestine are not subject to export tax and do not require licensing

The PNA has embarked on an extensive program of legal reform, in order to establish a healthy business environment. The policy makers are leaning towards a free market economy, where businesses are privately owned. With the assistance of the IFC, international legal experts and their local counterparts, the Legislative Council was able to pass the Investment bill, a new Taxation bill, and a bill regarding industrial estates and free zones. Preparation is underway for an intellectual property law, which will allow registration of patents and trademarks.

For additional analytical, business and investment opportunities information,
please contact Global Investment & Business Center, USA
at (703) 370-8082. Fax: (703) 370-8083. E-mail: ibpusa3@gmail.com
Global Business and Investment Info Databank - www.ibpus.com

The establishment of an independent Palestinian authority has enabled the WBGS to build trade links with a number of external markets under favorable terms, to set up a functioning civil service, and to remove many of the bottlenecks which previously hampered the development of its productive base.

2.3 Balance of Payments

The current account deficit in 1996 reached approximately one quarter of Gross Domestic Production (GDP). In figures, this amount translates into US$856 million. This number includes current transfers to government from the international donor community excluding these transfers, the deficit amounts to US$1.242 million, or more than one third of GDP. At US$1674 million in 1996, the imbalance in the visible trade account (including goods but excluding services) was noticeably negative. The capital account consists almost exclusively of capital transfers, i.e. unrequited transfers related to capital goods in Palestine. In 1996 a surplus amounting to US$271 million was recorded in this account.

This surplus is quite large and suffices to finance approximately a third of the current account deficit. The bulk of capital transfers is receivable by government, but the total amount also includes an estimate of capital transfers receivable by the private sector in association with construction activities. Under change in reserve assets are recorded changes in international assets held by the PMA. In 1996, these assets increased considerably (in line with standard norms; in book-keeping this is represented by a minus sign in the table), leading to a surplus in the overall balance. The increase amounted to US$83 million, and occurred in spite of the large current account deficit.

Item	1996
CURRENT ACCOUNT	-856.2
Goods (net)	-1773.7
Services (net)	-112.1
Income (net)	468.9
Current Transfers (net)	460.7
CAPITAL ACCOUNT	271.3
Capital transfers (net)	270
Acquisition/disposals of non-produced, non financial assets	1.3
FINANCIAL ACCOUNT	227.5
Direct investment (net)	147.2
Portfolio investment (net)	-16.2
Other investment (net)	96.5
Error and omissions	440.4
OVERALL BALANCE	83.0

THE ECONOMIC ENVIRONMENT

1.1 Introduction

A basic requirement for sustained economic development is the presence of a suitable economic environment. Attracting investment depends to a great extent on favorable and fair laws and regulations that govern business. It is also affected by the degree of political and economic stability, the adequacy of the infrastructure, and the development of the financial sector.

The Palestinian economic environment during the years of Israeli occupation was clearly deficient and was described as being 'ambiguous, complex and unpredictable' (World Bank, 1993).

Laws that go back to the British Mandate era remained in force in the Gaza Strip, with amendments that were introduced by Israeli military orders after 1967. As for the West Bank, Jordanian laws amended by Israeli military orders were in force. Researchers, politicians and observers agree that this legal framework is not adequate, that it does not take into consideration Palestinian public interests, and that it has been reshaped so as to serve the interest of Israel.

In addition, the Israeli Occupation Authorities neglected the Palestinian infrastructure, rendering it inadequate for the needs of economic development, and prohibited the development of the financial sector, closing all the banks that were in operation before occupation. Banks remained closed until 1981, when Israel allowed the opening of the Palestine Bank in Gaza, followed in 1986 by the reopening of the Cairo - Amman Bank in Nablus.

Aggravating the situation even further, the Occupation Authorities offered the least possible in terms of public services. These services sunk to dismal levels, which motivated local and foreign NGO's to focus on providing a good part of the missing services.

This was the situation when the PNA took over the self-government areas in the West Bank and Gaza Strip in 1994 and 1995. In order to prevent a legal void, the first decree by the PNA was to declare valid the laws that were in force in the Palestinian areas before June 5, 1967, until the two legal systems are unified.

The PNA set out to assume the powers and responsibilities of a governing authority and to establish the institutions of the self-government and its departments. Some laws that pertain to economic activities were enacted and other economic legislation and procedures were drafted. But this process is still in the initial stage and there is a great deal that needs to be done in the area of economic laws and legislation and trade procedures.

As for the infrastructure, only limited investment has taken place so far in the sectors of electricity, water, sewerage and pavement of roads Because of Israeli impediments, there is a limit to what the PNA can do. Israel still controls the borders of the West Bank and the Gaza Strip and this enables it to close-off the Palestinian areas and sever their ties to the outside world. This causes a state of uncertainty to prevail among local and foreign investors, making them reluctant to invest in the Palestinian economy, and leading to prolonged stagnation.

In addition, Israel still controls about 40% of the area of the Gaza Strip and more than 74% of the area of the West Bank (Area C), which leaves zoning and building in these areas under Israeli jurisdiction, thus limiting Palestinian ability to build and develop in these areas. Land registration procedures in these areas as well as in Area B, which constitutes 23 % of the area of the West Bank, are also under Israeli control. The suspension of land registration procedures by Israel in 1967 has resulted in leaving more than 70% of the lands of the West Bank and 10% of the lands of the Gaza Strip without registration. This constitutes an important obstacle to various economic activities that depend on land ownership, such as using land as a collateral for bank loans. The PNA could resume land registration operations in Area A, which it ought to do as soon as possible. Resuming such operations in 40% of the Gaza Strip and in Areas B and C in the West Bank is subject to approval by the Israeli authorities.

In the next section, the most important features of the legal environment and the changes that have taken place since the PNA took over its responsibilities are presented. Next, the most prominent economic and trade regulations and measures that have been introduced by the PNA are examined. Finally, the Israeli closures and land confiscation, which cause serious harm to the Palestinian economy, are discussed.

1.2 The Legal Environment

An important role for the state in a free market economy is the provision of a legal environment that promotes economic and commercial activities essential for economic growth and for the improvement of standards of living. A sound legal environment creates an atmosphere that provides the greatest certainty possible for investors, traders and the financial sector. It is not possible to achieve economic growth in a legal environment that is complicated and lacks transparency because these lead to an atmosphere of uncertainty toward investment, which is an additional cost that is difficult to assess making investment risky. A crucial component is the freedom and independence of the judiciary. It is not possible to attract investors and businessmen if the rule of law and respect for the law are lacking.

Although there is not a legal void in the literal sense of the word (since there were laws that existed before the PNA took over), and although the commercial laws are relatively modern, there are many problems in the body of commercial laws that need attention (Birzeit University Law Center). Most important of these problems are those pertaining to the legal dichotomy resulting from the existence of laws and regulations in the Gaza Strip that differ from those in the West Bank. This stems from the differing historical backgrounds of the two regions, as mentioned earlier. Many legal experts believe that this dichotomy is not a problem in itself, but that problems arise because of the separation of the two systems and the lack of a mechanism for mutual recognition. In addition, the different legal treatments affect the geographic distribution of businesses and investments.

Opinions differ as to what would be an adequate mechanism for changing the situation, but within the conditions in which the PNA operates, a slow transition may be the safest. The process of change has already started through the laws and regulations that were passed and enacted by the elected legislative Council and the PNA, which are valid in all the areas that are under the jurisdiction of the PNA. But there is an urgent need for issuing the Palestinian Basic Law and for new laws to deal with the differences arising historically between the two regions. There is also a need for the establishment of a higher judicial body that would rule on legal differences and settle legal disputes, and that would coordinate the two court systems in the West Bank and the Gaza Strip.

The PNA has enacted some economic and trade laws and it has drafted other laws that it intends to place before the Legislative Council for passage. Most important of these laws is the Encouragement of Investment Law, which was passed on May 14, 1995 (Al Waqa'i Al-Filistiniyah, 1995),(look somewhere else on this page). The Encouragement of Investment Law relies on tax exemptions as an incentive for attracting foreign investments and for encouraging local investments.

Economic experts consider this reliance on exemptions its main drawback because experience in developing countries has demonstrated the failure of such an incentive to attract investment. In addition, although the law stipulates the setting up of an independent board to oversee its enforcement, this board consists mainly of government officials. The private sector's role is very small, thus limiting the board's independence. Furthermore, there is the issue of unnecessary complications and lack of transparency in the articles and in the procedures prescribed by the law. Other criticisms pertain to the rights of investors and the setof disputes between them and official and unofficial parties. As a result of all these criticisms, the PNA has suspended the enforcement of the original law and is now working on drafting a new version, and it is hoped that this new version will resolve the problems encountered in the original version .

Other draft laws still being studied are the Income Tax Draft Law, Banking Draft Law, Establishment of Small and Medium Economic Ventures, and the Development Authority Draft Law, in addition to a draft law on the General Budget and another on Social Security. There are also laws pertaining to car rental and goldsmiths that are being considered.

There are many laws that are necessary for economic development that have not been addressed yet and do not appear in the list of laws under preparation. Most important among these laws are the Companies Law, Antitrust Law, and Proprietors and Tenants Law. There is an urgent need for unifying the Companies Law in the West Bank and Gaza Strip, especially since the two areas form one economic unit and companies have the right to operate in both regions.

For example, banks in the West Bank must be public share holding companies, whereas in the Gaza Strip this is not required, which creates problems for branches of banks registered in one region when operating in the other. Also, the present law governing proprietors and tenants constitutes a burden on the housing and building sector. The law keeps the rents fixed and does not allow the period of rental to be terminal. This issue requires the attention of the executive as well as the legislative authority, especially since the housing and building sector has the potential to take the lead in Palestinian economic development during the transition period. For this reason, this law must be amended in a way that creates a balance between the rights of the proprietors and the rights of the tenants. The absence of a basic law for the general budget, which would regulate public spending and revenue collection as well as the mechanism for preparing and approving the general budget, leads to disorder in the area of public spending. Therefore, a budget law is urgently needed. There is also an urgent need for the enactment of laws that prohibit monopolistic practices and prepare the ground for healthy competition. Furthermore, the economic role of government must be defined in way that minimizes its involvement in production and limits it to mainly providing an appropriate economic environment for the private sector.

1.3 Regulations and Procedures

The PNA has introduced many changes to the procedures relating to economic and commercial activities and plans to introduce additional changes. But the procedures still suffer from a general lack of clarity and rely heavily on licensing. Some of the requirements seem unnecessary and it is hoped that they will be abolished with time. The assumption is that the investor should be the one to decide on the choice of investment. If the PNA chooses to encourage a certain sector of the economy, that could be achieved by providing incentives for investment in that sector.

In external trade, all exporters to the Palestinian market now need to deal with Palestinian agents or distributors, which helps to limit the monopoly that Israeli importers of goods from abroad and exporters to WBCS exercise over the Palestinian market. Importing goods that are listed in lists Al and A2 requires a special license from the Palestinian Ministry of Trade. The issuance of a license depends largely on the discretion of officials in the Ministry, and although the Ministry asserts that no request for a license has so far been denied and that the waiting period is usually short, issuing import licenses without establishing transparent criteria for granting them may lead to problems in the future. The fact that such problems have not surfaced yet may be due to the limited amount of direct imports to date, as a result of Israeli impediments. Until the present, the quantities that Palestinian merchants have requested to import do not exceed the quantities allowed under the Economic Protocol, and therefore, there was no need to introduce quotas. But in the case of quantities exceeding the allowed limit, it may become necessary to distribute the total quantity among those applying for import licenses by auction, as it is done in many countries. Emphasis must be placed here on transparency and lack of nepotism.

As for public safety and consumer protection, the PNA made it mandatory that the labels on local and imported products be clear and in Arabic. The Department of Inspection in the Ministry of Trade is currently ensuring that goods are in proper condition and properly labeled. The Ministry of Labor established a department for occupational safety and health that aims to protect the worker in the work place. The officials of this department make field visits to work places, but as of December 1996, the department was still lacking regulations or laws that set the general conditions for occupational safety and health, the penalties for breaches of these conditions, and the mechanisms for enforcement.

The Department of Economic Activities in the Ministry of Labor and the Palestinian Petroleum Agency have begun licensing domestic gas refilling stations and setting conditions for their operation in order to reduce accidents involving exploding gas bottles.

Finally, the establishment of an Institute for Specifications and Standards was decreed by the President of the PNA in 1994 . This is an important step on the road to controlling Palestinian specifications and standards. But the Specifications and Standards Law is still under preparation and discussion. There is also a draft Jewelry Law as well as ongoing research on the possibility of establishing laboratories to test gold and jewelry.

1.4 Closure

In spite of the launching of the peace process in Madrid and the signing of the Oslo, Taba and Cairo agreements, Israel has persisted in practices that put economic and political pressure on the Palestinians. It has even developed a new method for economic blockade under security pretexts, which is the closure. The closure includes banning movement of goods, factors of production and people between the Palestinian areas and Israel and settlements, between the West Bank and the Gaza Strip, and between the rest of the West Bank and Jerusalem. Closure also often entails banning movement between the West Bank and Jordan and between the Gaza Strip and Egypt. Jordan and Egypt are the only entry points for the Palestinian economy to the Arab World and to the rest of the world, especially during closure.

Closure is usually accompanied by strict measures at the border crossings, which hamper the movement of people and goods. Many imported and exported goods have been spoiled because of these practices. In some cases, closure entails banning of movement between Palestinian towns and villages, in addition to banning of travel to Israel and to the outside world. In other cases, the closure is confined to a certain area, town, or village.

Available data show that the number of days of closure per year has increased during the last four years, reaching an overall total of 342 days in the Gaza Strip and 291 days in the West Bank. 1996 was the worst year: the number of days of closure reached 138 in the Gaza Strip and 132 in the West Bank. The 1996 figures indicate an increase of 35% in the Gaza Strip and 57% in the West Bank, as compared to 1995. What distinguishes the 1996 closures is that they were in effect during most of the months of that year (Figure 1.2), which had a significant effect on the continuity and the regularity of production, marketing and income generation. This exacerbated the confusion and distortion that affected Palestinian economic activities in general.

In addition to the days of closure , there were periods of closure that were limited to certain areas in the West Bank, effectively sealing them off from the rest of the West Bank, Jordan and Israel. Ramallah was sealed off twice, first in Jul1996 for one day and then in November for five days. The closure of Nablus, in the wake of the September 1996 clashes, continued two weeks beyond the lifting of the closure on the rest of the West Bank. Bethlehem was closed off for one day in January and for another in February.

A closure has a devastating effect on the Palestinian economy because it deprives thousands of workers of their only source of income-particularly work inside Israel-and consequently lowers the Palestinian GNP. The purchasing power of those workers and their families diminishes appreciably because of closure, which has negative repercussions on the macroeconomy. The labor market is the most affected by closure. As soon as such a measure is announced, thousands of workers become immediately unemployed as the permits they hold that allow them to reach their work places in Israel and in settlements become invalid. This practice has led to the spread of poverty and other negative social phenomena. The banning of the movement of goods from one region in the West Bank to another, between the West Bank and Gaza, and between the rest of the West Bank and Jerusalem obstructs the marketing process and increases the pressure on the Palestinian market, thus frustrating the hopes for increased productivity and a better exploitation of the unemployed production capacity. This also requires additional investments and mechanisms for storage and transportation that reduce profit and add to the obstacles facing production and -investment in Palestine.

Looking at another aspect, the banning of export of Palestinian manufactured goods and agricultural products to Israel causes a great loss in the short run and impedes production plans, which might lead to losing the Israeli market in the long run as the Israeli importer turns to more stable markets. The situation is particularly bad when it comes to agricultural products, which cannot endure long shipping delays and require special arrangements for storage. In addition, the delay in arrival of raw materials from Israel to the West Bank and Gaza leads to the upsetting of production plans and to a lowering of capacity utilization.

Closure also has a very negative effect on investment. The economic environment that accompanies closure is not conducive to attracting investments, foreign or local. Furthermore, closures have forced the PNA to divert funds that were allocated for spending on investments in order to cover recurrent expenditures and emergency employment programs.

1.5 Land Seizure

Ever since Israel occupied the West Bank and Gaza Strip in 1967, it has pursued a policy of controlling Palestinian natural resources, in particular land and water. The establishing of Israeli settlements has been employed as a means of imposing a *fait accompli* and dismembering the Palestinian Territory in order to make it easier to control the land and the life of its inhabitants. Israel has employed several methods to seize Palestinian land and forbid its inhabitants from using it. These methods include the following: declaring a certain area of land to be abandoned property, declaring a certain area as 'state land', compulsory acquisition of land by recourse to Jordanian Law and Israeli military orders, purchase of land, usually by impersonation or other subterfuge and with the help of restrictions on sale of land between Palestinians, and requisition of land for military or for settlement purposes and for the building of infrastructures that serve the settlements.

The proportion of land in the West Bank seized by Israel, using various methods, was estimated at 60% of the total area of the West Bank by mid-l 991 (Coon, 1995, Arabic translation). In the Gaza Strip, the proportion reached more than 40% of the total area of the Strip by the end of 1993 (Palestinian Ministry of Information, 1996, in Arabic).

Israeli seizure of land has continued during the last three years in order to expand existing settlements and build by-pass roads. The land that has been confiscated since 1993 is more than 85,000 dunums (PHRIC, 1996). land areas that have been confiscated for the purpose of opening by-pass roads since the Oslo Accords has amounted to about 30,000 dunums (Tufakji, in Arabic).

The number of settlers has increased substantially since the launching of the peace process, rising from 105,000 in 1992 to 145,000 in 1996, i.e. an increase of around 38%. This increase took place during the rule of the Labor Party in Israel which signed the Oslo Accords

FINANCIAL INSTITUTIONS

The Palestinian financial system expanded substantially in the last three years. This expansion was particularly large in the banking sector, which increased its deposits by almost 700% in this period. Some expansion has also taken place in the equity market. In contrast, lending NGO's which accounted for most lending in the WBGS before 1994, saw a decline in their relative weight in the financial system. Pension funds and insurance companies, which account for a significant share of investable funds in many countries, do not presently play important roles in the WBGS financial system and their roles are not expected to increase significantly in the near future.

4.2 Bank Penetration

The sudden and rapid increase in banking activity over the previous three years is significant. At the end of 1993, only two Arab banks with 13 branches were operating in the WBGS. By the end of 1996, there were 16 banks and 71 branches. Of total branches operating in the WBGS at the end of 1996, 49 were in the West Bank and 22 were in the Gaza Strip.

The WBGS banking system is dominated by foreign branches. Most of the foreign banks operating in the WBGS are owned, at least partially, by Palestinians in the Diaspora, and one, the Arab Bank, actually started its operations in Jerusalem. However, these banks report to foreign monetary authorities and their operations in the WBGS are subject to the approval of these authorities, thus limiting Palestinian regulatory control over them. In this sense, they are branches of foreign banks and are referred to as such in this chapter. Of the 16 banks operating in the WBGS at the end of 1996, only four were locally chartered. Of the 71 branches, locally chartered banks accounted for only 20. The dominance of foreign branches is particularly strong in the West Bank, where they accounted for 39 of the 49 in operation at the end of 1996. In comparison, foreign branches accounted for 12 of the 22 branches in the Gaza Strip.(Additional Information on Banks are available somewhere else on this page.)

At the end of 1996, the number of persons per branch (NPPB) for the WBGS was 35,699. Separate figures for the West Bank and the Gaza Strip were 32,741 and 43,774, respectively. Compared to other countries in the Middle East, the NPPB for the WBGS is lower than Egypt (47,831), Yemen (135,657) and Syria (155,194). It. is however, substantially higher than Israel (3,464), the UAE (11,260), Lebanon(11,924), Jordan (13,024), and Saudi Arabia (19,755).

Based on a survey conducted at the end of June 1996,15% of individuals over 18 years old in the WBGS have deposit bank accounts

This ratio, referred to from now on as the bank account ratio (BAR), is higher among men (17.5%) than women (12.4%). The BAR is highest among urban residents (1 7.8%), followed by residents of the rural areas (1 4.1 %)and refugee camps (11.5%). It varies considerably between occupations: it is 38.5% for professionals, such as doctors and engineers, and 48.3% for businessmen. In comparison, the BAR for laborers, farmers, students and housewives is 10%, 9.1%, 7.4% and 8.9 %, respectively.

Regionally, the BAR is substantially lower in the Gaza Strip (6.4%) than the West Bank (20.2%). Within the West Bank, it is highest in the middle districts (23.8%), followed by the northern districts (20.5%) and then tsouthern districts (17.6 Within the Gaza Strip, it is higher in Gaza City (7.4%) than the rest of the Gaza Strip (5.9%).

Based on branch and number of accounts data, a recent study (Hamed, 1996) concluded that the Palestinian banking system still has some room to grow. However, the study calls for a slow down of bank expansion to give bank regulators the chance to build the necessary supervisory capacity.

4.3 Deposits

While banks began operating in 1981 in the Gaza Strip and in 1986 in the West Bank, the combined bank deposits in the WBGS at the end of 1993 was only $219 million. By the end of 1996, these deposits reached $1,711 million, which represents an increase of almost 700% in 3 years. However, the growth rate of deposits seems to be slowing down. Of total deposits at the end of 1996, $462 million were in the Gaza Strip and $1,249 million were in the West Bank. In percentages, the respective shares of the West Bank and the Gaza Strip were 73% and 27%. The share of the Gaza Strip in the WBGS total is significantly *lower than its share of total* population, which is estimated at 38% (PCBS, 1996c). Despite recent expansion, the WBGS still has a relatively low deposit-GDP ratio. At the end of 1996, this ratio was around 57.5. Comparable ratios for Jordan, Kuwait, Israel, and Egypt were 82.5%, 77.1%, 73.4%, and 72.8%, respectively. If this ratio is to become equal to Jordan's, total bank deposits in the WBGS can potentially reach $2,455 million. This is, however, not expected to take place before a successful conclusion of final status negotiations, because political uncertainties may force many WBGS residents to maintain bank accounts abroad.

WBGS bank deposits are denominated in three main currencies: the Jordanian dinar), the New Israeli Shekel (NIS), and the US dollar. The relative shares of the three currencies in the Gaza Strip were more or less stable in 1996 . The share of the NIS in the West Bank was also stable. The shares of the JD and the dollar in the West Bank, on the other hand, changed significantly in 1996, with the dollar gaining at the expense of the JD . At the end of 1996, the shares of the NIS, JD and the dollar in total deposits in the West Bank were 20.5%, 45.3%, and 33.2%, respectively. Comparable figures for the Gaza Strip were 17.9%, 17.2%, and 64.3%, respectively.

For additional analytical, business and investment opportunities information,
please contact Global Investment & Business Center, USA
at (703) 370-8082. Fax: (703) 370-8083. E-mail: ibpusa3@gmail.com
Global Business and Investment Info Databank - www.ibpus.com

At the end of 1996, the share of checking accounts in total customer deposits in the WBGS was 34.4% Comparable figures for the West Bank and the Gaza Strip were 35.2% and 32.4%, respectively. While these shares have declined substantially in the last few months, they are still relatively high. In contrast the shares of current accounts in total deposits in Jordan and Israel are 19.3% and 5.5%, respectively.

4.4 Lending

Domestic lending by the WBGS banking system is still quite limited.

At the end of 1996, bank loans accounted for less than 19% of total assets in the WBGS. Other uses of funds at the time were deposits with the head offices outside the WBGS (44.8%), deposits with other banks outside the WBGS (17.6%), and deposits with other banks in the WBGS (2.4%). As a percentage of deposits, total loans at the end of the same month represented 23.9%. In comparison, the loan deposit ratios for Jordan and Israel are around 0.95 and 0.80, respectively.

The loan-deposit ratio in the WBGS varies considerably between currencies. At the end of 1996, it was 0.354 for the NIS, 0.37 for the JD and 0.148 for the dollar. The low dollar loan-deposit ratio can be attributed, at least partially, to the fact that most local bankers are the product of the Jordanian banking system where, until a few months ago, dollar lending was discouraged in order to reduce pressure on the national currency. Hence, despite the absence of a national currency, it is going to take a change in the local banking culture for dollar lending in the WBGS to increase significantly.

A relatively high share of loans extended by banks operating in the WBGS is in the form of overdraft facilities. Despite a significant decrease in the last few months of 1996, the share of overdraft facilities in total bank lending in the WBGS at the end of that year was still 64.3% . On a currency basis, such shares were 94.9% for the NIS, 57.4% for the JD and 36.9% for the dollar.

THE SITUATION OF THE PALESTINIAN ECONOMY

Middle Eastern regional economic development schemes now include Palestine in future plans for co-operation, integration, and development. But what is the situation of the Palestinian economy? The Palestinian economy has suffered more than twenty years of stagnation under administrative policies that have been effectively anti-developmental. Further economic declines occurred as a result of the Intifada and the Gulf war (1990-91), and, most recently by the ongoing Israeli closure policy of the West Bank and Gaza. Therefore, the Palestinian economy is an underdeveloped, low performance, dependent, subsistence economy, dominated in all spheres by Israel. The same is more or less true for single economic sectors, and no sector is progressing significantly either in terms of numbers employed or their contribution to the Gross Domestic Product, although there are some differentiation's to be made. The agricultural sector, which formed the economic base in Palestinian society, has been almost completely devastated by Israeli policies. As well as restricting Palestinian agriculture on paper, huge amounts of agricultural land have been confiscated and there has been a considerable amount of agricultural sabotage - hundreds of thousands of trees uprooted and orchards and vineyards burned. Consequently, there is no longer a strong Palestinian agricultural base from which economic recovery could have been built.

Economic growth and development in the Occupied Territories is restricted through the lack of infrastructure and investment, the restriction and control of Palestinian trade, the absence of authorities promoting development, the domination of the Occupied Territories' markets by subsidized Israeli products and the absence of an adequate monetary system. All of these factors have had disastrous effects on the Palestinian economy and have also created economic hardships that induce emigration and the exploitation of human as well as natural resources in the West Bank and Gaza.

Industry consists of primarily small-scale enterprises, and since the Israeli occupation, no significant changes in productive output, number and size of establishments, their contribution to the GDP, or the rate of employment are noticeable. The industrial sector has suffered with downturns in the Israeli economy but has not benefited when there have been upswings and expansion. Consequently, there can be no implementation of comprehensive development plans in which the growth of the industrial sector would be used to stimulate other sectors and promote stable development.

Trade is restricted from the Occupied Territories into Israel despite the fact that the West Bank and Gaza currently provide a market for Israeli products which is second only to the US. Tourism is one of the few areas in the Palestinian economy which still has a solid base but which will need to be further developed and made more efficient in the future. In the larger regional picture, the Occupied Territories are vulnerable to external economic shocks, in particular those originating in the Arab countries which have large Palestinian communities and through which income transfers and remittances back home have often kept living standards tolerable in the West Bank and Gaza. At the same time, all are aware that the economic price of the Arab-Israeli confrontation has been high and that a real solution of the conflict will bring with it significant potential for future development. The future economic conditions and development in the Occupied Territories will be determined by both economic and political factors. With the continuation of the peace process and the numerous difficulties, many Israelis and Palestinians remain skeptical about the future. While the Israeli side fears a Palestinian state and military attacks against Israel, the Palestinians are worried that the talks will lead to nothing more than a modified form of occupation.

Palestinians desire developing their infrastructure and economy as independently as possible. Self reliance has a high priority and once a degree of independent development has taken place, the potential for development and co-operation on a regional basis will increase. The West Bank has more chance of independent success than Gaza, which, because of its infrastructure weakness, seems to have little choice in the immediate future but to remain highly dependent on Israel and international financial support.

The Palestinian literature on the economy produced in the 1980s was very much influenced by the notion of sumud or 'steadfastness' which was regarded as the key element characterizing Palestinian resistance to occupation during that time.

Since the Intifada, and particularly since the events of 1993, the literature has become much more concerned with future potential and the possibilities of co-operation and development.

A considerable amount of material is also available on education and the future. Researchers have expressed the need for further research in this area to investigate what the needs of the future are and how educational programs can begin to prepare sectors of the population to fulfill these needs.

The most recent period has witnessed a plethora of research and feasibility studies on future economic prospects, development potential, regional co-operation potential, restructuring of the economy and the need for adequate planning. Future plans are clearly for increased co-operation and expansion of economic sectors in whatever way feasible; however, more activity is needed to promote co-operation and integration in different areas. One suggestions for this is that there should be an increase in economic workshops and consultation.

Palestine has to deal not only with the building and development of its economy, but also with would be returning refugees and their absorption into local markets. In addition, the special difficulties facing the Palestinian economy must be considered. No other country in the area lacks the experience of trade and even local co-operation as does Palestine. As all other Middle East nations, Palestine must ultimately find specialized economic niches and develop them to create a competitive economy and to play its role in Middle East regional co-operation.

ECONOMIC TRENDS AND OUTLOOK

MAJOR TRENDS AND OUTLOOK

With the White House signing of the "Declaration of Principles on Interim Self-Government Arrangements" in September 1993, Palestinians in WB/G began a new era of increasing political and economic responsibilities. Subsequent Israeli redeployment from most of Gaza and the major urban areas of the West Bank including Jericho, Nablus, Jenin, Tulkarem, Ramallah, Bethlehem, Qalqilya and most of Hebron extended PA control over a majority of the Palestinian population in WB/G. In democratic elections in January 1996, Yasser Arafat won 90% of the vote for the position of *Ra'ees* (which is translated variously as "chairman" or "president"). His political party, Fatah, won more than 80% of the vote for seats in the 88-member Council.

Under the terms of the Protocol on Economic Relations ("Paris Economic Protocol" or "Paris Agreement") signed on April 29, 1994, the PA has responsibility for key economic spheres. Within certain parameters, this document gives the PA the lead on trade, investment, internal transportation and infrastructure, banking, industry, taxation, and other economic and commercial issues. The PA inherited a hodge-podge of Jordanian, Egyptian, Turkish, and Israeli laws and a basket of regulations, some dating from the period of the British Mandate and has made progress in drafting and instituting a modern, unified legal and regulatory structure to stimulate private-sector activity and investment.

Despite the markedly enhanced responsibilities and capabilities of PA ministries and other institutions, WB/G remain highly dependent on Israeli supplies, labor markets and export opportunities. About 85% of Palestinian annual imports are purchased from Israel and all Palestinian exports must go through Israel or Israeli-controlled checkpoints. Israeli currency (New Israeli Shekel-NIS) is used for most day-to-day transactions, although the Jordanian dinar is also considered to be legal tender and is frequently used for large purchases, such as real estate. Most savings are held in U.S. dollars. Repatriated wages from Palestinian day laborers in Israel provides cash that sustains many local businesses, so the Palestinian economy in WB/G is highly vulnerable to Israeli policies. Since 1993, travel of Palestinians and their vehicles into Israel has been limited to those able to obtain an Israeli permit or those willing to skirt the checkpoints and enter Israel illegally. During periods of heightened security concern, usually after terror attacks, even those with permits are prevented from entering. This latter situation is known as "comprehensive closure." Given WB/G's overwhelming dependence on Israel, closure — particularly comprehensive closure -— is devastating to the Palestinian economy.

The outbreak of the Al-Aqsa Intifada in September 2000 has had a profound impact on the operations of the private sector in West Bank/Gaza (WB/G). Terrorist activity and violence has usually been directed at Israeli, not international or Palestinian, targets. The GOI has responded by imposing severe external and internal closures on WB/G since the end of September 2000. These measures have limited or obviated the movement of goods and workers within WB/G, between West Bank and Gaza, and into Israel; the import and export of raw materials and finished products; and the ability of Palestinians to leave and return to WB/G from abroad.

Political-economic conditions make hard statistical data problematic. Gross Domestic Product (GDP) in WB/G was estimated at $4.175 billion in 2000, about 3.8% of Israel's $110 billion economy. Compared to real growth from the 1970's to the mid-1980's, GDP significantly declined during the period of the first Intifada, which began in December 1987, as well as from 1993 to 1997. Several factors came into play: dislocations caused by the first Intifada, the loss of remittances from the Gulf following expulsion of Palestinians after the Gulf War, a reduction in work permits for Israel, and the economic impacts of closures. Beginning in 1998, the economy began to recover strongly, with GDP growing an impressive 7.0%. This recovery continued in 1999 with GDP growth of 6.0%, and through the first three quarters of 2000. According to UN figures, unemployment in WB/G in 2000 fell to 10%. Since the outbreak of the Al-Aqsa Intifada, however, GDP growth has plummeted and unemployment has risen to nearly 40%. In general, unemployment and poverty levels tend to be higher in the Gaza, an area about twice the size of the District of Columbia, where population density and scarce resources exacerbate economic problems occasioned by closure.

Prior to the Al-Aqsa Intifada, there had been a substantial increase in imports of consumer goods, particularly small electronic appliances, food products, clothing, and shoes. This increase may have been

For additional analytical, business and investment opportunities information,
please contact Global Investment & Business Center, USA
at (703) 370-8082. Fax: (703) 370-8083. E-mail: ibpusa3@gmail.com
Global Business and Investment Info Databank - www.ibpus.com

fueled by a growing "gray market" based on unreported production and income as well as to closer ties between Palestinians living in WB/G and those living in the U.S. Moreover, since the beginning of reconciliation between Israelis and Palestinians in September 1993, diaspora Palestinians had begun to transfer funds to WB/G for investment and residential/commercial construction. The closures in place since September 2000 have had a substantial, deleterious effect on both trade and investment.

Investment in housing has been strong since the 1980's. The sector comprises 20% of GDP compared to 7% in similar societies. Most housing construction is privately financed and benefits middle- and upper-class professionals, including many diaspora Palestinians.

Affordable housing is a serious problem for the lower middle-income and working-class Palestinians, particularly in Gaza. Land prices in urban areas of the West Bank have skyrocketed since September 1993 mainly because only 5% of land is zoned for development. In Gaza, land prices remain high because of the dense population and extreme land scarcity. Virtual integration of Palestinian labor into the Israeli economy and a legislated minimum wage in Israel makes wages in WB/G, while low compared to Israel, relatively high for the region.

PRINCIPAL GROWTH SECTORS

Continuation of the Israeli-Palestinian peace process and the gradual assumption by Palestinians of greater control over their own economy will almost certainly encourage continuing international donor efforts to support economic and social needs in WB/G. Infrastructure development, both publicly and privately financed, will be a major growth sector in WB/G over the next five years. Projected major projects include a port in Gaza; electric power generation; and the expansion of telecommunications infrastructure, equipment, and services. Public and private investment is needed for upgrading and expanding sanitation, waste disposal, and water services, as well as upgrading WB/G roads. Private and public contractors will be seeking suppliers of competitively priced equipment, machinery, and raw materials for these major infrastructure projects.

Private housing construction should also rebound with the continuing high demand for working class and lower middle-income families. While local builders and engineers can meet much of this demand at comparatively low prices, innovation in low-cost, multi-family housing construction is needed from outside sources. There is a growing trend, particularly in Gaza, toward building large commercial and residential towers rather than one- or two-story buildings. Companies that can produce low-cost construction inputs in high volume should consider marketing and distribution options in WB/G.

Investment in productive assets is extremely low, only 1-4% of GDP. In 1990, manufacturing made up only 7.4% of per capita GDP, compared to 13% in Jordan. Manufacturing employment accounts for about 15% of total employment in WB/G. Capacity utilization averaged 56% prior to the Intifada, but has fallen substantially due to the economic slowdown.

Companies in WB/G are small by world standards; 90% of all firms employ fewer than eight people. The manufacturing sector is projected to show increased growth, as Palestinians assume greater control over their political and economic lives. Widening regional cooperation should open export markets for Palestinian goods having the best prospects for regional sales.

Expansion is expected in light industry and low-tech electrical assembly, such as car dashboard and electronic goods assembly, as well as in the manufacture and export of processed foods, pharmaceuticals, textiles, shoes, hardware, wood and cane furniture, plastics, and housewares. Construction inputs such as cement and steel products also will be in heavy demand. The relatively high education level of the workforce in comparison to that in Jordan and Egypt should give WB/G a competitive advantage in industries requiring technical expertise.

The agricultural sector employs about 12% of the WB/G workforce and accounts for 15% of WB/G GDP. The sector has excellent growth potential, particularly for providing inputs to the local food-processing industry.

Entrepreneurial talent, climatic conditions, and a sound technological base are all relative strategic advantages in agriculture. However, the ultimate growth potential for this sector depends in part upon the willingness of Israel and neighboring countries to lower agricultural trade barriers or, at least, to allow the transit of Palestinian agricultural goods to Europe and the Gulf.

Penetration of the European market with out-of-season vegetables and fruits such as strawberries will require producers to improve the quality of their product. Unless exporters can reach IS-9002 standards, their product will not be accepted in the EU. Among other factors, this may require integrated pest management, reduction of quantities of pesticide applied and special care in the choice of pesticides used.

Non-government services account for 40% of WB/G GDP. Tourism in WB/G, as in Israel, has potential as a growth industry, but in both places it depends heavily on security issues and, in the West Bank, on whether the PA can obtain land and building permits from Israel. Franchising and distributorships are becoming more popular, with the best prospects in hardware, computers, electronics and office equipment, fast food, amusement and "theme" parks, and small business services like copying and printing.

Some Arab and other foreign banks have set up WB/G offices, but the financial services market remains relatively undeveloped. Correspondence and other international banking relationships are on the rise, and some observers believe that banking services in the WB/G will show especially strong growth in the offshore sub-sector because the PA maintains no restrictions on the holding of foreign currency accounts.

GOVERNMENT ROLE IN THE ECONOMY

The PA has pledged to promote the private sector, which accounts for over 80% of WB/G GDP, and to allow private management of major infrastructure systems, like power and telecommunications.

Unlike other developing regions, WB/G have no history of government ownership of large sectors of the economy, though the PA has been active in the commercial sector via the Palestinian Commercial Services Company, a PA-owned investment firm. Under pressure from foreign donors and domestic private sector companies, the PA has begun to implement a significant economic reform program, part of which includes a strategy for the eventual privatization of PCSC's commercial activities.

The PA leadership, including Chairman Arafat and various ministers, plays a major role in the approval process for large-scale private commercial projects. Often, several ministries oversee the same major projects, so U.S businesses must be sure to talk to all relevant ministries when competing for contracts.

Current investment law requires that new investments be registered with the PA and approved by the relevant ministries. Prior approval by the PA Council of Ministers is required for certain types of investments.

BALANCE OF PAYMENTS

Statistical trade data is imprecise due to the nature of the Israeli-Palestinian border, but clearly a large -- and growing -- WB/G trade deficit exists, one estimated by the respected Palestinian Central Bureau of Statistics (PCBS) at nearly 50% of GDP in 1997. PCBS estimates that WB/G merchandise exports declined from a peak of $403 million in 1981 to $381 million in 1997. With 1997 imports climbing to $2.164 billion, this leaves a trade deficit of $1.783 billion. One particularly vexing problem is the growing difficulty of conducting trade between the West Bank and Gaza Strip because of Israeli policies. Up to now, nearly 85% of all WB/G imports comes from Israel; 3% comes from other Arab countries, and about 9% comes from the U.S. and the EU. For the same period, about 94% of WB/G exports go to Israel and only 5% to Arab countries.

INFRASTRUCTURE

Infrastructure -- especially water/power systems; and sanitation, road, and telephone networks -- needs substantial upgrading and expansion, although a recent World Bank study indicated that the situation has improved greatly over the past few years.

Utilization of WB/G water resources must be expanded to sustain private sector development. Electricity consumption is low compared to per capita income: kWh per capita is 680 in WB/G, compared to 1,054 per capita in Jordan and 815 per capita in Egypt.

The ratio of telephone subscribers to population is estimated at 1:23 in WB/G compared to 1:15 in Jordan and 1:36 in Egypt. Lack of adequate physical infrastructure for electric power and an insufficient power supply cause work stoppages in most WB/G firms.

For additional analytical, business and investment opportunities information, please contact Global Investment & Business Center, USA at (703) 370-8082. Fax: (703) 370-8083. E-mail: ibpusa3@gmail.com Global Business and Investment Info Databank - www.ibpus.com

INTERNATIONAL ECONOMIC ASSISTANCE

US ASSISTANCE

For the past 13 years, USAID has funded programs that help the 3.8 million Palestinians living in the West Bank and Gaza lead healthier and more productive lives. The United States is committed to a two-state solution to the Israeli-Palestinian conflict. Because the new Hamas-led Palestinian government has failed to accept the Quartet principles of non-violence, recognition of Israel and respect for previous agreements between the parties, the United States is suspending assistance to the Palestinian government's cabinets and ministries.

Despite this, the U.S. is concerned about the basic human needs of the Palestinian people. The basic humanitarian assistance, including health, food and education, will increase by 57 percent over previous years. The United States will also help strengthen civil society and independent institutions. Assistance will be administered through the United Nations Relief and Works Agency, and non-Palestinian Authority actors, including local and international NGOs.

PROGRAMS

Meeting Basic Human Needs
To help the Palestinian people, USAID will provide food, health care, and education programs, as well as Avian Influenza prevention and containment assistance. The U.S. Government will also contribute to the UN Relief and Works Agency's emergency fund and general fund for refugees.

Securing and Expanding Democracy
USAID's goal is to protect and promote moderation and democratic alternatives to Hamas. Work will include training for independent media and assistance to civil society organizations.

HIGHLIGHTS OF PAST ACCOMPLISHMENTS

Injecting New Life into Underserved Communities
Since 1993, Palestinians have received more than $1.7 billion in U.S. economic assistance via USAID - more than from any other donor country. Some $371 million of that went to humanitarian aid and emergency response to alleviate the suffering caused by the latest Intifada. Below are some of highlights from USAID's work.

Bringing Palestinians Clean, Piped-in Water
USAID's programs to build reservoirs, drill production wells and repair water systems have brought fresh, clean, piped-in drinking water to 1.2 million people in 80 communities throughout the West Bank and Gaza.

Creating Jobs and Revitalizing the Private Sector
With nearly 26 percent of Palestinians unemployed, USAID emphasizes job creation. Thus far, USAID's programs have generated more than 3.5 million days of employment. USAID has also assisted 1,000 businesses in penetrating new markets, generating $25 million in exports.

Injecting New Life into Underserved Communities
USAID has built or renovated more than 3,200 classrooms and kindergartens, and constructed and equipped 200 youth, sport and computer centers. USAID has devoted more than one million hours to vocational training for women and youth.

Giving Mothers and Children Priority Health Care
USAID has upgraded and equipped more than 80 health clinics, distributed medicines to 150 health facilities and trained health care providers to educate women on birth spacing, family planning and well-baby care. USAID has also trained social workers and teachers to help some 230,000 children cope with the trauma of the current conflict.

Promoting Democratic Reform
USAID strengthened and equipped the Palestinian Legislative Council to enable it to fulfill its legislative, representative and oversight responsibilities. USAID provided the Palestinian judicial system with training, equipment and information technology.

Nurturing Leaders through Higher Education
USAID has awarded 160 scholarships for Master's degrees in U.S. universities and has provided scholarships to hundreds of talented, Palestinian students studying at accredited universities, community colleges and technical institutes in the West Bank and Gaza.

SUSTAINED PRIVATE SECTOR ECONOMIC OPPORTUNITIES

DEVELOPMENT CHALLENGES

- The Palestinian economy is characterized as risky, fragmented, and non-competitive in many sectors. Palestinian firms are less competitive than many of their rivals in Asia and the Middle East, resulting in low sales, a loss of local market share to cheap imports, and high unemployment. Frequent border closures increase transportation costs and distort investment incentives thus undermining competitiveness.
- The Intifada has also exacerbated low- income levels and high unemployment. Half of the population lives in poverty on less than $2 per day and per capita.
- Palestinian laborers that previously depended on work in Israel are now restricted from entering Israel.
- The West Bank and Gaza has a weak institutional and regulatory framework to support economic transactions.
- The Palestinian banking system expanded from 2 to more than 20 banks in less than four years -- a ten-fold increase -- creating an immediate need for improved bank oversight.

USAID RESPONDS

USAID/West Bank and Gaza's Economic Growth portfolio focuses on:
(1) increasing access to financial services (2) increasing access to markets, and (3) effective operations of selected economic regulatory institutions. The portfolio of $68 Million reflects a cognizance of the need to combine relief objectives with longer term economic development goals. It recognizes that the future of the Palestinian Economy will be determined by the emergence of a critical mass of Palestinian companies that can compete in the global markets and participate as partners in the global trading community.

USAID's Economic Growth Program broadly promotes exports, stimulate investment and create jobs. To do so, USAID is engaged in 11 different activities, including supporting microfinance service delivery, promoting commercial transparency, promoting trade and private sector development, supporting business revitalization and advancing economic reform and restructuring initiatives.

Special Emergency Program for the Private Sector

In response to the recent economic deterioration related to the political crisis, USAID's economic growth program has added some new activities and tailored several existing activities to mitigate the losses associated with prolonged closure. Through this short-term $11 Million program, USAID continues to promote the private sector as the engine for sustainable growth and stability in the West Bank and Gaza. Two emerging themes of the program are business revitalization and support for reform of Palestinian institutions and economic processes.

RESULTS

- Since inception of the activity in December 2001, CHF has disbursed $2,600,750 in 615 home improvement loans in the West Bank and Gaza, thus creating 4,471 person months of employment.
- Palestinian firms have sold more than $100 million in goods to new export markets.

- USAID has helped more than 50 Palestinian firms adopt international quality standards, such as ISO 9000 and international accounting standards.
- Palestinian high technology firms now participate in international information technology trade shows and they also have access to international venture capital for expansion.
- Palestinian pharmaceutical companies now export to more new markets than ever before, increasing sales and boosting employment in the sector.
- More than 50% of Palestinian accountants now using international standards, up from only 10% when USAID initiated its Accounting & Auditing program.

PROGRAM BUDGET

FY 96	FY 97	FY 98	FY 99	FY 00	FY 01	FY 02	FY 03 AS OF 03/31/03	TOTAL
4,100	11,100	9,004	8,576	16,631	8,039	14,650	7.376	79,476

(Disbursed in thousands of dollars)

PROGRAM PARTNERS

ACTIVITY	PARTNER	AGREEMENT TYPE	LOCATION
Microenterprise Program	Chemonics International, Inc. **Tel:** 972-2-234-4510 **Fax:** 972-2-234-4511	Contract	Dahiet Al-Barid, Al-Ram
Market Access Program	Development Alternatives, Inc. (DAI) **Tel:** 972-2-298-7187 **Fax:** 972-2-295-220	Contract	Ramallah
Market Access Program	PALTRADE **Tel:** 972-2-240-8383 **Fax:** 972-2-295-9449	Grant	Ramallah
Bank Supervision Activity	Barents Group **Tel:** 972-2-295-9920 **Fax:** 972-2-295-9922	Contract	Ramallah
Auditing & Accounting Standards	Deloitte, Touche, Tohmatsu **Tel:** 972-2-296-4782 **Fax:** 972-2-296-4898	Contract	Ramallah
PRIZIM Industrial Estate	The Services Group **Tel:** 972-8-283-4556 **Fax:** 972-8-283-4044	Contract	Gaza
Capital Markets Program	Financial Markets International **Tel:** 972-2-296-6252 **Fax:** 972-2-296-6255	Contract	Ramallah
Financial Management Services	El-Yousef & Co **Tel:** 972-2-298-2416 **Fax:** 972-2-298-2444	IQC	Ramallah

GREATER ACCESS TO AND MORE EFFECTIVE USE OF SCARCE WATER

DEVELOPMENT CHALLENGES

- The West Bank and Gaza suffer from a chronic water shortage, preventing sustained economic growth and damaging the environment and health of Palestinians. Further losses are caused by old, deteriorated infrastructure.
- Palestinians have a very low water consumption rate - generally using about half of internationally recommended daily amount of water for consumption, hygiene, and cleaning needs. One ten minute shower in the U.S. equals a day's water consumption for an average Palestinian.
- Hundreds of rural villages across the West Bank have no piped water, and hundreds more have it only in the winter. Residents typically use less than 30 liters per capita per day because of the high costs of water delivered by truck. Fewer and fewer families can afford basic water supplies.
- Water quality is not being tested in villages, and much of the water being used is untreated, largely because closures and curfews prevent of access to chlorine and safe water sources. About two-thirds of drinking water in rural households is contaminated with bacteria.
- Palestinian ground water supplies have increasingly become polluted as a result of agricultural chemicals, inadequate sewage treatment and over-pumping of wells. Untreated sewage is dumped in valleys and the Mediterranean Sea, decreasing the quality of the already inadequate groundwater supply, and polluting the soil, sea, and coastline.

USAID RESPONDS

USAID/WBG has remained steadfast in implementing a multi-year program that combines the rapid development of new water sources, improved systems for water distribution and management, and wastewater treatment. Despite the challenges posed by the Intifada (including shortages of critical building materials, limited access to the work site, and physical danger to workers), well drilling, pipeline construction, and delivery of essential water infrastructure continues with impressive results.

USAID, through its $42 million contracts with CH2M HILL and Contrack International, is constructing one well near Nablus and four wells, two pump stations, and 17 kilometers of pipeline in the Bethlehem/Hebron region that will add new sources of water. In the Hebron region, new transmission lines will deliver this water to more than 25 villages. An aquifer modeling tool, design by CH2, will enable the Palestinian Water Authority (PWA) to manage these resources efficiently.

In Hebron, the interests of Palestinians and Israelis have merged and led to the design of the Hebron Wastewater Treatment Plant. This $50 million USAID project will address the Israeli's concerns to protect the shared aquifer and eliminate stream pollutants in the northern Negev. For the Palestinians, the plant will protect public health, clean-up the environment, and develop agricultural uses for water that is now wasted.

In the West Bank, the heightened security situation and economic crisis have decreased access to water for the people in rural villages. Through USAID's Village Water and Sanitation program, a $9 million activity implemented by CDM's Environmental Health Project (EHP), construction of new water systems for under-served villages west of Hebron will begin later this year, and construction near Nablus will begin in 2004. In the meantime, USAID is providing water via tanker trucks to severely affected areas.

The Mission's $20 million Coastal Aquifer Management Program (CAMP), implemented by Metcalf & Eddy, supports activities to improve the management of Gaza's water system. A computerized model of the coastal aquifer highlights the dangers of over-pumping and points the way to sustainable water management. Desalination of seawater will be an essential element of Gaza's future water needs, and USAID will provide a plant to produce 60,000 cubic meters of water a day, equivalent to 40% of Gaza's current municipal supply. Other important achievements of CAMP include a monitoring system to help prevent over-pumping, rehabilitation of existing wells to improve efficiency and water quality, and re-use of treated wastewater through aquifer recharge.

The Emergency Water Operations Center, implemented by the EHP, provides immediate emergency response to damaged water systems in the West Bank and Gaza, including well repair, pipeline repair, and new water infrastructure. Municipalities and the West Bank Water Department are being provided pipes, pumps, generators, and related materials to replace facilities damaged during "operation desert shield."

RESULTS

- USAID wells and pipelines have nearly doubled the amount of water available for about 400,000 residents of Bethlehem and Hebron in the West Bank.
- USAID expanded a Jenin area well and provided for piped-in and cleaner drinking water for 11 villages in the Jenin area of the northern West Bank. Previously, the 40,000 people living in these villages had to rely on expensive deliveries of poor-quality water by truck.
- In early 2001, USAID financed a water distribution system for the Ein Sultan refugee camp near Jericho, bringing reliable running water to the 3,000 refugees for the first time ever.
- In Gaza, USAID built wastewater treatment capacity and sewers for about 400,000 Palestinians in Gaza City.
  USAID upgraded the existing treatment plant and increased its capacity to handle the city's wastes. The water treated in the plant is of high enough quality to recharge the shrinking Gaza water table.

ACTIVITIES

Activity Name: West Bank Water Supply Program

Start Date: 2/19/1999

Estimated Completion Date: 2/25/2003

Status: On-Going

Budget and Resources Obligated to Date: $53,014,739

General Description

Since it began working in the sector in 1995, USAID has dramatically increased the amount of water available to Palestinians in the West Bank. In a region chronically short of this vital resource, USAID continues to address this problem by drilling new wells; constructing reservoirs and transmission systems to take water from wells to towns and cities; and building distribution systems to deliver water to homes. USAID is also working to improve the capacity of the Palestinian Water Authority to monitor and manage wells and aquifer use in accordance with an integrated Master Plan. Also, as part of this effort, the Mission is working to build the capacity of the PWA to manage water utilities through operations and maintenance training sessions and has organized hands-on exercises for water professionals.

Notable Achievements

- In 2003, USAID completed the drilling of 3 large production wells, 7 monitoring wells, inaugurated 4 pump stations and laid the transmission lines to bring more than 6 million cubic meters per year in additional water resources to the residents of Bethlehem and Hebron.
- Between 1998 and 2000, USAID provided more than $20 million to develop village water networks which, for the first time, brought potable water to 11 villages in the Jenin area. Previously, more than 40,000 people in these villages had to rely on expensive deliveries of trucked-in water.
- USAID financed a water distribution system for the Ein Sultan refugee camp near Jericho, bringing reliable running water to 3,000 refugees for the first time ever. All construction occurred during the period following the outbreak of violence, overcoming many logistical obstacles, but demonstrating that a well-planned infrastructure project is possible even under the current circumstances.

PROGRAM BUDGET

FY 96	FY 97	FY 98	FY 99	FY 00	FY 01	FY 02	FY 03 AS OF 03/31/03	TOTAL
29,500	40,000	40,206	40,117	46,882	26,939	23,436	10,011	257,091

(Disbursed in thousands of dollars)

PROGRAM PARTNERS

ACTIVITY	PARTNER	AGREEMENT TYPE	LOCATION
Gaza CAMP	Metcalf & Eddy **Tel:** 972-8-284-8757 **Fax:** 972-8-284-2435	Contract	Gaza
Water Resources: Phase II & III	CH2MHill **Tel:** 972-2-234-4616 **Fax:** 972-2-240-4063	Contract	Ramallah
Ein Sultan I	General Contracting Group **Tel:** 972-2-277-7272 **Fax:** 972-2-274-5796	Contract	Bethlehem
Ein Sultan II	ANERA **Tel:** 972-2-627-7076 **Fax:** 972-2-626-4351	Agreement	Jerusalem
Gaza Piezometers	Metcalf & Eddy **Tel:** 972-8-284-8757 **Fax:** 972-8-284-2435 Saqqa & Khoudary **Tel:** 972-8-282-3164 **Fax:** 972-8-286-2934	Contract	Gaza
West Bank Bulk Water	CONTRACK **Tel:** 972-2-628-1596 **Fax:** 972-2-628-1547	Contract	Jerusalem
Ein Sultan Water System	Afaq-GCG **Tel:** 972-2-298-1090 **Fax:** 972-2-296-0542	Contract	Ramallah

For additional analytical, business and investment opportunities information,
please contact Global Investment & Business Center, USA
at (703) 370-8082. Fax: (703) 370-8083. E-mail: ibpusa3@gmail.com
Global Business and Investment Info Databank - www.ibpus.com

PRACTICAL INFORMATION FOR BUSINESS AND INVESTMENTS

Palestine is an Arab state with a democratically elected government. The process of institutional development began with signing of the Oslo Accord in 1993. This accord established the Palestinian National Authority as the executive representative of the Palestinian Liberation Organization (PLO). The Oslo agreement defines the interim rules of administration and security during the period leading up to a final status agreement.

The status of Palestine during this period is defined in the Declaration of Principles on Interim Self-Government (DOP), signed in Washington in September 1993. In the agreement, the Palestinian National Authority is defined geographically as the self-ruled territories, and administratively as the two main organizations, the Palestinian Legislative Council (PLC) and the Council of Ministers.

With respect to sovereignty during the interim period, the Palestine Territories area is divided into three different areas according to the level of Palestinian Authority. Israel maintains external security in all three areas.

·   Area "A" covers all Palestinian urban areas where the PNA has full autonomy. The PNA is responsible for administration and enforcement of the law on all levels. This includes civilian and police powers.

·   Area "B" covers Palestinian rural areas where the PNA has civilian jurisdiction but no police powers. Israeli and Palestinian police patrol together

·   Area "C" includes Israeli settlements, military areas and open areas. These areas are under complete Israeli control.

Palestinian government structure

The Palestinian Legislative Council (PLC) is the representative legislative body, or parliament of Palestine. It is a unicameral legislative council comprised of the President, elected to a 4-year term by direct popular vote, and 132 members, directly elected on a multi-member constituency basis. The current President, Mr. Mahmoud ABBAS, became President of the Palestinian National Authority in January 2005.

The Council of Ministers reports to the PLC. Due to the geographical separation between Gaza strip and the West Bank (approximately 1.5 hours by car), each ministry maintains two offices.

Palestinian National Authority

President: Mr. Mahmoud ABBAS elected by the Palestinian people in the West Bank, Gaza strip, and East Jerusalem

Prime Minister: Position appointed by the President. Current Prime Minister Dr. Rami Hamdallah

Palestinian Legislative Council (PLC): One hundred and thirty two members elected by Palestinian population voting in the West Bank, Gaza strip and East Jerusalem.

INVESTMENT LEGISLATION

The majority of Palestine's foreign trade is with Israel, followed by some of the Arab countries, the European Union, Turkey, South and East Asia and the United States. Like all countries that have a high trade dependence on one particular country, Palestine's dependence on Israel has both positive and negative consequences. On one hand, exporters know their markets very well and benefit from their advanced technology, but adversely, any shock to the Israeli economy can have strong effects on the Palestinian markets. Therefore, the Palestinian Authority and the private sector are cooperating to increase the rate of direct trade transactions with less dependency on Israeli intermediation.

Economic Agreement with Israel (Paris Protocol)

Free Trade Agreements
Current Foreign Trade Indicators
Import Laws and Procedures
Export Laws and Procedures

Free Trade Agreements

The Palestinian Authority benefits from free trade arrangements with the United States, Canada, the European Union (EU) and the European Free Trade Association (EFTA). A trade agreement signed with Russia grants a reciprocal Most Favored Nation treatment for Russian products in the Palestinian market and vice versa. Both Egypt and Jordan have signed trade agreements stating bilateral duty-free status and reduced duties on certain products, while Saudi Arabia has granted some Palestinian products preferential treatment.

SPECIAL INVESTMENT ZONES

Palestine is characterized of many features and preference provided to investors, especially in the existence of attractive investment structure and climate for business . The State of Palestine is seeking to provide facilities for investment and is keen to provide infrastructure and incentives in the industrial cities and industrial free zones in Palestine.

The industrial and agricultural zone of Jericho
The Industrial zone of Gaza
The Industrial zone of Bethlehem
The Industrial zone of Jenin

The industrial and agricultural zone of Jericho

It will contribute to the strengthening of the food industry, it's execution agreement has been signed with Jordan and Japan in 2006. It has 2 phases ,the first phase (150 dunams) , followed by two stages on an area (500 acres) each.

Geographic Location: it is located at the south of Jericho, 4.5 km far from the city center, and 7 km from the Jordanian-Palestinian border.
A partnership with(PRIDE), (PIEFZA), and (JIPA).

Objectives:

Create new markets.
Improve the quality of products.
Reduce the cost of the products.
Create new jobs and investment climate.
The project will be managed and operated by General Authority for Industrial Estates and industrial free zones and Jericho Company to develop Palestine Real Estate Investment (Prico), and Jordan Valley and the Dead Sea development company of the Palestinian Investment Fund - with the support of the Japanese government.

For more information:
• Telefax: +970 2 2960361
• Email: info@pride.ps
• Website: www.pride

Development Company agro-industrial city of Jericho:
• Phone: +970 2 2986505
• Fax: +970 2 2986506
• website: www.jaipark.com

The Industrial zone of Gaza:

It's considered the first industrial city in Palestine and one of the most important cultural manifestations, both environmental and development in terms of its key role in ending the problems of installations offense within residential communities on the one hand and achieving the possibility of setting up small and medium enterprises, which are the arteries of the large industries on the other hand. It is also confronted to attract investment and facilitate the establishment of projects.

Geographic Location: It's located at the east of Gaza City, 4 Km to the east away from Martyrs Square (Palestine Square) .
industrial buildings and their specifications:
The industrial buildings in Gaza City are Classified and divided based on the type of industry, major, medium industries, and private industries.
spaces needed for these industries ranges between 500 m2 to 2000 m2. The factory area is determined according to the industry needs and investor's demand.

Number of the established factories in the industrial zone are so far 72 factory with different sizes according to international standards:
a roof with thermal insulator to maintain the temperature inside the factories, transparent panels for roofs and walls for lighting and ventilationand concrete floors with extended breaks which bear the high pressure. install lation of transparent panels ceilings and walls for lighting and ventilation needed for factories and concrete floors that bear high pressure and by the expansion joint.
The length of the stores walls is 6.20 m and the central to rise length is 7.70 m .
Interior and the administrative divisions are left to the owner of the factory to create it based on his need. created by his need for it.
Existing industries in the region:

Sewing and textile industry.
Food industries.
Wood industries.
Aluminum and plastic industry.
For more information:
General Authority for Industrial Estates and industrial free zones
• Telephone: +9702 2960351/70/71
• Fax : +970 2 2960355

The Industrial zone of Bethlehem:

It's a result of Donors Conference which was held in Paris in December 2007. This project is implemented by French-Palestinian committee of the General Authority for Industrial Estates and industrial free zones and Bethlehem multidisiplanry industrial park - and the Palestinian Water Authority.

Project Objectives:
facilitate the development of of the industrial companie Network.
create between 500 to 1000 jobs through building a sustainable industrial area at south of the city.
support small and medium-sized businesses in order to develop new practices that will enhance its position in the domestic market and for exporting, in addition to improving the performance of its environmentally-friendly industries.

Achievements:

The completion of a major power station to equip the industrial zone with electricity
The establishment of the power line carrier to feed the RTS capacity 2 MW.
The establishment of a high water tank with a capacity of 500 cubic meters to meet the needs of the region's water.
Specify the location of the central processing unit. (CPU) in collaboration with the developer companyand is being supplied to choose a company processing unit after the international tender.
The opening of the first of the company's headquarters in Schnaider Electric Industrial Zone and is currently working on holding training courses for engineers.
The establishment of an office building consisting of two floors includes the offices of the company and the Commission services firms.
 For more information:
General Authority for Industrial Estates and industrial free zones
• Telephone: +9702 2960351/70/71
• Fax: +970 2 2960355

The Industrial zone of Jenin
It's located on the most prominent strategic locations (Marj Bin Amer) with an area of (933 acres), it's close to the infrastructure and raw materials.

Geographic Location: it is 25 km far from Haifa port, and 25 km far from the Jordanian-Palestinian border too.
Project organizers : The General Authority for Industrial Estates and industrial free zones
The project is funded by the German Government with 15 million Euros worth for infrastructure. .
Project execution: A Turkish Company will develop and operate the industrial city of Jenin.
Project importance: The project will create thousands of jobs and attract foreign investments; it will support the Palestinian economy.
The main objectives of the project:

For additional analytical, business and investment opportunities information,
please contact Global Investment & Business Center, USA
at (703) 370-8082. Fax: (703) 370-8083. E-mail: ibpusa3@gmail.com
Global Business and Investment Info Databank - www.ibpus.com

To Develop the Palestinian economy.
To Improve and promote Investments in Palestine.
 For more information:
General Authority for Industrial Estates and industrial free zones
Phone: + 970 2 2960351/70/71
Fax: +970 2 2960355

PROCEDURES FOR THE REGISTRATION OF COMPANIES

The Palestinian Government- including its ministries and intuitions , works together to facilitate the procedures of companies registration , through one stop shop that aim to achieve the best and easier services to investors by lower cost.

Service	Requirements for obtaining service	Attachments	Fees
Registration of Ordinary Company (public, ed)	Fill (3 copies) of the company's registration form with the required data, signed by the partners in the presence of the Companies' Controller or Notary public.	Choose a name for the company to be registered, fill it on the prescribed form used for verification of names and obtaining the approval in case the name is not identical with the name of another company on the register. Fill (3copies)of the company's registration form with the required data, signed by the partners in the presence of the Companies' Controller or Notary public. Submit (3 copies) of the company's Articles of Corporation and company's By-laws prepared by an attorney registered at the Palestinian Advocate Syndicate and signed by the partners. Submit copies of the shareholders' identity cards and an attorney's proxy. Copies Identities Partners.	493 NIS: Registration fees 84 NIS: Fee per shareholder in case of signature in the presence of the CompaniesController. 87 NIS: Fees for the verification of the company's name.
Registration of (Public / Private) Shareholding Companies	Fill (3 Copies) form Company Registration signed from Company Controller, or by Lawyer	Proxy attorney registered at the Palestinian Advocate Syndicate. Copies Identities Partners. Contract of establishment (3copies),Internal System of the Company)3copies), List of the partners. Choose a name for the	285 NIS: Registration fees 87 NIS: Fees for the verification of the company's name 84 NIS: Fee per shareholder in case of signature in the presence of the Companies Controller

For additional analytical, business and investment opportunities information,
please contact Global Investment & Business Center, USA
at (703) 370-8082. Fax: (703) 370-8083. E-mail: ibpusa3@gmail.com
Global Business and Investment Info Databank - www.ibpus.com

		company to be registered, fill it on the prescribed form used for verification of names and obtaining the approval in case the name is not identical with the name of another company on the register.	
Registration of Foreign Shareholding Companies	Obtain a work permit by the observer after the approval of the Minister. Application for registration of a foreign company (3 copies) signed by the lawyer by the original company or Commissioner appointed by the Company under the authorization letter certified by the Palestinian embassy or the Palestinian representation in the country of the company. Payment of fees.	Memorandum and an internal system of the original company certified by the Palestinian embassy or the Palestinian representation in the country of the company and whether the original contract language other than Arabic, are in addition to the translated legal translations and ratified by the Ministry of Justice and the State of Palestine. Check and Registration Company Name Approval of the Board of Directors appoints a representative for the company in the areas of the Palestinian Authority and the registration of a foreign company. The company's last budget; The names of the members of the Board of Directors and the nationality each of them.	493 NIS: Registration fees 87 NIS: Fees for the verification of the company's name 84 NIS: Fee per partner in case of signing in the presence of the Companies Controller.
Registration of Non-Profit Companies	Fill Registration form of Non-Profit Companies	Establishment Contract. Company Name including Non-Profit Company. Company Address. Company Capital. Authorized signatory. Names of shareholders and their Nationalities. Any documents that Controller needs it to register company. The Treatment of Non-Profit companies like private shareholding companies through procedures of registration and fees.	285 NIS: Registration fees. 84 NIS: Fee per shareholder in case of signature in the presence of the Companies Controller. 87 NIS: Fees for the verification of the company's name.
Registration of Civil Company	Fill Registration form of Civil Company	Establishment Contract Company Name including Civil Company	493 NIS: Registration fees 84 NIS: Fee per

		Company Address. Company Capital. Authorized signatory. Names of shareholders and their Nationalities. Any documents that Controller needs it to register company. The Treatment of Civil Company like Ordinary companies through procedures of registration and fees	shareholder in case of signature in the presence of the Companies Controller 87 NIS: Fees for the verification of the company's name
Registration of Holding Company	Fill 3 Copies from Company Registration Application signed from Company Controller, or by Lawyer.	proxy attorney registered at the Palestinian Advocate Syndicate if not signed by the partners. Copy of Partners ID Establishment Contract List of founders name Check and Registration Company Name. The Treatment of Holding Company like Public companies through procedures of registration and fees	493 NIS: Registration fees. 84 NIS: Fee per shareholder in case of signature in the presence of the Companies Controller. 87 NIS: Fees for the verification of the company's name.
How to get Service ?	Ministry of National Economy & Or Branch Offices		
Place of service ?	Customer Service Center at Ministry of National Economy & Branch Offices		

FINANCING A BUSINESS IN PALESTINE

The Palestine monetary authority was able to accomplish important steps in order to achieve safety, and high banking confidence in the recent years to reach efficiency and to achieve monetary and financial stability at the regional and international level.

Banking institutions in Palestine(local and foreign):

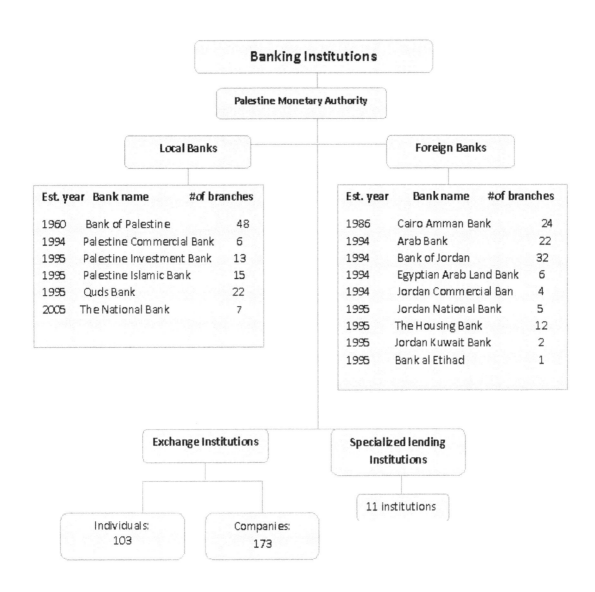

SPECIALIZED LENDING INSTITUTIONS

Most of the specialized lending institutions operating in Palestine are classified as non-profit financial institutions, aiming to contribute to the process of economic development, reduce poverty and unemployment in the community. This sector provides essential financial services to a wide segment of society, in return for guarantees and conditions of concessional credit to conform to simple economic ability of these sectors.

Source: Palestinian Network for Small and micro-lending (partnership).

Deep reforms have been implemented on the policy of these institutions that follow the supervision of the Monetary Authority and Control since 2011; this aims to maintain the safety and effectiveness of these institutions and to ensure the stability of the financial system in Palestine. During 2012, the Monetary Authority issued a number of instructions aimed at regulating management of these institutions, in addition to show the licensing mechanism, and the allowed and prohibited actions.

With the end of the year 2012, the number of specialized lending institutions, and the members in the Palestinian Network for Small and Micro-lending (partnership) are 8 institutions, operating through 62 branches and offices distributed in various areas in the northern and southern provinces.

The net credit portfolio of 84.2 million USD, distributed over different economic sectors that are naturally connected with these institutions and their goals; where in terms of trade and the service sector dominated approximately 38.5% of the loans granted, followed by the consumption sector of 31.3%, agriculture sector by 20.2% and Gaza Industry and Crafts of 10%.

Some programs and funding institutions and lending

More than 25 lending institution within a variety of programs provide facilities through easy and affordable packages to set up projects in Palestine, where these institutions facilitate the access to the necessary funding under flexible conditions and possibilities proportionate with the nature and the ability of the investor.

Institution Name	Telephone	Fax	Email	Website
Palestinian Businesswomen's Association (asala)	+970 2 2400532	+970 2 2402433	asala@palnet.com asala-g@palnet.com	www.asala-pal.com
Reyada	+970 2 2410510	+970 2 2410592	info@ryada.org	www.ryada.org
FATEN	+970 2 2961470/1/3	+970 2 2961472	-	www.faten.org
YMCA	+970 2 2956769	+970 2 2959986	ashalaldeh@ej-ymca.org	www.ej-ymca.org
Reef Finance	+970 2 2951071/84	+970 2 295173		www.reef.ps
Islamic Relief	+972 8 2833343 +970 8 2837889 +970 8 2862228	+970 8 2844606	info@irpal.ps m.east@irworldwide.org	www.irpal.ps
The Palestinian Network for Small and Microfinance - Sharakeh	+970 2 2959388	+970 2 2959395	info@palmfi.ps	www.palmfi.ps

UNDP-DEEP	+970 2 2976101			www.deep.ps www.undp.ps
SME's finance- unrwa	+970 2 2984831/2	+970 2 2984830	s.mshasha@unrwa.org	www.unrwa.org
Arab center for agricultural development-ACAD	+970 2 2409651/60	+970 2 2409652	info@acad.ps	www.acad.ps
Global Communities	+970 2 2413616	+970 2 2413614	info@globalcommunities.ps	www.globalcommunities.ps
Juhoud	+970 2 2811629	+970 2 2811831	info@juhoud.org	www.juhoud.ps
Palestinian banking Institution	+970 2 2969800	+970 2 2969801/11	info@palbabanking.com	www.palbanking.com
International Relief & Development	+970 9 2515199	+970 9 2515099	m_shriedy@yahoo.com ird@ird-dc.org	www.ird.org
Palestinian Economic Council For Development & Reconstruction (Pecdar)	+970 2 2974300 +970 9 2375575	+970 2 2974331	info@pecdar.pna.net ata@pecdar.pna.net	www.pecdar.ps www.pecdar.org
NGO Development Center	+970 2 2347771	+970 2 2347776	info@ndc.ps	http://www.ndc.ps
Palestine Investment Fund- PIF	+970 2 2974971	+970 2 2974976	info@pif.ps	www.pif.ps
Dutch Grant Program				http://www.mne.gov.ps/smes/dutsh.pdf
French Grant Program	+972258289 95		frenshgrant@dgtresor.govu.fr	www.mne.gov.ps/smes/frenches.pdf
Palestinian SME'S Development Program-ITALIAN Loan	+970 2 5327447	+970 2 5322904	sme@itcoop-jer.org	http://www.mne.gov.ps/smes/italy.pdf
Programme for Cooperation with Emerging Markets PSOM	+31 70 7788568			www.mne.gov.ps/pdf/psoma.pdf
USAID- Compete Project	+970 2 2988530	+970 2 2988528	Info_compete@dai.com	www.competeproject.ps
Palestinian Market Development Program-PMDP	+970 2 2986340	+970 2 2959220	info@pmdp.ps	www.pmdp.ps
The European Palestinian Credit Guarantee Fund (EPCGF)	+970 2 2400330 +970 2 2400327	+970 2 240082	info@cgf-palestine.com	www.cgf-palestine.com
PRIDE	+970 2 2960361		info@pride.ps	www.pride.ps

INVESTMENT AND BUSINESS CLIMATE - STRATEGIC INFORMATION AND CONTACTS FOR STARTING BUSINESS

Contact for More Information

NAME: Mary E. Vargas
TITLE: Economic Officer
TELEPHONE NUMBER: +972-2-622-6969
EMAIL ADDRESS: VargasME@state.gov

The Palestinian economy is small and relatively open, with several large holding companies dominating certain sectors. Palestinian businesses have a reputation for professionalism as well as the quality of their products. Large Palestinian enterprises are internationally connected, with partnerships extending to Asia, Europe, the Gulf, and the Americas. Due to the small size of the local market, access to foreign markets through trade is essential for private sector growth.

Since 2007, the West Bank's investment climate has improved significantly – primarily due to security, economic and legal reforms; international donor support, and the easing of some Government of Israel (GOI) restrictions. Many of these reforms, however, were only applicable to business concerns in the roughly 40 percent of the West Bank under the civil control of the Palestinian Authority (PA). Restrictions on the movement and access of goods and people between the West Bank, Gaza, and external markets imposed by the GOI continue to have a deleterious effect on the private sector and limit economic growth.

Opportunities for meaningful foreign direct investment in Gaza are few, due to Hamas's control and Israeli restrictions on the flow of imports and exports. Numerous consumer goods enter Gaza through Israel, but there are restrictions in place that limit the import of a number of dual-use items, including construction materials, which are only allowed to enter with advance coordination and approval from Israel. Likewise, only a few hundred truckloads of exports can exit each year.

Real Gross Domestic Product (GDP) increased by 2.9 percent in 2015: 1.8 percent in the West Bank and 6.5 percent in Gaza, where much of the growth was attributable to increased humanitarian and reconstruction assistance. This GDP growth followed a decline in 2014 that international organizations attributed mainly to that summer's conflict in Gaza, ongoing political disputes with the GOI, uncertainty over the PA's ability to pay salaries, and accumulation of high levels of private sector arrears. In 2015, donor countries provided the PA with USD 709 million to support its budget, about USD 510 million short of the amount needed to cover the PA's recurrent deficit of USD 1.219 billion. The PA covered this financing gap by increasing bank debt and accumulating new private sector and pension fund arrears.

Future economic growth depends on a series of factors: easing Israeli movement and access restrictions, further expanding external trade and private sector growth, improved PA governance on commercial regulation, political stability, the GOI's prompt release of customs and VAT revenues collected on behalf of the PA, and a general recovery of global and regional economic growth. Economic sectors that are not dependent on traditional infrastructure and freedom of movement, such as information and communications technologies (ICT), are able to grow somewhat independent of these factors and therefore have enjoyed greater success in the Palestinian economy during the past decade, although they are still impeded by factors such as GOI control of the electromagnetic spectrum.

According to the PA, the unemployment rate in 2015 was 17.3 percent in the West Bank and 41 percent in Gaza, or 25.9 percent overall. Among women, the overall unemployment rate was 39.2 percent and among youth aged 20-24 it was 36.5 percent (approximately 65 percent in Gaza). The workforce is expected to expand significantly in the coming years, as 50.5 percent of the population is currently below the age of 19. The labor force is relatively well educated, boasting a high literacy rate, with high technology penetration and familiarity with overseas markets. Wages are low relative to Israel but higher than neighboring Arab countries. In January 2013, the PA implemented the first Palestinian minimum wage, at NIS 1,450 (USD 389) per month. Palestinians remain dependent on the public sector, which employs 22.9 percent of the workforce. The PA depends primarily on the transfer of its customs and VAT revenue, which Israel collects on the PA's behalf, to cover its operational expenses, including its wage bill.

Significant sectors highlighted by the Palestinian Investment Promotion Agency (PIPA) and in the National Export Strategy for 2014-2018 include the following:

Stone and marble

Tourism

Agriculture, including olive oil, fresh fruits, vegetables, and herbs

Food and beverage, including agro-processed meat

Textiles and garments

Manufacturing, including furniture and pharmaceuticals

Information and communication technology (ICT)

This report focuses on investment issues related to areas under the administrative jurisdiction of the PA, except where explicitly stated. Where applicable, this report addresses issues related to investment in the Gaza Strip, although Hamas's implementation of PA legislation and regulations may differ significantly from the West Bank. In contrast to the West Bank, Gaza was controlled by Egypt rather than Jordan from 1948-1967, while Israel controlled both the West Bank and Gaza from 1967-1993. For issues where PA law is not applicable, Gazan courts typically refer back to Israeli and Egyptian laws; however, the *de facto* Hamas-led government in Gaza does not consistently apply PA, Egyptian, or Israeli laws. In 2014, Fatah (a major political party) and Hamas initiated a reconciliation process; however, at the time of writing the PA does not exercise operational control within Gaza.

Due to the changing circumstances, potential investors are encouraged to contact the PA Ministry of National Economy (www.mne.gov.ps), Palestinian Investment Promotion Agency (http://www.pipa.gov.ps), the Palestine Trade Center (www.paltrade.org), and the Palestinian-American Chamber of Commerce (www.pal-am.com); as well as the U.S. Consulate General in Jerusalem (http://jerusalem.usconsulate.gov) and the U.S. Commercial Service (http://export.gov/westbank) for the latest information.

Table 1

Measure	Year	Index or Rank	Website Address

TI Corruption Perceptions index	2014	N/A	transparency.org/cpi2014/results
World Bank's Doing Business Report "Ease of Doing Business"	2015	129 of 189	doingbusiness.org/rankings
Global Innovation Index	2015	N/A	globalinnovationindex.org/content/page/data-analysis
U.S. FDI in partner country ($M USD, stock positions)	2015	N/A	BEA/Host government
World Bank GNI per capita	2014	$3,060	data.worldbank.org/indicator/NY.GNP.PCAP.CD

Millennium Challenge Corporation Country Scorecard

The Millennium Challenge Corporation, a U.S. Government entity charged with delivering development grants to countries that have demonstrated a commitment to reform, has not produced a scorecard for the West Bank and Gaza.

1. OPENNESS TO, AND RESTRICTIONS UPON, FOREIGN INVESTMENT

Attitude toward Foreign Direct Investment

The PA continues to rank poorly in the World Bank's Ease of Doing Business report, receiving a ranking of 129 out of 189 in 2016 (compared to 127 in 2015) due to a challenging business environment affecting domestic and foreign investors alike. The 2016 Doing Business Report scored the Palestinian economy particularly low in the categories of Resolving Insolvency (189 of 189), Staring a Business (170 of 189), and Dealing with Construction Permits (162 of 189), while the PA performed relatively better with respect to Paying Taxes (56 of 189) and Getting Electricity (75 of 189). However, there are no significant PA laws or practices discriminating against foreign investors. In 2007, the PA began implementing reforms aimed at stimulating growth through private sector investment as well as consolidating public finances. The current 2014-2016 National Development Plan (NDP), like its predecessor, focuses on four sectors: economic development and employment, governance and institution building, social protection, and infrastructure. Within the economic sector, the NDP actively seeks to encourage private sector and foreign investment, improve Palestinian infrastructure, increase the competitiveness of Palestinian companies, and encourage entrepreneurship in the West Bank and Gaza, among other goals. The NDP caveats that any economic progress is inextricably linked to resolution of the political conflict with Israel, as well as overcoming internal divisions between the West Bank and Gaza. The PA is currently preparing a National Policy Agenda (NPA) to replace the NDP and outline priorities beyond 2016.

Since June of 2010, the PA has not hosted any major investment conference, although it did so in previous years. The 2010 conference attracted over 1,000 potential investors and business representatives. Over 100 projects were presented at the conference. Further information on these and other projects is available at www.pic-palestine.ps.

Beginning in 1995, the PA took steps to facilitate and increase foreign trade by signing free trade agreements with the European Union, the European Free Trade Association (EFTA), Canada, and Turkey. The PA also is eligible for the benefits of the Free Trade Agreement signed between the United States and Israel. The PA has finalized other trade agreements with Russia, Jordan, Egypt, the Gulf States, Morocco, Tunisia, Mercosur, Vietnam, and Germany. On July 31, 2012

Israel and the Palestinian Authority reached an understanding on trade and taxation designed to facilitate the flow of goods between Israel and the PA, reduce smuggling, and increase tax revenues to be shared by both parties. Additionally, the PA is preparing to seek permanent observer status in the World Trade Organization (WTO); it participated in the 2005, 2009, 2011, 2013, and 2015 WTO Ministerial meetings as an ad hoc observer.

Other Investment Policy Reviews

Beginning in 2013, the Office of the Quartet (OQ), an international organization working to support the Palestinian people on economic development, rule of law and improved movement and access for goods and people, began work on the Initiative for the Palestinian Economy (IPE), a multi-year plan to engage the private sector to drive economic growth and job creation across the Palestinian territories. Based on rigorous analysis of the Palestinian investment climate, the IPE focuses on catalyzing private sector-led growth by leveraging new financing and investment into the Palestinian economy, continued and expanded Israeli easing measures, and increased institutional capacity within the PA. The IPE centers on eight sectors: (1) agriculture; (2) construction; (3) tourism; (4) information and communication technology (ICT); (5) light manufacturing; (6) building materials; (7) energy; and (8) water.

During the current impasse in political negotiations, OQ has continued to work on advancing economic development and application of the rule of law, giving priority to areas where accomplishments are most viable under current conditions. Looking ahead, OQ's forward priorities focus on five strategic pillars that represent the fundamental impact areas that contribute to economic growth and capacity building: (i) movement and trade; (ii) investment promotion; (iii) reliable infrastructure; (iv) unlocking value of land and human capital; and (v) strengthening government. A summary overview of the Initiative for the Palestinian Economy is available at http://blair.3cdn.net/a0302ab9e588825b29_1bm6yhjay.pdf.

The Organization for Economic Cooperation and Development (OECD), the World Trade Organization (WTO), and the United Nations Conference on Trade and Development (UNCTAD) do not provide investment policy reviews for the West Bank and Gaza.

Laws/Regulations on Foreign Direct Investment

Since 2006, there have been no general elections, and the Palestinian Legislative Council (PLC) has not met since April 2007. This means that any new laws or amendments must be issued by presidential decree. In the absence of a renewed political mandate or the endorsement of a legislative body, the PA has been reluctant to issue new laws that it does not view as immediately necessary. For amendments and changes to business regulations, the PA normally engages in a series of consultations involving ministry officials, the private sector, donors, and other stakeholders, resulting in lengthy delays for many key pieces of legislation. The United States Government (USG), through the U.S. Agency for International Development (USAID) and other agencies, is providing technical assistance to the PA to improve the investment climate and strengthen the trade regime through legislative reforms, improved regulations, and capacity building.

The legal framework for foreign investment in the West Bank and Gaza is based on the 1998 Law on the Encouragement of Investment in Palestine (Investment Law) No. 1, which was amended by Presidential Decree in 2011 and subsequently in 2014. All business entities must be registered with PIPA's registry of investments either in the West Bank or in Gaza. There is minimal executive or other interference in the court system. According to existing PA company laws, three different types of companies may be incorporated:

General Partnership: The liability of each partner in a general partnership is unlimited. All partners are personally responsible for the liabilities of the partnership. The name of at least one of the partners must be included in the title of the General Partnership.

Limited Partnership: This includes two different types of partners: general and limited. A limited partnership must have at least one general partner who is personally responsible for the liabilities of the company. There is also at least one limited partner whose liability is limited to the amount of the capital.

Local Companies (Limited Liability Company (LLC) and Public Liability): Most investors prefer to use LLCs for the purposes of conducting commercial affairs.

Business Registration

Foreign companies may register businesses in the West Bank and Gaza according to the Jordanian Companies Law Number 12 of 1964. The Ministry of National Economy (MONE) and the PIPA provide information online about the business registration process at http://www.mne.gov.ps/compreg.aspx?lng=1&tabindex=100 and http://www.pipa.ps/page.aspx?id=BMfDyia1843545561aBMfDyi, but the PA does not offer a business registration website. The PA is working to simplify the process of starting a business, which currently requires an average of nine steps and 44 days to complete, according to the World Bank's 2016 Doing Business Report. This includes two days to register the company, one day to pay registration fees, two days to register for taxes, one day to register with the Chamber of Commerce, and 36 days to obtain the business license from the Municipality. Foreign investors must obtain approval from the MONE and submit the application for registration through a local attorney. The procedures required to register this form of company are as follows:

Search for company name and reserve proposed name.

Submit company incorporation papers to MONE and sign document pledging to deposit initial capital within three months, if applicable (Jordanian Dinars (JD) 250,000 for a public shareholding company, JD 10,000 for a private shareholding company, or JD 10,000 for a nonprofit; other companies are exempt from this requirement). Obtain certificate of registration from the MONE.

Register with the Companies Registry and pay registration fee.

Register for income tax and value added tax.

Register with the Chamber of Commerce.

Obtain business license from the municipality.

Obtain approval from fire department.

In addition to applicable fees, public and private companies must submit the following documents to the Companies Registry:

Articles of Association (3 copies)

Company Bylaws (3 copies)

Shareholders Identification (copies)

Verified company name

Registration application (3 copies)

Powers of attorney

Foreign companies may work with PIPA to obtain the investment registration certificate and investment confirmation certificate. In addition, foreign companies seeking to open branches in the West Bank or Gaza must submit registration documents certified by the Palestinian Liberation Organization (PLO) representative in their home country. According to PIPA, the majority of Palestinian companies are small- and medium-sized enterprises (SMEs), and the PA has sought to support SME development and financing. SMEs are categorized according to staff size: small enterprises employ up to nine people, while medium enterprises employ 10-19 people.

Industrial Promotion

The PA's 2014 amendments to Promotion of Investment in Palestine Law No. 1 of 1998 shifted promotional incentives from a focus on those that benefit from industrial projects providing large capital investments to a focus on employment growth, development of human capital, increased exports, and local sourcing of machinery and raw materials. (See "Investment Incentives" below.)

Limits on Foreign Control and Right to Private Ownership and Establishment

Under the Jordanian Company Law of 1966, the foreign investor should own no more than 49 percent of a company, with a local partner holding at least 51 percent. However, foreign investors can readily obtain exceptions to this policy by working with PIPA and the MONE, which issues exceptions promptly. Foreign and domestic private entities may establish and own business enterprises in areas under PA civil control.

Privatization Program

There is no PA privatization program for industries within the Palestinian Territories.

Screening of FDI

Certain investment categories require pre-approval by the Council of Ministers (PA Cabinet). These include investments involving (1) weapons and ammunition, (2) aviation products and airport construction, (3) electrical power generation/distribution, (4) reprocessing of petroleum and its derivatives, (5) waste and solid waste reprocessing, (6) wired and wireless telecommunication, and (7) radio and television. Purchase of land by foreigners also requires approval by the Council of Ministers.

Competition Law

There is no competition law for the Palestinian territories at this time. The PA drafted a law in 2003 that was not enacted, and in 2012 the PA prepared a new draft law that has not yet been issued. Because of the geographic division between businesses in East Jerusalem, the West Bank and Gaza, many firms in disparate geographic locations within the Palestinian territories

For additional analytical, business and investment opportunities information,
please contact Global Investment & Business Center, USA
at (703) 370-8082. Fax: (703) 370-8083. E-mail: ibpusa3@gmail.com
Global Business and Investment Info Databank - www.ibpus.com

have little to no competition, causing variations in both pricing and firm productivity between regions and sometimes cities within a region.

2. CONVERSION AND TRANSFER POLICIES

Foreign Exchange

The PA does not have its own currency. According to the 1995 Interim Agreement, the Israeli Shekel (NIS/ILS) freely circulates in the Palestinian territories and serves as means of payment for all purposes including official transactions. The exchange of foreign currency for NIS and vice-versa by the Palestinian Monetary Authority (PMA) is carried out through the Bank of Israel Dealing Room, at market exchange rates.

Remittance Policies

The Investment Law guarantees investors the free transfer of all financial resources out of the Palestinian territories, including capital, profits, dividends, wages, salaries, and interest and principal payments on debts. Most remittances under USD 10,000 can be processed within a week. In addition to the Israeli Shekel (ILS), U.S. dollars (USD) and Jordanian dinars (JD) are widely used in business transactions. There are no other PA restrictions governing foreign currency accounts and currency transfer policies. Banks operating in the Palestinian territories, however, are subject to Israeli restrictions on correspondent relations with Israeli banks and the ability to transfer shekels into Israel, which occasionally limit services such as wire transfers and foreign exchange transactions.

3. EXPROPRIATION AND COMPENSATION

The Investment Law, as amended in 2014, prohibits expropriation and nationalization of approved foreign investments, except in exceptional cases for a public purpose with due process of law, which shall be in return for fair compensation based on market prices and for losses suffered because of such expropriation. The PA must secure a court decision before proceeding with expropriation.

PA sources and independent lawyers say that any Palestinian citizen can file a petition or a lawsuit against the PA. In 2011, the PA established independent, specialized courts for labor, chambers, customs, and anti-corruption. These courts are composed of judges and representatives from the Ministries of National Economy and Finance. While general confidence in the judicial system is improving and businesses are increasingly using the courts and police to enforce contracts and seek redress, alternative means of arbitration are still used to resolve some disputes.

4. DISPUTE SETTLEMENT

Legal System, Specialized Courts, Judicial Independence, Judgments of Foreign Courts

The Investment Law, as amended in 2014, provides for dispute resolution between the investor and official agencies either through binding arbitration or in Palestinian domestic courts. In 2010, the International Chamber of Commerce Palestine began work to establish the Jerusalem Arbitration Center (JAC) to provide a forum to resolve business disputes between Palestinian and Israeli companies; it officially launched in November 2013.

Commercial disputes can be resolved by way of conciliation, mediation, or domestic arbitration. Arbitration in the Palestinian territories is governed by Law No. 3 of 2000. International arbitration is accepted. The law sets out the basis for court recognition and enforcement of arbitral awards. Generally, every dispute may be referred to arbitration by agreement of the parties, unless prohibited by the law. Article 4 of the law states that certain disputes cannot be referred to arbitration, including those involving marital status, public order issues, and cases where no conciliation is permitted. In the event that parties do not agree on the formation of the arbitration tribunal, each party may choose one arbitrator and arbitrators shall then choose a presiding arbitrator, unless the parties agree to do otherwise.

Judgments made in other countries that need to be enforced in the West Bank/Gaza are honored, according to the prevailing law in the West Bank, mainly Jordanian Law No. 8 of 1952 as amended by the PA in 2005. Gazan courts refer back to Israeli and Egyptian laws, which were in force prior to 1993, for matters not covered by PA law; however, the *de facto* Hamas-led government in Gaza does not consistently apply PA, Egyptian, or Israeli laws. The law covers many issues in relation to the enforcement of foreign judgments.

Bankruptcy

The World Bank's 2016 Doing Business Report did not cite any cases involving a judicial reorganization, judicial liquidation, or debt enforcement procedure (foreclosure) in the previous five years. According to that report, no priority is assigned to post-commencement creditors, and debtors may file for liquidation only. The PA MONE, with the assistance of international donors, is in the process of drafting a number of proposed laws related to bankruptcy, but no bankruptcy reform has been enacted.

Investment Disputes

The Investment Law, as amended in 2014, provides for dispute resolution between the investor and official agencies by binding independent arbitration or in Palestinian courts. It has been reported that some contracts contain clauses referring dispute resolutions to the London Court of Arbitration. The Jerusalem Arbitration Center (JAC) provides a forum to resolve business disputes between Palestinian and Israeli companies. Commercial disputes may be resolved by way of conciliation, mediation, or arbitration.

International Arbitration

International arbitration is permitted and governed by governed by Law No. 3 of 2000. The law sets out the basis for court recognition and enforcement of awards. Generally, every dispute may be referred to arbitration by the agreement of the parties, unless prohibited by the law. Article 4 of the law states that certain disputes cannot be referred to arbitration, including those involving marital status, public order issues, and cases where no conciliation is permitted. In the event that parties do not agree on the formation of the arbitration panel, each party may choose an arbitrator and arbitrators shall choose a casting arbitrator unless the parties agree to proceed otherwise. Arbitral awards made in other countries that need to be enforced in the West Bank/Gaza are honored, according to the prevailing law in the West Bank, mainly Jordanian Law Number 8 of 1952 as amended by the PA in 2005. The law covers many issues in relation to the enforcement of foreign judgments.

ICSID Convention and New York Convention

The PA signed the Convention on the Recognition and Enforcement of Foreign Arbitral Awards (New York Convention) in January 2015, and the Convention entered into force in April 2015. The PA is not a member of the Convention on the Settlement of Investment Disputes between States and Nationals of Other States (ICSID Convention).

Duration of Dispute Resolution – Local Courts

In 2014 the IMF reported an average of 540 days to resolve a standardized commercial dispute through the courts, with 44 separate procedures required for a dispute resolution. Litigants suggested that the decisions at different levels of the courts were inconsistent, prompting more appeals and a larger overall caseload.

5. PERFORMANCE REQUIREMENTS AND INVESTMENT INCENTIVES

WTO/TRIMS

The PA is not a member of the World Trade Organization (WTO), but is actively preparing for eventual permanent observer status, and participated in the 2005, 2009, 2011, 2013, and 2015 WTO Ministerial meetings as an ad hoc observer.

Investment Incentives

In 2014, by presidential degree, PA President Abbas, in order to align the PA's development priorities with the investment incentives provided by Palestinian law, enacted amendments to the Promotion of Investment in Palestine Law No. 1 of 1998, the investment and tax law. These amendments extended tax incentives to small and medium companies, exporters, and agriculture and tourist businesses; and shifted the focus towards incentives on human capital instead of fixed assets. The amendments add tourism and agricultural projects to qualifying industries, and removed real estate development projects from the industries promoted through the incentives. The amendments also gave additional authority to the PIPA to create incentive packages targeted to individual business needs (www.pipa.ps). PIPA expects the changes to create streamlined investment and incentive processes to circumvent some PA bureaucratic red tape to obtain investment project licenses. For example, if any step in the business registration process takes longer than 30 days, PIPA can intervene and issue a business license or registration on its own authority.

The 2014 amendment to Article 23 of the Promotion of Investment in Palestine Law No. 1 of 1998 granted the following incentives and exemptions for projects approved by PIPA:

Income tax of zero percent for producers of agricultural products whose income is directly generated from land cultivation or livestock.

Income tax of five percent for a period of five years commencing from the date of realizing profit but not exceeding four years, whichever is earlier.

Income tax of ten percent for a period of three years commencing from the end of the first phase. It will thereafter be calculated based on the applicable and in-effect percentages and segments.

Projects that may be targeted for taxation incentives and support services include the following:

Industrial sector projects;

Tourism sector projects;

New projects within any sector that employ at least 25 workers during the period of benefit;

Projects that increase their production exports ratio by more than 40 percent;

Projects within any sector which use approximately 70 percent locally-sourced machinery and raw materials;

Any existing project that adds 25 workers to the number of already existing workers;

Developmental expansions of projects (to be based on percentage of paid-in capital but not land value);

Projects in which the PIPA Board of Directors provides specific incentive packages that comply with special criteria, meet international environment conditions or alternative energy services, or are projects located within areas of developmental priorities.

Any project determined by PIPA's Board of Directors to advance the public interest (subject to the nature of a project's activity, geographical location, the extent to which the project contributes to increasing exports, creating job opportunities, advancing development, transferring knowledge, and supporting research and development for the purposes of enhancing the public benefit).

Excluded from the incentives are:

Commercial projects;
Insurance companies;
Banks;
Money changers;
Real estate projects;
Some electricity projects;
Telecommunication services;
Commercial services;
Crushers;
Quarries;

Any companies that obtained concessions contracts from the Council of Ministers and operate as monopolistic companies.

Research and Development

U.S. and other foreign firms are able to participate in partnerships with the PA for research and development programs. (Note: Because of the PA's budgetary restrictions, much of the financing for such projects typically comes from donor countries or NGOs and not the PA itself.)

Performance Requirements

The current performance requirements for investment incentives have reduced the focus on a capital investment requirement and now focus on job growth and locally-sourced production.

For additional analytical, business and investment opportunities information,
please contact Global Investment & Business Center, USA
at (703) 370-8082. Fax: (703) 370-8083. E-mail: ibpusa3@gmail.com
Global Business and Investment Info Databank - www.ibpus.com

While the PA does not require foreign nationals working in the West Bank to seek work permits, the GOI does require foreigners to obtain Israeli visas in order to enter the West Bank and Gaza via Israel. Israel generally grants foreign passport holders from countries that have diplomatic relations with Israel three-month tourist visas upon arrival, but longer-term business visas may only be obtained by businesses or organizations with an Israeli presence. Israel often requires foreign passport holders of Palestinian descent to apply for Palestinian ID cards. Israeli authorities may consider as Palestinian anyone who has a Palestinian identification number, was born in the West Bank or Gaza, or was born in the United States (or elsewhere) but has parents or grandparents who were born or lived in the West Bank or Gaza. Any such U.S. citizen may be required to use a Palestinian travel document and enter via the Allenby Bridge crossing on the Jordanian border instead of Ben Gurion Airport in Tel Aviv. If they decide not to obtain a PA travel document, such Americans may be barred from entering or exiting Israel, the West Bank or Gaza, face long delays, or be denied entry at the ports of entry. Palestinian-Americans holding Palestinian IDs and PA exit permits may depart via the Allenby Crossing between Jordan and the West Bank, provided they have valid Jordanian visas in their U.S. passports.

According to the GOI, foreign nationals working in the West Bank should either apply for work visas at Israeli embassies in their countries of origin or seek adjustment of status through the Israeli Coordinator of Government Activities in the Territories (COGAT) after their arrival in the West Bank. This process, however, is opaque, time consuming, and may not result in issuance of a work visa. As a result, many foreign passport holders depart and reenter the West Bank every three months to receive new three-month tourist visas upon re-entry. The GOI has placed a stamp reading "Judea & Samaria Only" on the visas of some U.S. citizens working in the West Bank, thereby prohibiting them from entering Israel or Jerusalem from the West Bank. The United States government continues to press the GOI to cease this policy.

Data Storage

There are no data storage requirements under PA law for IT companies. The PA does not follow a forced localization policy, and there are no requirements for foreign IT providers to turn over source code or provide access to surveillance.

6. PROTECTION OF PROPERTY RIGHTS

Real Property

The Acquisition Law in the West Bank, which regulates foreign acquisition and the rental or lease of immovable properties, classifies foreigners into three categories:

Foreigners who formerly possessed Palestinian or Jordanian passports shall have the right to own certain properties sufficient to erect buildings and/or for their agricultural projects.

Foreigners who hold other Arab passports have the right to own certain property that suffices for their living and business needs only.

Other foreigners, including Jerusalem ID holders, must receive permission from the PA Cabinet to own buildings or purchase land.

The permission process can be lengthy and includes clearances from the intelligence and preventive security agencies. It is critical that potential purchasers of land or buildings perform a title search to ensure that no outstanding violations or unpaid penalties exist on the properties. Under current law, outstanding violations and penalties are transferred to the new owners.

For additional analytical, business and investment opportunities information,
please contact Global Investment & Business Center, USA
at (703) 370-8082. Fax: (703) 370-8083. E-mail: ibpusa3@gmail.com
Global Business and Investment Info Databank - www.ibpus.com

Title searches can only be obtained from the PA Land Authority (al-Taboh). Land registration is done through the Land Registries in Hebron, Ramallah, Qalqiliya, Tulkarem, Nablus, Bethlehem, Jericho, Jenin, and Gaza City. In order to purchase land in the West Bank or Gaza, an application that includes supporting documents, such as deeds to the property and powers of attorney, should be submitted to the land registry office having jurisdiction over the land.

The issue of land registration in the West Bank is complicated by overlapping, and sometimes conflicting, laws and customs derived from the Ottoman, British Mandate, and Jordanian periods of rule. In addition, there is no comprehensive registry of land ownership for the West Bank, and efforts to complete one are expected to take decades at the current pace. The majority of the land has not been registered; even where land is registered, titles are often more than a generation old, with unresolved rights to numerous inheritors, which affects the mortgage market. The Palestinian Land Authority has been working with support from the Government of Finland and the World Bank on land titling and registration. Israeli administrative control over 60 percent of the West Bank designated as "Area C" adds an additional layer of bureaucracy and restrictions with respect to sale and use of privately held lands in those areas.

Intellectual Property Rights

The West Bank and Gaza do not have modern intellectual property rights (IPR) regimes in place, and IPR legislation originates from a combination of Ottoman era, British Mandate, and pre-1967 Jordanian laws. The PA was indirectly committed to the General Agreement on Tariffs and Trade and the agreement of Trade Related Aspects of Intellectual Property Rights (GATT-TRIPS) when it signed the 1995 Interim Agreement on West Bank/Gaza according to Annex III (Protocol Concerning Civil Affairs), Appendix 1, Article 23.

Currently, intellectual property is governed by the Civil Claims Law of 1933 and the Palestinian Trademark and Patent Laws of 1938 in Gaza, and the Commercial Law No. 19 of 1953 and the Patent Law No. 22 of 1953 in the West Bank. Registration is very similar and, despite different authorizing legislation, there are few substantive differences between IPR laws in the West Bank and Gaza.

To register a trademark, four copies of the proposed trademark must be attached to the application, one of them in color, along with a copy of the company's Certificate of Registration. A foreign company is entitled to register its trademark in the Palestinian territories by giving power of attorney in this regard either to a trademark agent or to a lawyer. Trademarks can be registered unless they fall within the recognized prohibition, such as being similar or identical to an already registered trademark, are likely to lead to deception of the public, or are contrary to public morality. Trademark protection is available for registered trademarks for a period of seven years, which may be extended for additional periods of 14 years. The proprietor of a trademark in the West Bank/Gaza owns the sole right to the use of the trademark in association with the goods with which the trademark is registered. The trademark is open for opposition after being published in the Gazette for a period of three months. The holder of a trademark retains the right to bring civil action against any perpetrator in addition to criminal proceedings.

Trade names are registered by the PA according to specific procedures and conditions that are laid out in the Jordanian Trade Names Registration Law No. 30 of 1953, which is still applicable in the West Bank, and Law No. 1 of 1929 in Gaza.

The Patents and Design Law No. 22 of 1953 is applicable in the West Bank and the Patents Design Law No. 64 of 1947 is applicable in Gaza. A foreign company is entitled to have a patent or design registered by giving power of attorney in this regard to a patent agent or to a lawyer, with the requisite documents. Patent protection is provided for a period of 16 years from the date of filing the patent application.

Copyright in the West Bank and Gaza is governed by the Copyright Laws of 1911 and 1924. The protection lasts for a period of 50 years after the death of the author of the work. The law also deals with infringements, compulsory licenses, and many other procedural issues as well.

The law prescribes imprisonment for a maximum period of one year or a fine not exceeding 100 Jordanian dinars for infringement of a registered mark.

There is minimal enforcement of IPR laws for music and movies in the West Bank/Gaza, while the PA has enforced some of these laws to protect the Palestinian pharmaceutical industry. The PA has drafted a modern law that will encompass IPR, including copyright, patents and designs, trademarks, and merchandise branding, but the law has not yet been adopted in the absence of a functioning legislature. The PA is keen to obtain membership in the different organizations and agreements concerned with intellectual property, such as the World Trade Organization (WTO) and the World Intellectual Property Organization; it has held observer status in the latter since 2005.

Resources for Rights Holders

Contact at American Consulate General in Jerusalem:
NAME: Mary E. Vargas
TITLE: Economic Officer
TELEPHONE NUMBER: +972-2-622-6969
EMAIL ADDRESS: VargasME@state.gov

Country/Economy resources:

NAME: The Palestinian American Chamber of Commerce
ADDRESS: PCS Bldg. 1st Floor, Al Ma'ahed St. Al Masyoun, Ramallah
TELEPHONE NUMBER: +972-2-297-4117
EMAIL ADDRESS: info@amcham.ps
WEBSITE: http://www.pal-am.com

7. TRANSPARENCY OF THE REGULATORY SYSTEM

The PA has worked to erect a sound legislative framework for business and other economic activity in the areas under its jurisdiction since its creation in 1994; however, implementation and monitoring of implementation needs to be strengthened, according to many observers. The PA MONE, with the assistance of international donors, is in the process of drafting a number of proposed laws related to business and commercial regulation, including licensing, intellectual property rights, business registration regulation of competition, secured lending, bankruptcy, and trademark and copyright. The MONE regularly holds stakeholder meetings for draft commercial legislation to gather input from the private sector, and publishes drafts of the proposed law. Because the Palestinian Legislative Council has not met since 2007, each law must be adopted as a presidential decree, an effort that often delays reform efforts. The proposed laws will likely need to be approved by the PLC, should it reconvene in the future. The PA Ministry of Justice, in cooperation with Birzeit University, publishes online the Official Gazette of all PA legislation since 1994 at http://muqtafi.birzeit.edu/en/index.aspx.

For additional analytical, business and investment opportunities information,
please contact Global Investment & Business Center, USA
at (703) 370-8082. Fax: (703) 370-8083. E-mail: ibpusa3@gmail.com
Global Business and Investment Info Databank - www.ibpus.com

The PA budget is publicly available, including on the Ministry of Finance website. A regulatory body governs the insurance sector, and the PA has adopted a telecom law that calls for establishment of an independent regulator. However, establishment of the telecom regulator has stalled due to disagreement over its proposed members and authorities.

8. EFFICIENT CAPITAL MARKETS AND PORTFOLIO INVESTMENT

In 2004, the PA enacted the Capital Markets Authority Law and the Securities Commission Law, and created the Capital Market Authority to regulate the stock exchange, insurance, leasing, and mortgage industries. In 2010, a banking law was adopted to bring the Palestinian Monetary Authority's (PMA) regulatory capabilities in line with the Basel Accords, a set of recommendations for regulations in the banking industry. The 2010 law provides a legal framework for the establishment of deposit insurance, management of the Real Time Gross Settlement (RTGS) system, and treatment of weak banks in areas such as merger, liquidation, and guardianship. It also gives the PMA regulatory authority over the microfinance sector. In 2013, the PA passed a commercial leasing law and in 2015 the MONE finalized a registry for moveable assets, intended to facilitate secured transactions, especially for small and medium-sized businesses. The PA is also working to finalize both a Companies Law and a Secured Transactions law, both of which are currently under review by interagency panels. Implementation of these laws would help improve the investment climate and the ease of doing business. The World Bank 2016 Doing Business report assigned the West Bank and Gaza a particularly low score for protecting minority investors, resolving insolvency, and obtaining credit. Founders of new SMEs complain that loan terms from Palestinian creditors are often too short in that they fail to allow the borrower enough time to establish a sustainable business. The new Moveable Assets Registry, coupled with the Commercial Leasing Law, is expected to improve the ranking.

The Palestine Exchange (PEX) was established in 1995 to promote investment in the West Bank and Gaza Launched as a private shareholding company, it was transformed into a public shareholding company in February 2010. The PEX was fully automated upon establishment – the first fully automated stock exchange in the Arab world, and the only Arab exchange that is publicly traded and fully owned by the private sector. The PEX operates under the supervision of the Palestinian Capital Market Authority. There are 49 listed companies on the PEX, which as of 2016 had a market capitalization of about $3.339 billion across five main economic sectors: banking and financial services, insurance, investments, industry, and services.

Money and Banking System, Hostile Takeovers

The Palestinian banking sector continues to perform well under the supervision of the PMA. The World Bank's reports to the Ad Hoc Liaison Committee (AHLC) have consistently noted that the PMA is effectively supervising the banking sector. The PMA continues to enhance its institutional capacity and is steadily building many of the capabilities of a central bank. It provides rigorous supervision and regulation of the banking sector, consistent with international practice. An Anti-Money Laundering law that was prepared in line with international standards with technical assistance from the International Monetary Fund (IMF) and USAID came into force in October 2007. In December 2015 the PA President signed the Anti-Money Laundering and Terrorism Financing Decree Law Number 20. Among its many improvements over the 2007 decree was to make terrorist financing a criminal offense and to define terrorists, terrorist acts, terrorist organizations, foreign terrorist fighters, and terrorist financing. It also makes terrorism and terrorist acts predicate money laundering offenses.

Credit is limited by uncertain political and economic conditions and by the limited availability of real estate collateral due to non-registration of most West Bank land. Despite these challenges,

For additional analytical, business and investment opportunities information,
please contact Global Investment & Business Center, USA
at (703) 370-8082. Fax: (703) 370-8083. E-mail: ibpusa3@gmail.com
Global Business and Investment Info Databank - www.ibpus.com

the sector's strong loan-to-deposit ratio continues to improve, moving from 56 percent in January 2015 to 59 percent in January 2016. The PMA has achieved this in part by encouraging banks to participate in loan guarantee programs sponsored by the United States and international financial institutions, by supporting a national strategy on microfinance, and by putting in restrictions on foreign placements. The MONE's draft Secured Transactions Law would allow use of moveable assets, such as equipment, as collateral for loans. Non-performing loans are around three percent of total loans, due to credit bureau assessments of borrowers' credit worthiness and a heavy collateral system.

Palestinian banks have remained stable despite the global economic crisis, but have suffered from deteriorated relations with Israeli correspondent banks since the Hamas takeover of Gaza in 2007, at which time Israeli banks cut ties with Gaza branches and gradually restricted cash services provided to West Bank branches. All Palestinian banks were required to move their headquarters to Ramallah in 2008. Israeli restrictions on the movement of cash between West Bank and Gaza branches of Palestinian banks have caused intermittent liquidity crises in Gaza and the West Bank for all major currencies: U.S. dollars, Jordanian dinars, but mainly Israeli shekels (ILS).

The PMA regulates and supervises 15 banks with 260 branches and offices in the West Bank and Gaza, several of which are foreign banks, mostly Jordanian; the top three banks have assets of more than USD 5.8 billion combined. No Palestinian currency exists and, as a result, the PA places no restrictions on foreign currency accounts. The PMA is responsible for bank regulation in both the West Bank and Gaza. Palestinian banks are some of the most liquid in the region, with net assets of USD 12.4 billion, total deposits of USD 9.7 billion and gross credit of USD 5.8 billion as of the end of January 2016.

9. COMPETITION FROM STATE-OWNED ENTERPRISES

Although there are no state-owned enterprises (SOEs), some observers have noted that the Palestine Investment Fund (PIF), an investment fund that essentially acts as a sovereign wealth fund for the PA, enjoys a competitive advantage in some sectors, including housing and telecom, due to its close ties with the PA. The import of petroleum products falls solely under the mandate of the Ministry of Finance's General Petroleum Corporation, which then re-sells the products to private distributors at fixed prices.

Sovereign Wealth Funds

The PIF acts as a sovereign wealth fund, owned by the Palestinian people. According to PIF's 2014 annual report, its assets that year reached USD 795 million; earnings before taxes were USD 44 million, and net income was USD 36.7 million. PIF's investments in 2014 were concentrated in infrastructure, energy, telecommunications, real estate and hospitality, micro/small/medium enterprises, large caps, and capital market investments. The overwhelming majority of PIF investments are domestic, but excess liquidity is invested in international and regional fixed income and equity markets. In 2014 the fund established the Palestine for Development Foundation, a separate not-for-profit foundation managing PIF's corporate social responsibility initiatives, which are primarily focused on support to Palestinians in the West Bank, Gaza, Jerusalem, and abroad. Since 2003, PIF has transferred over USD 728 million to the PA in annual dividends, but the PIF leadership does not report to the PA per PIF bylaws. International auditing firms conduct both internal and external annual audits of the PIF.

For additional analytical, business and investment opportunities information,
please contact Global Investment & Business Center, USA
at (703) 370-8082. Fax: (703) 370-8083. E-mail: ibpusa3@gmail.com
Global Business and Investment Info Databank - www.ibpus.com

10. RESPONSIBLE BUSINESS CONDUCT

Most large or multinational businesses in the West Bank include corporate social responsibility (CSR) in their business plans, mainly focusing on philanthropy related to education, health, and youth. Some medium sized enterprises, particularly in healthcare and the food industry, started CSR initiatives to create goodwill for their products. CSR engagement remains relatively low because most companies are small, family-run businesses – over 68 percent of Palestinian companies employ one or two people – and many of these do not have the budgetary resources for CSR.

11. POLITICAL VIOLENCE

The security environment remains complex in the West Bank, and Gaza. The security situation can change day to day, depending on the political situation, recent events, and geographic area. Potential investors should consult the State Department's latest travel warnings available at https://travel.state.gov.

Violent clashes between Israeli security forces, Israeli settlers, and Palestinian residents of the West Bank have resulted in numerous deaths and injuries. Demonstrations and violent incidents can occur without warning, and vehicles are sometimes damaged by rocks, Molotov cocktails, and gunfire on West Bank roads. During periods of unrest, the Israeli government may restrict access to and within the West Bank, and some areas may be placed under curfew. In June 2007, Hamas, a designated Foreign Terrorist Organization (FTO), violently seized control of the Gaza Strip, effectively removing the PA from government facilities. Following the Hamas takeover, the GOI implemented a closure policy that restricted imports to limited humanitarian and commercial shipments and cut off most exports. The economic situation and investment outlook in Gaza have continuously deteriorated since that time, especially following Israeli combat operations there in December 2008-January 2009 (Operation Cast Lead), November 2012 (Operation Pillar of Defense) and July-August 2014 (Operation Protective Edge). Even before the substantial physical damage sustained by the private sector during the military operations, the World Bank estimated as many as 90 percent of private sector businesses had closed. The GOI has from time to time eased its closure policy by lifting some restrictions on goods imported into and exported out of Gaza, but the measures have been largely symbolic and the situation remains unstable. The GOI allows limited exports to overseas markets, Israel and some sales to the West Bank. According to the 2014 World Bank Investment Climate report, political instability and the restrictions on movement and access to resource and markets remain the key obstacles to investment.

12. CORRUPTION

The Anti-Graft Law (AGL) of 2005 criminalizes corruption, and the State Audit and Administrative Control Law and the Civil Service Law both aim to prevent favoritism, conflict of interest, or exploitation of position for personal gain. The AGL was amended in 2010 to establish a specialized anti-graft court and the Palestinian Anti-Corruption Commission, which was tasked with collecting, investigating, and prosecuting allegations of public corruption. The Anti-Corruption Commission, appointed in 2010, has indicted several high-profile PA officials; these cases are now pending before the courts. However, the PLC, which is responsible for oversight of the PA's executive branch, has not met since April 2007. In May 2011, the World Bank reported that the PA had made significant progress in establishing a strong governance environment in many critical areas, but highlighted continuing areas of concern, including management of state land assets, transparency in licensing and business rights, and public access to government information. Palestinian civil society and media are active advocates of anti-corruption measures, and there are international and Palestinian non-governmental organizations that work to raise

For additional analytical, business and investment opportunities information,
please contact Global Investment & Business Center, USA
at (703) 370-8082. Fax: (703) 370-8083. E-mail: ibpusa3@gmail.com
Global Business and Investment Info Databank - www.ibpus.com

public awareness and promote anti-corruption initiatives. The most active of these is the AMAN Coalition for Integrity and Accountability, which is the Palestinian chapter of Transparency International. According to the World Bank 2014 Investment Climate Assessment report, Palestinian firms do not consider corruption to be one of the most serious problems they face. Seven percent of the firms surveyed reported having experienced a request from a government official for a bribe. Please see the AMAN website (http://www.aman-palestine.org/eng/index.htm) for further information.

During the past decade the perception of corruption involving political figures and institutions, once widespread, has significantly declined. Private sector businesses agree that the PA has been successful in reducing institutional corruption and local perceptions of line ministries and PA agencies are generally favorable in this regard. PA officials, businesses and representatives of service sectors note, however, that the largely discretionary authority given to Israeli military, police, and civilian officials in administering economic policy in the West Bank – touching on imports, checkpoint crossings, labor permits, and building licenses, among other things – create regular opportunities for low-level corruption on a range of daily decisions.

UN Anticorruption Convention, OECD Convention on Combatting Bribery

In April 2014 the PA acceded to the UN Anticorruption Convention. The PA is not a party to the OECD Convention on Combatting Bribery.

Resources to Report Corruption

Contact at American Consulate General in Jerusalem:

NAME: Mary E. Vargas
TITLE: Economic Officer
TELEPHONE NUMBER: +972-2-622-6969
EMAIL ADDRESS: VargasME@state.gov

Contact at government agency or agencies are responsible for combating corruption:

NAME: Dr. Ahmed Barak
TITLE: Acting Attorney General
ADDRESS: Al-Balua, opp. Foreign Ministry, Al-Bireh
TELEPHONE NUMBER: +972-2-242-8538
EMAIL ADDRESS: ag.office@pgp.ps

The Coalition for Accountability and Integrity - AMAN
TELEPHONE NUMBER: +972-2-298-9506
EMAIL ADDRESS: info@aman-palestine.org
WEBSITE: http://www.aman-palestine.org

13. BILATERAL INVESTMENT AGREEMENTS

Bilateral Taxation Treaties

The Palestine Liberation Organization (PLO), on behalf of the PA, has signed international trade agreements, which refer implicitly or explicitly to WTO rules. These include:

For additional analytical, business and investment opportunities information,
please contact Global Investment & Business Center, USA
at (703) 370-8082. Fax: (703) 370-8083. E-mail: ibpusa3@gmail.com
Global Business and Investment Info Databank - www.ibpus.com

Paris Protocol Agreement with Israel (1994) – free trade in products between Israel and Palestinian markets
Technical and Economic Cooperation Accord with Egypt (1994)
Trade Agreement between the PA and Jordan (1995)
Duty Free Arrangements with the United States (1996)
The EuroMed Interim Association Agreement on Trade and Co-operation (1997)
Interim Agreement between European Free Trade Area (EFTA) states and the PLO (1997)
Joint Canadian-Palestinian Framework for Economic Cooperation and Trade (1999)
Agreement on Commercial Cooperation with Russia – extends MFN status
Greater Arab Free Trade Area, to which PA is a party (2001)
Free Trade Agreement with Turkey (2004)
Trade Agreement with the EU – duty free access for Palestinian agricultural and fishery goods (2011)

Free Trade Agreement with Mercosur (2011)

Unilateral acts by other Arab trade partners extending preferential treatment to trade with the Palestinians

Since 1996, duty-free treatment has been available for all goods exported from the West Bank and Gaza to the United States, provided they meet qualifying criteria as spelled out in the U.S. - Israel Free Trade Area (FTA) Implementation Act of 1985, as amended. The duty-free benefits accorded under the FTA exceed those benefits which would be provided under the Generalized System of Preferences (GSP). It is worth noting that the benefits for imports provided in all of the trade agreements listed above are subject to application by the GOI, since all goods destined for the West Bank or Gaza must enter through Israeli-controlled crossings or ports. The GOI generally applies duties and tariffs consistent with its trade agreements, not with the PA's trade agreements.

The West Bank and Gaza do not have a bilateral taxation treaty with the United States.

14. OPIC AND OTHER INVESTMENT INSURANCE PROGRAMS

The Overseas Private Investment Corporation (OPIC) provides a variety of services to qualified investors with either U.S. partners and/or subsidiaries in emerging economies and developing nations. During the early stages of investment planning, U.S. investors may contact OPIC for insurance against political violence, inconvertibility of currency, and expropriation in the form of an insurance registration letter. OPIC has initiated a number of programs in the West Bank and Gaza to support private sector development, including a successful loan guarantee facility. Building on previous programs that disbursed over $117 million in loans from July 2007 to September 2015, OPIC launched a new Loan Guarantee Facility in April 2016 enabling pre-approved lenders to provide up to $143 million in loans to eligible SMEs. The new facility expands the parameters of its predecessor programs to broaden the range of guaranty products and technical assistance.

The World Bank, via a USD 26 million fund administered by its Multilateral Investment Guarantee Agency (MIGA), provides loan guarantees in the form of insurance against political risk for private investments in the West Bank and Gaza. Under the terms of the Fund, investors who are nationals of companies incorporated in a MIGA member country, or who are Palestinian residents of the West Bank or Gaza, are eligible to obtain guarantees for up to 15 years. The Fund currently has the capacity to issue guarantees for up to USD 5 million per project. This trust fund, administered by MIGA on behalf of the government of Japan and the PA, aims to encourage

For additional analytical, business and investment opportunities information,
please contact Global Investment & Business Center, USA
at (703) 370-8082. Fax: (703) 370-8083. E-mail: ibpusa3@gmail.com
Global Business and Investment Info Databank - www.ibpus.com

investment in the West Bank and Gaza by providing political risk insurance to both local and foreign investors. The fund is designed to facilitate small and medium-size investments, with a special emphasis on projects with high employment-generating capacity. The fund is currently backing the development of Mejdool date palm and herb farms, a dairy factory, a plastic manufacturing plant, and the expansion of a company that produces and distributes beverages.

15. LABOR

With its growing youth population, the West Bank and Gaza have an abundant labor supply with a high level of education and skills. According to the Palestinian Central Bureau of Statistics (PCBS), the total population of the West Bank and Gaza in December 2015 was about 4.75 million, including 2.9 million in the West Bank and 1.85 million in the Gaza Strip.

PCBS estimated there were 1.299 million people in the labor force as of the end of 2015, effectively 46.1 percent of the West Bank population and 45.2 percent of the Gaza population. Since 2001, when the GOI began restricting the number of labor permits available to Palestinians, areas adjacent to the Green Line between Israel and the West Bank, such as Jenin, Tulkarem, and Qalqiliya have seen their unemployment rates increase substantially above the West Bank average.

The most recent PCBS labor statistics estimate 2015 unemployment was 17.3 percent in the West Bank and 41 percent in Gaza. Unemployment disproportionately affects youth: when broken down, the highest unemployment rate in 2015 was 36.5 percent among youth ages 20-24 years. According to PCBS, at the end of 2014, the service sector was the biggest employer in the local market with 36.1 percent in the West Bank and 58.4 percent in Gaza Strip. The public sector employed 22.9 percent of the workforce in 2014 (16 percent in the West Bank and 41.5 percent in Gaza Strip). The average daily wage during the first quarter of 2015 in the West Bank was 94.1 ILS (USD 24.50) compared with 66.19 (USD 16.30) NIS in the Gaza Strip. The Palestinian minimum wage in 2014 was NIS 1,450 (USD 381.57) per month. The average daily wage for persons employed in Israel and Israeli settlements was NIS 187.5 (USD 48.50).

According to the most recent Labor Force Survey, labor distribution by sector is as follows:

36.1 percent - Services and Other Branches
20.2 percent - Commerce, Hotels, Restaurants
15.3 percent - Construction
12.6 percent - Mining, Quarrying, Manufacturing
10.4 percent - Agriculture, Forestry, Fishing, Hunting
5.4 percent - Transportation, Storage, Communication

The International Labor Organization reported in 2015 that increasing uncertainty and restrictions on labor institutions and practices in the West Bank and Gaza could lead to negative prospects for private economic activity. PA law does not expressly forbid forced or compulsory labor, and there have been reports of forced labor and child labor in the West Bank and Gaza, particularly in agricultural work and the informal economy. Despite widespread informality in the economy, most large Palestinian employers rely on standard, long-term employment contracts with minimal use of temporary workers. Israeli law applies to settlements in the West Bank, but authorities did not enforce it uniformly. Investors may encounter increasing reputational risks related to labor conditions in these settlements.

PA law provides for the rights of workers to form and join independent unions and conduct legal strikes. The law requires conducting collective bargaining without any pressure or influence but

For additional analytical, business and investment opportunities information,
please contact Global Investment & Business Center, USA
at (703) 370-8082. Fax: (703) 370-8083. E-mail: ibpusa3@gmail.com
Global Business and Investment Info Databank - www.ibpus.com

does not explicitly provide for the right to collective bargaining. Anti-union discrimination and employer interference in union functions are illegal, but the law does not specifically prohibit termination due to union activity. Labor unions were not independent of authorities and political parties in 2015.

The requirements for legal strikes are cumbersome, and strikers had little protection from retribution. The PA Ministry of Labor can impose arbitration; workers or their trade unions faced disciplinary action if they rejected the result. If the ministry cannot resolve a dispute, it can be referred first to a committee chaired by a delegate from the ministry and composed of an equal number of members designated by the workers and the employer, and finally to a specialized labor court. Teachers, who comprise the most significant portion of the public sector work force, participated in a large-scale strike with demonstrations in early 2016 protesting partial pay.

In early 2016, the PA President ratified a new Social Security Law, but the law had not been formally adopted or implemented at the time of this report. The draft law is expected to cover issues related to retirement benefits, maternity leave and disability payments, as well as compel employers to contribute to a Social Security Fund for employees.

16. FOREIGN TRADE ZONES/FREE PORTS/TRADE FACILITATION

There are no foreign trade zones or free ports in the West Bank or Gaza.

17. FOREIGN DIRECT INVESTMENT AND FOREIGN PORTFOLIO INVESTMENT STATISTICS

According to the PCBS, the stock of foreign investment in the Palestinian territories at the end of 2014 amounted USD 2.746 billion. This includes foreign direct investment, portfolio investments, and other investments.

Table 2: Key Macroeconomic Data, U.S. FDI in Host Country/Economy

	Host Country Statistical source		USG or international statistical source		USG or International Source of Data: BEA; IMF; Eurostat; UNCTAD, Other
Economic Data	Year	Amount	Year	Amount	
Host Country Gross Domestic Product (GDP) ($M USD)	2014	12,716	2014	12,737	Host source: PCBS, "Major National Accounts" International source: World Bank, Worldwide Development Indicators
Foreign Direct Investment	Host Country Statistical source		USG or international statistical source		USG or international Source of data: BEA; IMF; Eurostat; UNCTAD, Other
U.S. FDI in partner country ($M USD, stock	N/A	N/A	N/A	N/A	BEA data unavailable

positions)					
Host country's FDI in the United States ($M USD, stock positions)	N/A	N/A	N/A	N/A	BEA data unavailable
Total inbound stock of FDI as % host GDP	2014	19.9%	2014	19.5%	Host Source: PCBS Foreign Investment Survey of Palestinian Enterprises (stocks) at the end of 2014 available athttp://www.pcbs.gov.ps/Portals/_Rainbow/Documents/e-FIS-annual-2014.htm

International Source: IMF Coordinated Direct Investment Survey |

Table 3: Sources and Destination of FDI

The largest foreign company in the West Bank/Gaza is the Palestine Development and Investment Company (PADICO), which has invested over USD 250 million in the economy. Key PADICO investors include diaspora Palestinians from Jordan, the United Kingdom, and the Gulf. PADICO has made significant investments in telecommunications, housing, and the establishment of the Palestinian Securities Exchange. The Arab Palestinian Investment Company (APIC), headquartered in Ramallah, is a large foreign investment group with authorized capital of over USD 100 million. There are four private equity funds operating in the West Bank/Gaza, largely comprised of foreign investors: Riyada, Siraj, Sharakat, and Sadara. Other significant foreign investments include Qatari mobile operator QTel's projected USD 600 million investment in Wataniya Mobile over a 10-year period, and Qatari Diar's projected USD 1 billion investment in Rawabi, a mixed use/affordable housing real estate development. The largest U.S. investment is Coca Cola's 15 percent stake in the local bottler, Palestine National Beverage Company (PNBC), a company valued at USD 70 million. PNBC is currently investing USD 20 million in a bottling facility in Gaza, in addition to its three West Bank-based plants.

Direct Investment from/in Counterpart Economy Data					
From Top Five Sources/To Top Five Destinations (US Dollars, Millions)					
Inward Direct Investment			Outward Direct Investment		
Total Inward	2,487	100%	Total Outward		100%
Jordan	1,275	51%	Data unavailable		
Qatar	129	5%			
Egypt	54	2%			
United States	39	2%			
Cyprus	16	1%			
"0" reflects amounts rounded to +/- USD 500,000.					

LEADING SECTORS FOR US EXPORTS AND INVESTMENTS

BEST PROSPECTS FOR NON-AGRICULTURAL GOODS AND SERVICES

1 - TELECOMMUNICATIONS EQUIPMENT (TEL)

In 1997 the PA issued regulations governing wire and radio communications in WB/G, empowering the Ministry of Post and Communications to establish, manage, and operate wire and radio communications networks in WB/G. Under this law, all public wire and radio communication networks are subject to licensure. The Cabinet has the authority to grant a license by means of a franchise based on the Minister of Communication's recommendation.

Recognizing the need to mobilize sufficient capital to build a modern telecommunication system, Palestinian investment companies in 1997 joined with approximately 8,000 investors to launch the Palestinian Telecommunications Company (Paltel) on the Palestinian Stock Exchange in Nablus. This development followed the November 1996, PA decision to award Paltel an exclusive license to develop telecommunications infrastructure and digital cellular telephone services in WB/G.

Paltel, which is committed to open competition for service suppliers, seeks to offer value-added services like Internet and telephony. To date, it has issued tenders for wired and digital cellular telephone equipment and services in WB/G, signing supply and operating agreements with Nortel, Motorola, MCI-Worldcom, and Startec Global Communications. Interested U.S. telecommunications companies should contact the U.S. Consulate, Commercial Section in Jerusalem.

Paltel cellular phone service "Jawal" has been operational for the last two years and a half and has initial capacity of 70,000 lines, which is creating demand for cellular phone equipment. Furthermore, the cellular phone service license that the PA granted to Paltel for expires in 2001, when the market will be opened to competition.

Opportunities for US companies in this sector are in providing switches, transmission networks, microwave networks, earth stations, optic fiber cables, cellular phones and public payphones.

2- PROCESSED FOODS (FPP)

Although many food products in WB/G are imported from Israel, these are relatively expensive. Palestinian consumers know American brands and are willing to pay for good quality and internationally recognized names.

The potential for U.S. processed food exports is very promising. Good opportunities exist in snack foods, cereals, condiments and sauces, canned fruits and vegetables, cheese, dried fruits, tea and instant coffee, frozen meat, vegetable oil, candy, vegetable oil, and ghee. Excellent opportunities also exist for processed food products that do not require refrigeration during shipment or in storage.

3 - Franchising (FRA)

Palestinian Authority areas in WB/G provide new opportunities and niche markets for U.S. companies looking to expand their franchises, especially those in the fast-food sector, at competitive prices.

A growing low-cost fast-food sector, where American-style pizza parlors and hamburger and chicken chains such as Checkers and Pizza Inn, are already popular among Palestinians, may attract other American food franchisers looking to enter the WB/G market.

5 - COMPUTERS AND OFFICE EQUIPMENT (CPT)

PA and municipal offices, as well as expanding private companies, need a full range of office equipment including, but not limited to, computers, software, copiers, faxes, and supplies. The local market, particularly banks and other internationally oriented enterprises, values American expertise in the computer and software field. Arabic software and keyboards should be included in proposed sales.

For additional analytical, business and investment opportunities information, please contact Global Investment & Business Center, USA at (703) 370-8082. Fax: (703) 370-8083. E-mail: ibpusa3@gmail.com Global Business and Investment Info Databank - www.ibpus.com

6- Furniture (FUR)

Although only small quantities of American wood furniture have so far been imported into WB/G, its competitive pricing and good reputation for quality bode well for higher volume sales, especially for home furniture. Good opportunities exist for sitting room and bedroom sets, dining tables, recliners and sleepers, buffets, coffee tables, end tables, and TV tables.

Although American home furniture is relatively more expensive than other imported or locally made furniture, Palestinians appreciate its durability, classical appearance and quality. They generally prefer oak, birch, or mahogany and prefer to pay extra for quality furniture, which can be kept for a long time.

7- Textiles Fabrics (TXF)

There are good opportunities for textile fabrics such as denim and cotton. A total of 1650 large and small textile and apparel establishments operate in WB/GF and many work as subcontractors for Israeli companies. Fabrics are mostly imported from Southeast Asia, Turkey, Israel and the U.S.

Note: Statistics are currently not available on amount of imports for above listed products

BEST PROSPECTS FOR AGRICULTURAL PRODUCTS

1 – Wheat and Feed Grains (HS Code: 1000.0000)

Only a small proportion of annual feed grain consumption is WB/G-based, so U.S. grain exporters have ample opportunity to supply feed for local poultry and livestock. Of the recently commissioned flourmills, two are in Gaza and the other on the outskirts of Bir Zeit, near Ramallah on the West Bank. In addition, a number of smaller mills, whose production does not exceed 10,000 metric tons (mt) per year, operate in WB/G. These mills can satisfy the entire 250-300,000 mt annual demand of the PA for wheat.

By the terms of the Paris Protocol, Palestinian grain and meal purchasers, who generally seek low-cost sources, may import grain from anywhere. To date, the major flour mills, which import on their own account, have purchased only U.S. milling quality wheat. There are few importers of animal feeds although the annual feed mixing and grinding capacity is estimated at some 200,000 mt.

2 - Rice (HS Code: 1006.000)

WB/G import 20-30,000 metric tons of rice annually. Competitive pricing by U.S. sources could make this an attractive market and might enable U.S. exporters to capture a significant share of it from Asian suppliers.

3 - Dried Legumes (HS Code: 0713.0000)

WB/G account for an estimated 40 percent of all Israeli imports of peas, beans, chickpeas, and other legumes. 1994 WB/G imports totaled: white beans: $1.4 million; lentils: $920,000; dried peas: $368,000; and chickpeas: $312,000.

4 - Processed Oils (HS Code: 1500.0000)

WB/G locally produce and use large quantities of olive oil, but not other processed oils favored by Palestinian consumers, so moderate prospects exist for importing soy, corn, sunflower, and rapeseed oils. There are no crushing plants in WB/G but some crude vegetable oils are imported from various sources and refined locally.

5- Sugar (HS Code: 1701.0000)

WB/G sugar imports are up from around 30,000 mt in 1996. Sugar is now being transshipped to Jordan via Israeli ports to avoid higher shipping/transportation costs via the Jordanian port of Aqaba. In recent years WB/G has been importing about 130,000 mt of sugar via Israel.

6- Frozen Fish (HSCode: 0303.0000)

Israel and the Palestinian Authority import the majority of their fish requirements. They enjoy jointly a 4,000 mt duty-free import quota for frozen salt water fish from the U.S. In spite of this, only five percent of all frozen salt water fish imports are of U.S. origin. In recent years the Pacific Whiting has found a favorable market in WB/G although U.S. exporters have encountered difficulties in meeting the rigid Palestinian standards. At present, most of this type of fish is being imported from Argentina.

MAJOR INVESTMENT OPPORTUNITIES

The USG recognizes the major contribution that outward foreign direct investment -- increasingly viewed as a complement, or even a necessary component, of trade -- makes to the U.S. economy. U.S. firms with overseas operations account for about 60% of total U.S. exports, so the USG undertakes initiatives, such as Overseas Private Investment Corporation (OPIC) programs, investment treaty negotiations, and business facilitation programs that support U.S. export-promotion activities. Until the present situation improves many business people are postponing any investment.

FOOD AND BEVERAGE PROCESSING AND PACKAGING

Local and foreign businesses report that this established profit center continues to show excellent growth prospects. While agricultural products are plentiful in WB/G, local companies mostly manufacture products such as sweets, cookies, and snack foods. Accordingly, opportunities for U.S. companies exist over the full range of fruit and vegetable canning and processing as well as frozen food preparation. Other opportunities include joint ventures to manufacture snack foods, cookies, and sauces.

Gulf and European markets provide a natural merchandising opportunity for U.S.-Palestinian joint-venture food products.

PHARMACEUTICAL PRODUCTION

Four of the largest, best managed, and most successful West Bank companies produce pharmaceuticals; they also have substantial ready capital for expansion. Some multinationals are already working with these and other companies under distributorship arrangements, which will likely develop into joint manufacturing agreements. Some West Bank pharmaceutical companies have shifted to cosmetic production, while others are penetrating overseas markets in the Gulf, Eastern Europe, and the former Soviet Union. Good joint-venture opportunities exist in this sector: local firms can benefit from U.S. quality-control techniques and new technologies, while offering relatively low wage structures.

BUILDING MATERIALS

The building and construction materials industry, including stone and non-metallic minerals quarrying, employs 18% of all WB/G workers. A survey of local and international businesspeople rates this sector as having strong growth potential.

Stonecutting also rates high in international competitiveness and growth potential. Over 300 firms annually produce 250,000 square meters of cut stone, much of which is exported to Israel and Jordan, with an estimated value of $160 million. Housing and commercial construction should continue to grow along with private and public capital inflow.

LIGHT ASSEMBLY TECHNOLOGY

The relatively well-educated local Palestinian population should, with appropriate specialty training, contribute to a solid labor force for a wide variety of light assembly or electronics work. Many Palestinians have excellent computer/software training, and small computer programming firms already exist in Ramallah and Bethlehem.

Two major U.S. information technology companies have set up offices in the West Bank. One is carrying out a Research and Development project and has hired many Palestinian engineers. This field is developing fast and looks to expand over the next few years.

HOTEL CONSTRUCTION AND UPGRADING

Tourism, particularly by Diaspora Palestinians, is projected to increase over the next five years. Before 1967, Ramallah was an important regional summer resort, and it still has considerable potential for tourism development. Demand is estimated at slightly over 1 million tourists annually, including religious pilgrims, enough to maintain a viable industry. Visits to Bethlehem, by far the most important WB/G tourist site, are pegged at 2-3 million during and beyond 2000 during special commemorations of Jesus' birth. Tourist expenditures in 1995 in the West Bank and East Jerusalem were estimated at over $150 million.

A number of three-star hotels have opened up in the West Bank cities of Bethlehem, Ramallah and Hebron to cater to pilgrims and budget tourists while Jericho has a new three-star resort hotel. Recently Jericho and Bethlehem have seen the opening of the first two five-star Intercontinental hotels targeting business and upscale travelers. Most existing hotels in the West Bank are in the three-star category and need upgrading. Nablus and Gaza have two and four three-star hotels respectively. They both could support a number of new hotels, especially Gaza.

The current crisis has had a significant impact on the Palestinian Tourism industry. For instance, Bethlehem and Jericho that depend mainly on tourism sustained some heavy losses. Currently, the Oasis Casino, the Telepherique Tourist Center, and the Intercontinental hotel in Jericho are closed. At this time also, the first 5-star Intercontinental Hotel in Bethlehem is closed.

According to a report that published by the Palestinian Central Bureau of Statistics (PCBS) , the number of hotel guests who visited the PA areas during the fourth quarter of 2000 has dropped to 28,646 from 117,355 guests in the third quarter of the same year, a decline by over 75 percent. Also, since December 2000 most of the 116 hotels in the PA have been closed for lack of guests.

APPAREL AND TEXTILES

The approximately 1,650 large and small textile and apparel establishments in the PA areas mostly work as subcontractors for Israeli textile companies; they employ 25,000 people. A few factories have made agreements to manufacture apparel for major department stores and apparel companies in the U.S. like Calvin Klein and JC Penny's.

Investors in this sector can take advantage of the Gaza Industrial Estate. Opportunities for joint ventures in this sector are good in view of the high level of experience that Palestinians have doing subcontracting work.

JEWELRY, HANDICRAFTS, ETHNIC IMPORTS

WB/G are famous for olivewood, tiles and ceramics, mother-of-pearl, and needlework products.

With upgrading in design and quality, these products can be successfully marketed internationally. Small joint ventures with U.S. partners that focus on quality and developing ethnic designs, along with appeal to Western tastes, offer good investment opportunities.

The Government of the United States acknowledges the contribution that outward foreign direct investment makes to the U.S. economy. U.S. foreign direct investment is increasingly viewed as a complement or even a necessary component of trade. For example, roughly 60 percent of U.S. exports are sold by American firms that have operations abroad. Recognizing the benefits that U.S. outward investment brings to the U.S. economy, the Government of the United States undertakes initiatives, such as Overseas Private Investment Corporation (OPIC) programs, investment treaty negotiations and business facilitation programs, that support U.S. investors.

ENERGY (OIL & GAS ELECTRICAL POWER)

Energy (Oil & Gas Electrical Power) Three electricity distribution companies operate in the West Bank: the Jerusalem District Electric Company (JDECO) that serves East Jerusalem, Jericho, Ramallah and Bethlehem; the Northern Electricity Distribution Company (NEDCO) operating in the northern West Bank; and the Southern Electric Co. (SELCO) serving the southern areas. The three companies purchase 95% of the needed electricity from the Israel Electric Corporation (IEC), which they transmit over a grid that is currently owned by IEC. The remaining 5% of electric power used in the West Bank comes from Jordan. In Gaza, the Palestine Electric Company (PEC) operates a power station, which currently generates 70MW covering 30% of the 240 MW demand. Egypt supplies Gaza with 20 MW and Israel supplies the remaining 150 MW.

For additional analytical, business and investment opportunities information,
please contact Global Investment & Business Center, USA
at (703) 370-8082. Fax: (703) 370-8083. E-mail: ibpusa3@gmail.com
Global Business and Investment Info Databank - www.ibpus.com

The electricity systems in the West Bank require substantial upgrading and expansion to meet current demand. Over the next few years, infrastructure development, including upgrading of the electricity network and establishing a national electricity distribution company in the West Bank, will be a major growth sector of the Palestinian economy. Also, another opportunity exists for establishing a solar energy generation plant in the West Bank.

The West Bank and Gaza, like other developing countries, depend on oil as the main source of energy. Palestinians import all their petroleum products from Israel. Prices are high due to heavy taxation. Several years ago, natural gas was discovered off the Gaza coast. British Gas holds a license to explore the gas fields and the company has been involved in negotiations to secure a supply agreement with Israel, the main potential customer for the gas. Once an agreement is reached and the infrastructure to transport the gas is developed, the Gaza power station will begin to operate on natural gas. Future demand for gas is estimated at 1.1 BCM/pa.

For more information, please contact Assad Barsoum directly at Tel: 972-2-625-4742, Fax: 972-2-623-5132, or E-mail:Assad.Barsoum@trade.gov

TELECOMMUNICATIONS EQUIPMENT AND SERVICES

Telecommunications Equipment and Services Telecommunications is the most vibrant sector in the Palestinian economy. The sector was fully privatized in 1997 with the establishment of Paltel - Palestine Telecommunications Company, as the fixed line operator. In 1998, Jawwal – Palestine Cellular Communication Company was established as the first Palestinian cellular company. In 2009, Wataniya Mobile launched its commercial operations to become the second cellular operator.

Paltel is the fixed line operator in the West Bank and Gaza that offers subscribers with local and international telephone services, Internet access and payphone services. Paltel's capital is estimated at $200 million and the company has 357,000 subscribers. Jawwal, the first cellular company, was established in 1998 as a spin-off from Paltel to develop cellular communications in the West Bank and Gaza. Jawwal has invested over $700 million in establishing a cellular network and the company currently has 2 million subscribers. In 2009, the second mobile operator Wataniya Mobile launched operations in the West Bank only. Wataniya Mobile has invested $240 million in license fees and network building. The new company was established in partnership between Wataniya Group which owns 57% of Wataniya Mobile and the Palestine Investment Fund which owns 43%. In 2010, Wataniya's mobile subscribers reached 300,000.

Many Voice over Internet Protocol (VOIP) and broadband companies that offer international calls and wireless Internet service have also recently entered the Palestinian market. The new entrants are expected to result in increasing demand for cell phones and telecommunication equipment in the West Bank. Finally, the Palestinian Ministry of Telecommunications and Information Technology MTIT plans to announce a tender for the third mobile operator in 2013.

For more information, please contact Assad Barsoum directly at Tel: 972-2-625-4742, Fax: 972-2-623-5132, or E-mail:Assad.Barsoum@trade.gov

SAFETY AND SECURITY EQUIPMENT AND SERVICES

Safety and Security Equipment and Services The West Bank and Gaza (WB/G) is home to approximately 4 million Palestinian and has a population growth estimated at about 3.6%. Despite ongoing political conditions, the influence of Palestinians familiar with American culture opens the door to numerous export opportunities for American companies in establishing agents, distributors, and partners.

The market for safety and security equipment in the WB/G is estimated at $2 million and is dominated by imports coming from Taiwan, U.K., France, and the United States. The market for such equipment has shrunk sharply in recent years due to the outbreak of the Intifada in October

For additional analytical, business and investment opportunities information,
please contact Global Investment & Business Center, USA
at (703) 370-8082. Fax: (703) 370-8083. E-mail: ibpusa3@gmail.com
Global Business and Investment Info Databank - www.ibpus.com

2000. However, as the political conditions improve in the short-term, the demand for security equipment will grow considerably.

There are no restrictions on importing safety and security equipment into the WB/G and the Palestinian Authority is beginning to develop a formal tendering and bid process for government contracts. However, the WB/G has no indigenous ports or freight-handling airports and all goods must transit Israeli ports. The Palestinian Ministry of Interior (the Palestinian Police in particular) is the main end user of security equipment followed by banks, hotels, big companies, and foreign representative offices. Good export opportunities exist for CCTV, ID systems, data cards, surveillance systems, fire alarms, sirens, burglar alarms, metal detectors, and access control.

For further information about the Palestinian market for safety & security equipment, please contact Assad Barsoum directly at Tel: 972-2-625-4742, Fax: 972-2-623-5132, or E-mail: Assad.Barsoum@trade.gov

INFORMATION AND COMMUNICATIONS TECHNOLOGIES

The Palestinian Information and Communication Technology (ICT) sector employs around 4,500 individuals in 300 companies in the West Bank and Gaza (WB/G). All types of ICT companies exist including: computer hardware and office equipment importers, software development houses, business consulting services, Internet Service Providers, and telecommunication companies. Total investment in the ICT sector is estimated at $700 million. The sector contributes 13% of GDP and has an estimated 30% annual growth rate. With the development of the Palestinian ICT sector, the demand for computers and peripherals, telecommunication equipment, mobile handsets, and web designing services is growing.

The telecommunications sector was privatized in 1997 with the establishment of Paltel- the Palestine Telecommunications Company as the fixed line operator in the West Bank and Gaza. In 1998, Jawwal was established as the first Palestinian cellular company. In 2009, Wataniya Mobile entered the market as the second mobile operator in the West Bank only. Also, a number of VOIP and broadband companies have recently entered the West Bank. Currently, Paltel has 375,000 fixed line subscribers and 78,000 ADSL customers. Jawwal has 2 million mobile subscribers and Wataniya Mobile has 300,000 subscribers.

Internet serves as an important communication tool within the West Bank and with the outside world. Today, an estimated 1.2 million people use the Internet in the WB/G, representing approximately 30% of the population. Most of Palestinians use the Internet for knowledge, research, studying, business-to-business activities, and entertainment.

The percentage of Palestinians in the WB/G who own a computer is 50%. Most of the computer hardware companies import directly from international vendors. Exports are limited to software, research and development, and outsourcing services. Some software companies have outsourcing and developing projects for regional and international companies.

The Palestinian ICT sector is represented by PITA, the Palestinian IT Association of Companies; a membership-based non-for-profit organization. With its 130 members, representing 43% of the ICT sector, PITA has been very active in representing the interests of its members, in developing the Palestinian ICT sector, and in increasing the partnership between the public and private sectors.

For additional information on the Palestinian market for information and communication technology, please contact Assad Barsoum directly at phone: 972-2-625-4742, fax: 972-2-623-5132 or e-mail: Assad.Barsoum@.trade.gov

EDUCATIONAL SERVICES

Educational Services Summary Palestinian students represent a distinct opportunity for American suppliers of post-secondary educational services. In 2003, more than 7,000 Palestinian students

For additional analytical, business and investment opportunities information,
please contact Global Investment & Business Center, USA
at (703) 370-8082. Fax: (703) 370-8083. E-mail: ibpusa3@gmail.com
Global Business and Investment Info Databank - www.ibpus.com

in the West Bank and Gaza requested information about studying in the United States. In 2002, 38,411 Palestinian students graduated from 554 high schools.

Student Demographics 1. The West Bank and Gaza (WB/G) have a population of around 4 million and boast one of the highest per capita rates of university graduates in the Arab world. Palestinians have a long-standing tradition of spending generously on higher education, regarded as an asset. 38,411 students graduated from WB/G high schools in 2002. About 18,000 enrolled in local institutions for advanced studies. There are ten universities and twenty community colleges in WB/G. Enrollment in these schools reached 89,668 students in 2002. The Open University accounts for 29,845 students. In 1999, revenues of local universities and community colleges reached $45.1 million. During 2003, 7,235 Palestinians requested information from AMIDEAST and the U.S. Consulate Jerusalem about studying in the United States.

Opportunities for American Providers of Higher Education Services 2. There is an excellent niche opportunity for American universities, colleges and other educational organizations to capture a larger part of the Palestinian higher education services market. The opportunity is greatest in the Ramallah, Bethlehem and Jerusalem areas, where there are many private schools that graduate students with high English proficiency, prime candidates to continue higher education in the United States. Family incomes in these areas are the highest in the West Bank and Gaza (WB/G).

Market Background and Characteristics 3. Until local universities were established in WB/G in the early 1970's, Palestinian students enrolled at universities in the United States, Lebanon, the U.K., Jordan and Eastern Europe. The early university graduates established themselves in the job markets in the Arab world, particularly in the Gulf States, since the early sixties and became role models for Palestinian high school graduates. In the past ten years, however, Jordan has become the primary choice for a large number of Palestinian students because of its proximity and the proliferation of Jordanian private universities. Tuition fees at these universities are high, comparable to, and in some cases higher than, those at some American universities.

U.S. Special Scholarship Programs 4. The vast majority of Palestinian undergraduate students who go to study in the United States pay their own way. However, several graduate and postgraduate scholarship programs are available to Palestinians. They include the Fulbright Scholarship Program (FSP), the Presidential Scholarship Fund (PSF) and the Ford Foundation's International Fellowships Program (FFIFP).

5. AMIDEAST, an American education NGO based in Ramallah, runs the Fulbright Scholarship Program (FSP) and the Ford Foundation's International Fellowship Program (FFIFP) programs. The Presidential Scholarship Fund (PSF) is another relevant program, funded by USAID that provides scholarships to Palestinian graduate students. The (PSF) is managed by the Academy for Educational Development (AED), which has a contract from USAID to run the program through 2007. The most active program is the Fulbright Scholarship Program, which has been running in WB/G since 1970.

Preferred Specializations 6. Palestinian undergraduate students select a wide range of specializations, but the greatest demand is for business administration, computer science and technology, pharmacology and the various engineering fields. Graduate students' preferences also cover a wide range of majors, mainly business administration, chemistry, education and civil engineering.

Level of Interest in American Education 7. Palestinians in WB/G are interested in American undergraduate, graduate, postgraduate, high school, short-term study, non-degree, and correspondence study programs, but graduate and undergraduate studies are the two most popular choices. According to 2003 AMIDEAST statistics, a total of 5,938 Palestinians requested information and showed interest in graduate studies, while 1,297 requests were made for information on undergraduate studies programs.

Matriculation Exams and the School System in WB/G 8. Out of a total of 554 high schools in the WB/G, 64 are private. In Ramallah, there are 10 private schools that operate on the American curriculum. Many Ramallah students are related to Palestinian immigrants living in the United States. Missionaries run many private schools in Jerusalem and Bethlehem, where great emphasis is placed on foreign language skills.

9. All public school students have to sit for the matriculation exam known as "Tawjihi" at the end of twelve years of schooling. The results of this exam are the sole criterion for getting accepted at a university and the choice of major in WB/G and Jordan. Private schools on the other hand offer students the choice of two curricula, the "Tawjihi" or the General Certificate of English (GCE). The (GCE) exam entitles passing students to be accepted at universities in the U.K. At the ten private schools in Ramallah that run the American curriculum, senior students sit for the (SAT) exam.

Why do Palestinian Students Study in the USA? 10. Palestinian students choose to study in the U.S. because of the quality of education, the wide choice of specializations and the experience of living in the United States. Family connections also play a major role, especially in the Ramallah area. It is estimated that around 60,000 Palestinian immigrants in the United States are related to residents of Ramallah and its environs. These immigrants have maintained strong family ties with their hometown, and the United States has become the natural choice for university education for many high school graduates in this city.

11. WB/G universities are limited in the scope of specializations currently offered. Studies have often been interrupted over the last four years because of the current unrest in the area. Public universities in Jordan are subsidized by the government and have always been the first choice for Palestinian students. However, when a quota system was introduced at Jordanian universities, the number of eligible students from WB/G sharply decreased, and Palestinians started enrolling in the private universities that have mushroomed in Jordan in the last ten years. Private universities have more limited fields of specialization and do not always carry the same level of prestige considered important for landing the best good jobs after graduation. The "Tawjihi" scores also limit acceptance and the choice of major. Acceptance at universities in Lebanon and Egypt has also become more difficult because of travel restrictions currently imposed by those two countries on Palestinians coming from WB/G.

12. Palestinian high school graduates are proficient in English language and academically prepared to study in American universities. In WB/G, English language is a must, starting from first grade in all public and private schools. There are also several private schools that run American or English curricula, particularly in the cities of Ramallah, Bethlehem and Jerusalem. High school graduates of these schools are good candidates to enroll in American universities.

Israeli Arab Students' Demographics 13. Another niche market that American institutions of higher learning can tap into is the Israeli-Arab sector. Statistics reveal that in 2002 the number of Israeli Arab students in the senior class was 13,019. Out of that, 11,640 sat for the Israeli Matriculation Certificate (Bagrut) exam and 6,843 passed. That same year 4,151 high school graduates became eligible to study at local universities after passing the unified Israeli university entrance exam known as (Psychometric). Also in 2002 the total number of schools in the Israeli Arab sector, (secondary and elementary), was 123 while the schools' population stood at 56,514 students. Israeli-Arab students and their families will be encouraged to attend either the Tel Aviv or the Jerusalem events.

For further information on the topic, please contact Issa Noursi directly at Tel: 972-2-625-5201, Fax: 972-2-623-5132, or E-mail: Issa.Noursi@trade.gov

Back to top

AUTOMOTIVE AFTERMARKET PRODUCTS

Automotive Aftermarket Products Market Overview The automotive aftermarket sector in the West Bank and Gaza is made up of the Original Equipment Manufacturer (OEM) parts and their

**For additional analytical, business and investment opportunities information,
please contact Global Investment & Business Center, USA
at (703) 370-8082. Fax: (703) 370-8083. E-mail: ibpusa3@gmail.com
Global Business and Investment Info Databank - www.ibpus.com**

substitute. According to figures released by the Palestinian Central Bureau of Statistics (PCBS) imports of auto parts totaled $17 million in 2002. It is estimated that the total number of vehicles in WB/G is 150,000 including trucks, buses and other commercial vehicles and only 2% are from the U.S. and the rest from Europe and Asia.

There are ten authorized importers of new cars in the WB/G and they use OEM parts. They import European, Asian and American vehicles. Leading the list of new car imports is VW, followed by Audi and then Peugeot.

Because of generally lower incomes, there is considerable demand for competitively priced auto parts and used cars in the Palestinian market. Imports of three years old cars are allowed and they come mostly from Israel and used car markets in Germany. Used and refurbished auto parts however cannot be imported and expensive parts are refurbished locally. Demand for refurbished and competitively priced new parts has increased in the last three years due to the prevailing economic conditions.

The city of Nablus in the West Bank is considered the hub for importers and distributors of auto spare parts of European and Japanese make especially Mercedes Benz and VW/Audi. All commercial and transport vehicles like buses and minivans for passengers transport run by diesel fuel and the majority of passenger cars run on gas.

Imports of auto spare parts come mostly from Europe and the Far East yet American made parts are recognized for their high quality and are now more competitive with the rise in the value of the Euro versus the U.S. dollar.

Opportunities for U.S. Exporters of aftermarket products and services The Palestinian market is currently price sensitive and Palestinian importers look for competitively priced products.

Best Prospects:

Service parts: disk brake pads, shock absorbers, front suspension parts, filters for oil lubrication, air conditioning parts

Car body: front and rear lamps, bumpers, radiator grills, hood and trunk lids

Replacement service parts: tires, fan belts, water hoses, water pumps, brake components, engine and transmission components, electrical components

Vehicle accessories: car care products, polish, wax, upholstery spray

Water-cooling (Glycol) for radiators

Universal lubricants: lubricating oils, wax, glycol

For further information on the topic, please contact Issa Noursi directly at Tel: 972-2-625-5201, Fax: 972-2-623-5132, or E-mail: Issa.Noursi@trade.gov

HEALTHCARE PRODUCTS & SERVICES

Healthcare Products & Services The population in the Palestinian West Bank and Gaza is 4 million. The population growth rate is 3.9% and around 47% of the population is 14 years or younger. GDP in 2006 was $4.394 billion and in 2009 the local economy grew by 8%.

The size of the medical equipment and supplies market in the West bank and Gaza has been estimated to $20 million annually. The figures change depending on international donors' support for specific health projects carried out in the area. The market is made up of medical capital equipment, medical supplies, and lab equipment and lab disposable supplies. There is no domestic production of medical equipment and supplies, so Palestinians depend 100% on imports. Germany and the UK are the primary sources, and are followed by European and Asian countries, the United States and Israel.

The U.S. share of the market is roughly 15% of the total, but two factors are expected to change the percentage: the falling value of the U.S. dollar vs. the Euro that makes U.S. exports more competitive and the continued support by USAID of healthcare projects in the West Bank and Gaza. USAID regulations stipulate that funds can be spent on American-made equipment only, and the Agency has pledged $86 million for the coming five years to help reform the Palestinian healthcare sector.

There are no import duties on U.S.-made goods entering the West Bank and Gaza, however products are subject to value added tax that is currently 14.5% and purchase tax. In order to benefit from duty free entry, products must have a U.S. certificate of origin for exporting to the West Bank and Gaza. Also prior to shipping approvals must be obtained from both the Palestinian and Israeli ministries of health for any medical product coming into the area.

The majority of the Palestinian population relies on medical services provided by public hospitals that are run by the Palestinian Ministry of Health under a general health insurance program. The Ministry is in charge of providing all medical equipment and supplies that are paid for mostly through international donors support programs. The total number of public and private hospitals in West Bank and Gaza is 72 and total number of beds is 5,000.

For more information, please contact Issa Noursi directly at Tel: 972-2-625-5201, Fax: 972-2-623-5132, or E-mail:Issa.Noursi@trade.gov

BUILDING AND CONSTRUCTION SECTOR

The building and construction industry is one of the leading economic sectors in the West Bank and Gaza. Home building makes up the bulk of investments. Although spending in this sector has somewhat diminished over the past four years, it is estimated that in 2002 total output in this sector amounted to $300 million. From a high of 5,803 new building licenses in 1999, the number came down to 1,913 at the end of 2002. The current number of housing units is estimated at 676,029 and is expected to reach 973,761 by 2010.

Over the past 30 years, the growth rate in the home construction sector lagged behind the 3.9% population growth rate of the Palestinian West Bank & Gaza. Demand for housing also grew after the return of expatriate Palestinians soon after the Oslo Peace Agreement and, in 2002, home construction amounted to 57% of total construction spending in WB/G. Construction of office buildings also increased, spurred by demand from new local companies that were set up, and the Palestinian Authority that started renting out premises for its different ministries and agencies.

Preferences for house ownership are for individual homes with large spaces, while living in apartment buildings is the least desirable. The average size of a Palestinian family in the WB/G is 6 persons. In Gaza however, because of scarcity of land, the trend has been to build high-rise office and apartment buildings.

The situation in Gaza should significantly change after Israeli settlements were razed down that freed more land for construction. A lot of investments are expected to be made in building new houses especially for citizens who had their homes demolished by the Israeli army and to alleviate the housing shortage in Gaza. Gaza is one of the most densely populated tracts of land in the world: population count is approximately 1.5 million living in an area of 360-square/km and growth rate of 3.90%.

The private sector leads the construction sector and according to Palestinian Central Bureau of Statistics' figures; there are 348 enterprises in the construction contracting business that employ 3,500 workers. In the public sector, most projects are geared towards infrastructure and are financed by international donors mostly USAID. These projects mostly focus on the provision of potable water, sewage disposal and road construction.

Stone is used in construction in the WB/G because it is readily available and cheaper than wood. It is estimated that there are 297 quarries and 5633 stone and marble cutting operations in West

Bank and Gaza. Also climatic conditions make wood less desirable as the winter season is relatively short, and mild to hot weather prevails throughout most of the year. All other materials are imported and the list includes; lumber wood used to make doors, furniture and kitchens; steel, cement, aluminum profiles, glass, heavy equipment and machinery used in construction, and elevators.

For more information, please contact Issa Noursi directly at Tel: 972-2-625-5201, Fax: 972-2-623-5132, or E-mail:Issa.Noursi@trade.gov

ENVIRONMENTAL WATER TECHNOLOGIES

Environmental Water Technologies Short and medium-term environment sector opportunities in the West Bank and Gaza are very small and limited to public projects that are undertaken by municipalities. These are small wastewater treatment or solid waste removal projects that are funded by international donor agencies like USAID and World Bank. However given the scarcity of water resources in the region, long-term prospects for water treatment for reuse could become a viable prospect. Solid waste removal and recycling could also become a viable industry but needs huge investments in equipment and educating the public.

An Overview of Some Water Projects Undertaken by USAID in West Bank and Gaza The Environmental Sector in the West Bank and Gaza is being developed with financing from international donors, mainly USAID, World Bank and the EU. Projects are being undertaken to increase the amount of fresh water available to the population by digging new wells in the West Bank, and desalination of seawater and wastewater treatment for reuse in Gaza. This creates an attractive niche market for U.S. exporters of environmental technologies particularly in desalination and wastewater treatment.

The Gaza Coastal Aquifer Management Program Between 1999 and 2005, USAID will provide $100 million to support a program of activities to protect and better manage the Coastal Aquifer, the only local source of fresh water in Gaza. Overuse and pollution endangers the aquifer, and intrusion of urban and agricultural pollutants and seawater is further limiting the amount of water that can be used. The cornerstone of this work will be construction of a desalination plant that will purify up to 20 million cubic meters of sea water each year, equivalent to nearly 40% of Gaza's current municipal consumption. A water carrier project will also be constructed to distribute the water and finally a wastewater treatment and reuse system is planned for Gaza over the next three to five years. On a fee-for service basis, farmers will reuse wastewater after it has been treated. To date, this ongoing program has been obligated a budget of $26 million.

Construction of a New Wastewater Treatment Facility is planned for the Hebron area in the West Bank, home to more than 120,000 Palestinians. Currently, municipal sewage is dumped untreated into neighboring streambeds. The plan also includes pilot projects to improve the treatment of industrial waste. $12 million has been obligated to date.

The West Bank Water Supply Program aims to increase the amount of water available to Palestinians in the West Bank region chronically short of this vital resource. The program involves the drilling of new wells, construction of reservoirs and transmission systems to take water from wells to towns and cities; and building distribution systems to deliver water to homes. Budget obligated to date: $53 million.

For more information, please contact Issa Noursi directly at Tel: 972-2-625-5201, Fax: 972-2-623-5132, orIssa.Noursi@trade.gov

MARKETING PRODUCTS AND SERVICES

IMPACT OF CURRENT EVENTS ON DISTRIBUTION AND SALES CHANNELS

The current events have greatly impacted the distribution and sales channels in the PA because of the new facts on the ground created by the Intifada. Gaza has become almost inaccessible for Palestinian distributors based in the West Bank because movement of trucks and people within and outside of the West Bank has been significantly curtailed.

Palestinian businesses in the West Bank are using alternative unpaved roads to access cities and villages and often distribution programs are altered on a daily basis depending on the evolving facts on the ground.

On the other hand crossing points with Jordan and Egypt at Allenby Bridge and Rafah have been either closed or out of bound for Palestinian businesses for the past nine months. Also PA bound goods have been held up for extended periods at Israeli ports for inspection or because there is no access to West Bank and Gaza.
Demand for goods and services in the PA has generally dropped due to the significant decreased in income, which forced Palestinian businesses to reduce their stock and putt off new orders.

DISTRIBUTION AND SALES CHANNELS

The WB/G population is heavily concentrated in or near the urban centers of Gaza City and Khan Yunis in Gaza and four major towns of Nablus and Ramallah in the northern part of the West Bank and Bethlehem and Hebron in the southern part of the West Bank. The area has no indigenous ports or freight-handling airport, so goods must transit either Israeli, Jordanian, or Egyptian ports. The PA, Israel, Jordan, and Egypt have concluded agreements to allow goods through the Rafah Crossing from Egypt into Gaza and across the Allenby Bridge from Jordan into West Bank markets.

Delays for products entering or exiting WB/G are common, due in large part to Israeli security checks. Most products entering or exiting Gaza transit the Erez/Beit Hanoun or Qarni/al Muntar checkpoints. Time-consuming Israeli security checks can cause delays. Both Israelis and Palestinians recognize the need to move goods faster and in greater quantities, while fully addressing Israeli security concerns. Several options are under study.

Most goods are sold in small retail outlets in WB/G towns. Local consumers are price-conscious, although American brand names are more important than price for more westernized upper-middle class consumers. Moreover, even with shipping costs, American-made consumer products are sometimes cheaper than relatively high-priced comparable Israeli items currently being sold in Palestinian stores.

In 1997 the PA issued a regulation requiring that products intended for sale in WB/G be labeled in Arabic. Wholesale channels and generic sales are not well developed. We expect these channels to expand over the next several years, as they have in the neighboring Israeli market.

U.S. companies are strongly advised to work with local clearing agents to expedite goods through the customs-clearing process. Currently, only Israeli firms are licensed as customs-clearing agents, a situation that may change in the future.

USE OF AGENTS AND DISTRIBUTORS; FINDING A PARTNER

Given the complexity of the local economic and commercial environment, U.S. exporters wishing to market their goods in WB/G are strongly encouraged to use local agents and distributors to obtain maximum sales exposure to the local market. From 1967 through 1995, Israeli companies and Israeli affiliates and franchisees of foreign companies held almost all rights for agencies and distributorships in WB/G.

The establishment of the PA and its increasing control over the Palestinian economy caused many companies to begin reorienting their marketing efforts and to acknowledge the Palestinian market as culturally distinct from the Israeli one.

In 1997 the PA required that foreign companies selling goods in WB/G operate through a PA-registered local direct importer, distributor, or agent. While the USG broadly considers such agency/distributorship decisions to be commercial arrangements best made by the respective companies, it strongly supports Palestinian economic development and encourages direct commercial arrangements between Palestinian and U.S. companies when most practicable to the business parties concerned.

There are several small- and mid-sized WB/G distributorships available for select U.S. food products, cigarettes, household products, computer equipment, medical supplies, and pharmaceuticals. Local distributors now import goods on their own, carry limited stocks sufficient to satisfy immediate needs, and maintain their own sales organizations.

When concluding a representation agreement, U.S. companies should include the following elements:

--Contract duration;
--Exclusivity (if applicable);
--Compensatory amount as a function of contract duration, in case of termination of exclusivity;
--Promotional input by agent and volume of sales; and
--Dispute settlement mechanism, if possible.

The U.S. Commercial Service (CS) and U.S. Foreign Agricultural Service (FAS) at the U.S. Embassy in Tel Aviv and the U.S. Consulate General in Jerusalem provide agent/distributor search services for Gaza and the West Bank, respectively, to assist U.S. companies in establishing themselves in the local market. Interested firms should contact the USG personnel listed at the end of this report.

FRANCHISING

The number of direct franchises is still very small, but three U.S. fast food franchisers -- Checkers and Pizza Inn -- have opened in WB/G over the last few years. Pepsi has had a bottling franchise in Gaza for many years, and, more recently, Coca-Cola, too, has invested in its own WB/G bottling franchise.

In addition, there is great potential for other franchises in sectors including fast food restaurants, computer training, automotive supplies and service, hardware, garments, retailing, and office supplies. As with agency/distributorship arrangements, the USG supports the expansion of the Palestinian economy in WB/G and the deepening of bilateral commercial relations through direct franchise arrangements between Palestinian and U.S. companies.

The key to successful franchising in WB/G will be cost competitiveness in relation to comparable items, brand recognition, strong management and marketing, and initial and ongoing training programs. Due to the relatively small local population, the best franchising potential exists in sectors where specific dietary, language, or usage patterns differ from those in neighboring countries. U.S. companies that want to develop local franchising arrangements should contact the U.S. Commercial Service at the U.S. Embassy in Tel Aviv or the U.S. Consulate general in Jerusalem. (See Chapter 5.)

DIRECT MARKETING

Direct marketing in WB/G has been recently introduced by the Ramallah based Coke bottling franchise and Unipal, a Palestinian company that imports American-made products from major US companies like Phillip Morris and Procter and Gamble. Other local companies are also picking up on this new trend.

JOINT VENTURES/LICENSING

Local Palestinian businesses are eager to develop joint-venture arrangements. Larger local companies, particularly those with export experience, will be reliable partners for U.S. companies. Several small-scale joint ventures with U.S. companies currently operate in WB/G, and discussions on a few larger collaborations are in progress.

The 1998 "Encouragement of Investment Law," which applies to both foreign and local businesses, establishes certain tax breaks and financial incentives for investments in specific industry sectors.

STEPS IN ESTABLISHING AN OFFICE

Given the complexity of jurisdictional authority between the PA and Israel, U.S. businesses should work both with local partners and the U.S. Embassy in Tel Aviv and/or U.S. Consulate General in Jerusalem.

Foreign companies wishing to conduct business in WB/G have the same registration requirements as locally established companies. They must file copies of both their certificate of incorporation and memorandum and articles of association, all authenticated by the registrar of companies located where they are incorporated. These documents must be translated into Arabic. Registration fees for foreign companies are not the same as those for locally established companies. All new WB/G commercial enterprises must register with the PA

**For additional analytical, business and investment opportunities information,
please contact Global Investment & Business Center, USA
at (703) 370-8082. Fax: (703) 370-8083. E-mail: ibpusa3@gmail.com
Global Business and Investment Info Databank - www.ibpus.com**

Ministry of Justice, the Ministry of Economy and Trade, and the Customs Authority, as well as open income tax and value-added tax (VAT) accounts.

SELLING FACTORS/TECHNIQUES

U.S. businesses should note the influence of a comparatively large formerly U.S.-based Palestinian community that has transferred American consumer preferences and buying habits to WB/G. These cultural and consumption links are important factors in local Palestinian knowledge of U.S.-made products. Although price is critical for successful sales in WB/G, local purchasers increasingly seek American quality, particularly for computers, electronic equipment, and consumer items.

ADVERTISING AND TRADE PROMOTION

U.S. products face stiff competition from European, Israeli, and locally made goods. Competitively priced U.S. brand names are popular, particularly with well-to-do Palestinian consumers. Most advertising is done through local Arabic newspapers, although an expansion of advertising through newly established Palestinian radio and television stations is possible. A few companies have begun billboard advertising, which should expand over the next few years. Advertising in WB/G is comparatively cheap by world standards: prime-time Palestinian radio time costs about $35 per minute.

The USG, through the programs of the U.S. Commercial Service and Foreign Agricultural Service, organizes several trade events and catalog shows each year.

Major Newspapers and Business Journals:

Al Quds (Arabic daily) www.alquds.com
Al Ayam (Arabic daily) www.al-ayyam.com
Al Hayat Al Jadida (Arabic daily) www.alhayat-j.com
Jerusalem Times (English weekly) www.jerusalem-times.net

Local Television Stations:

PBC, (All PA)
Wattan , (Private Ramallah area)
El Mahed, (Private Bethlehem area)
Nablus, (Private Nablus area)
El Salam, (Private Tulkarem area)

PRICING PRODUCT

Price is a major factor affecting purchasing decisions by Palestinian companies and consumers. U.S. companies may want to gain market share by introducing products into the Palestinian market at locally competitive prices.

SALES SERVICE/CUSTOMER SUPPORT

Both after-sales service and customer support are important in the WB/G market. They are strong selling points for U.S. goods, as well. However, competitive pricing will remain the key to building a customer base.

SELLING TO THE GOVERNMENT

The PA is beginning to develop a formal tendering and bid process for government contracts. U.S. companies with questions about transparency in bidding procedures for PA contracts or having additional concerns about doing business in WB/G should contact one of the U.S. Commercial Service officers or other Commercial Service personnel listed in Appendix E. When in doubt, please contact these USG employees and local national employees at the U.S. Embassy in Tel Aviv or the U.S. Consulate General in Jerusalem.

PROTECTING YOUR PRODUCT FROM IPR INFRINGEMENT

While WB/G do not have a modern intellectual property rights (IPR) regime in place, the respective authorities are well aware of the problem and are beginning to address the issues involved. The World Bank

For additional analytical, business and investment opportunities information,
please contact Global Investment & Business Center, USA
at (703) 370-8082. Fax: (703) 370-8083. E-mail: ibpusa3@gmail.com
Global Business and Investment Info Databank - www.ibpus.com

and other international donor organizations have developed and are conducting programs to promote awareness of the financial and trade benefits to be derived from observing IPR standards. The legal regime with regard to IPR can be expected to change in the future, as several donor countries and the World Bank are currently assisting in the development of a modern IPR law.

To date, 1967-era Jordanian laws concerning trademarks, patents, and designs are applicable in the West Bank.
In Gaza, the Palestinian Trademark and Patent Laws of 1938, adopted during the British Mandate, are applicable. Registration under the two laws is very similar, and, despite different authorizing legislation, there are few substantive differences between the West Bank and Gaza Strip laws.

Patent protection in WB/G is provided for a period of 16 years from the date of filing the patent application. Furthermore, both systems allow compulsory licensing of anything already patented to be ordered if the "reasonable requirements" of the public under the applicable law have not been met. In Gaza the novelty requirement for patenting may be met if the invention has not been previously published or used. In contrast, the novelty requirement in the West Bank is met if there has been no prior publication, use, or sale in the West Bank.

Trademark protection is available for registered trademarks for a period of seven years, which may be extended for additional periods of 14 years. Prevailing WB/G laws prohibit the registration of a trademark that is contrary to public morals.
Unpublished new and original designs may be protected under WB/G laws. Both applicable legal systems prohibit the registration of designs that are contrary to morality or public order. In Gaza a registered design may be compulsorily licensed under certain circumstances. Compulsory licensing of designs is not allowed in the West Bank. U.S. firms should note that there is minimal enforcement of IPR laws in WB/G.

NEED FOR A LOCAL ATTORNEY

U.S. companies should seek professional legal and/or accountancy advice whenever engaged in complicated contractual arrangements in WB/G. These activities include establishing an office, investing, or applying for IPR registration. Companies may also wish to seek legal assistance when encountering trade or payment problems. A list of local law firms is available from the U.S. Commercial Service offices.

TRADE REGULATIONS, CUSTOMS AND STANDARDS

Import and export procedures for WB/G remain tied in large part to Israeli regulations. Ostensibly, the PA has primary control over imports into WB/G, with Israel retaining quantitative control over some imports in key industries such as dairy products. Most WB/G-bound products pass through Israeli ports and so are subject to Israeli customs and security inspection. U.S. companies should work with Palestinian agents and/or the U.S. Embassy in Tel Aviv and U.S. Consulate General in Jerusalem to determine specific import and export requirements for their goods.

TRADE BARRIERS: TARIFFS, NON-TARIFF BARRIERS, AND IMPORT TAXES

In accordance with duty-free arrangements between the U.S. and the PA, the PA theoretically should not impose tariffs on U.S. products. However, as the PA and Israel are a customs union, and Israel does impose duties and quotas on some U.S. goods, the same conditions apply to U.S. goods destined for WB/G.

The 1994 Paris Protocol provides that the PA not impose tariffs on goods of Israeli origin, but it does impose purchase taxes on many durable goods imported from other countries, generally at Israeli rates. Like Israel, the PA imposes a Value-added Tax (VAT) of 17% on all goods sold in WB/G, whether imported or locally made. By the terms of Palestinian-Israeli agreements, VAT paid to Israel on WB/G-bound goods is rebated to the PA.

CUSTOMS REGULATIONS

The PA does not impose customs tax on U.S. imports, which are, however, taxed as they enter Israeli ports.

For additional analytical, business and investment opportunities information, please contact Global Investment & Business Center, USA at (703) 370-8082. Fax: (703) 370-8083. E-mail: ibpusa3@gmail.com Global Business and Investment Info Databank - www.ibpus.com

IMPORT LICENSES

Import Licenses for WB/G, when required, are issued by the PA. The importer must be a trader registered with the PA and must present a pro-forma invoice and certificate of origin.

The Paris Agreement mandates that the PA must inform the Israeli Ministry of Industry of each import request. While the PA may import some items freely, other items are subject to quantitative restrictions set forth in the Paris Agreement.

The importer is required to submit an application for an import license issued by the Ministry of Economy and Trade available through offices of the Chamber of Commerce. Upon approval, and after the application is stamped and signed, it becomes the import license. Each import shipment must also be authorized by the Ministry and so is subject to quota controls and labeling requirements. Depending on the product, it may also be subject to testing by the Standards Institute of Israel.

In some instances of differing standards, Israeli standards authorities will defer to their Palestinian counterparts on the condition that the importer provides satisfactory assurance that the product(s) in question will remain inside WB/G.

Israel imposes licensing requirements and quantitative restrictions on a wide range of foods and agricultural products. Items subject to quotas – mainly agricultural produce and processed foods – are negotiated annually. The Palestinian share is determined on the basis of estimated consumption requirements and past quota utilization.

All health-related imports, such as food and pharmaceuticals, require approval by both the Israeli Ministry of Health and the Palestinian Ministry of Health, whose standards are the same.

TEMPORARY ENTRY OF GOODS

The PA has not yet established specific provisions for temporary entry of goods. It is currently using Israeli regulations.

IMPORT/EXPORT CONTROLS AND DOCUMENTATION

Some specific items entering WB/G, totaling approximately 15% of total imports, must be accompanied by a pro-forma invoice, packing list, certificate of origin, and import license request.

The remaining 85% of imported items may be imported directly with a permit from the relevant PA ministry. U.S. exporters should check with relevant personnel at the U.S. Embassy in Tel Aviv or the U.S. Consulate General in Jerusalem regarding specific items.

For exports, the PA requires an invoice and certificate of origin signed by the local Chamber of Commerce and the Ministry of Economy and Trade. Permission to export is virtually automatic. However, Israeli security controls apply to Palestinian goods.

No further documentation is required to transit the Allenby Bridge into Jordan and the Rafah Crossing into Egypt, but security checks are conducted. Goods transiting Israeli ports require Israeli port documentation.

LABELING AND MARKING REQUIREMENTS

Goods entering WB/G may be subject to marking and labeling requirements in order to prevent leakage back into Israel. Some goods such as cigarettes and laundry powders now have Arabic or Arabic/English stamps labeled "Only for sale in the West Bank and Gaza." U.S. businesses should check with a Palestinian importer for exact specifications.

As of January 1, 1997, all products imported or brought into WB/G must carry labels in Arabic in addition to the original labels. The labels must carry information on the product ingredients, production and expiry dates, and consumer warnings for hazardous products such as cigarettes and inflammable materials.

PROHIBITED IMPORTS

Although the PA has no published import prohibitions, U.S. companies should check with local Palestinian distributors to see if restrictions apply in certain cases (e.g., food products, firearms, etc.).

STANDARDS

The PA has pledged to apply international standards requirements (e.g., ISO 9000 usage) to all imports. Currently, the PA uses Israeli standards codes for the import of all products that could affect health (e.g., food, especially meat, and pharmaceuticals). Most standards testing is conducted in Israeli labs, although the Palestinian Ministry of Health has begun to institute some testing procedures of its own. Concrete and construction materials as well as some food products are being tested at Bir Zeit University.

FREE TRADE ZONES/WAREHOUSES

The PA, Israel, and the international donor community are establishing industrial zones in WB/G to stimulate local economic activity and employment. Efforts are focused on a pilot zone, the Gaza Industrial Estate (GIE) at Qarni/Al Muntar. The GIE, which was inaugurated in November 1998, will initially house export-oriented industries. However as a result of the current crisis many companies located there have closed shop due to violence in the vicinity of the GIE and road closures that have prevented the transport of goods and people.

In the future, and with the help of donor countries, several additional zones may be established containing 200,000-600,000 square meters of industrial and commercial construction space and, when fully developed, employing 5,000 to 10,000 workers. The management of the zones will probably offer investment-incentive and tax-relief packages. In Tulkarem, the USG plans to support the creation of a High Technology Development Park that would develop links with the nearby Israeli high technology sector. However, all these projects have been put on hold due to the current crisis.

MEMBERSHIP IN FREE TRADE ARRANGEMENTS

In October 1996, President Clinton signed a proclamation granting duty-free import status to items produced in or imported from WB/G.

The European Union has a preferential trade agreement with WB/G similar to that of the U.S. Generalized System of Preferences program. The PA has more restrictive trade agreements with Jordan and Egypt.

Under the terms of the Paris Protocol, there are no restrictions on trade between WB/G and Israel. However, WB/G exports entering Israel face significant barriers, principally as a result of Israeli security measures.

To the best of our knowledge, the information contained in this report is accurate as of the date published. However, the Department of Commerce does not take responsibility for actions readers may take based on the information contained herein. Readers should always conduct their own due diligence before entering into business ventures or other commercial arrangements. The Department of Commerce can assist companies in these endeavors.

TRADE AND PROJECT FINANCING

BRIEF DESCRIPTION OF THE BANKING SYSTEM

The Palestinian Monetary Authority (PMA) has the power and responsibility to regulate and implement monetary policies. It is sole holder and manager of the PA's and Palestinian public-sector entities' foreign currency reserves.

With 23 commercial banks comprising 114 branches now operating in WB/G, the local banking sector has undergone rapid growth since the establishment of the PA in May 1994. Two foreign banks have returned to take up operations abandoned after the 1967 war, and a number of new Palestinian banks have been established and begun operating. Israeli banks do not operate in the West Bank and Gaza.

For additional analytical, business and investment opportunities information,
please contact Global Investment & Business Center, USA
at (703) 370-8082. Fax: (703) 370-8083. E-mail: ibpusa3@gmail.com
Global Business and Investment Info Databank - www.ibpus.com

Cairo-Amman Bank, the largest bank operating in WB/G, has 20 branches and over 700 employees. It handles accounts for most PA ministries, including the Ministry of Finance, the Palestinian Economic Council for Development and Reconstruction (PECDAR), and the Ministry of Planning. It offers extensive overdraft privileges to the PA.

The Palestinian-owned Arab Bank, the largest in the Arab world, has 17 branches in WB/G. Arab Bank offers a wide array of international banking privileges and is highly regarded among the local and international business communities.

West Bank and Gaza banks routinely deal in the Israeli shekel and Jordanian dinar. Banks in WB/G may hold dollar accounts, and they are beginning to develop some offshore banking services.

Israeli shekels are preferred for business dealings, while U.S. dollars and Jordanian dinars are preferred for savings. To offer Israeli shekel accounts, local banks must maintain correspondence relationships with Israeli banks. Most local banks currently have a relatively conservative approach, primarily because the lack of legal remedies and absence of a commercial regulatory banking structure make it nearly impossible to recoup non-paying loans.

Local banks generally offer savings and checking accounts; some do either personal or commercial lending or both. The annual interest rate for Jordanian dinar loans is 11.5–12% (8-9% in interest with a 3.5% "service charge."), while Israeli shekel loans average about 13.5% annually. Most commercial and private lending is done on a short-term basis, of one to three years and one to four years, respectively, with shorter terms the norm. Firms often must put up the full amount of the loan -- or more -- as collateral. The lending to deposit ratio, however, remains low at 32.1 compared to regional standards. Interest rates on both dinar and shekel deposits are around 6%.

FOREIGN EXCHANGE CONTROLS

Under the Interim Agreement, the PMA authorizes foreign exchange transactions within WB/G. West Bank banks must use the Bank of Israel (shekels) and Central Bank of Jordan (dinars) for all foreign exchange transactions. The New Israeli Shekel (NIS) circulates in the area, and so this currency, too, is a legal means of payment.

GENERAL FINANCING AVAILABILITY

As noted above, local bank credit is scarce due to both the lack of a legal code to enforce loan collection and generally conservative local banking practices. Most local businesses use their own capital to finance operations or else work with one of the European credit agencies described below. Some firms seek out international joint-venture partners.

HOW TO FINANCE EXPORTS/METHODS OF PAYMENT

Most local importers use Letters of Credit. U.S. firms should use contractual arrangements to ensure fulfillment of payment obligations, particular when beginning a business relationship.

The U.S. Export-Import Bank (EXIM) offers insurance, loan, and guarantee programs to facilitate export financing of U.S. goods and services. Export financing through EXIM must be done with an obligor/guarantor from outside WB/G in a country with which EXIM has an agreement (e.g., Jordan). EXIM is currently performing a rating of the WB/G as a first step towards deciding whether to provide export financing without requiring an outside obligor/guarantor in the future.

Export credit insurance programs can be obtained from the U.S. Export-Import Bank's (EXIM BANK) Insurance Division. Two short-term (maximum 180 days) policies are designed for small new-to-export businesses. Each provide 95% of the commercial risk and 100% of the political risk involved in extending credit to U.S. exporters' overseas customers. The pre-export working capital program is administered in cooperation with the Small Business Administration (SBA).

EXIM also provides direct loans to foreign buyers of U.S. products and intermediary loans to fund commercial lenders who extend loans to creditworthy foreign buyers of U.S. capital goods and related services. These guarantees cover 100% of principal and interest.

For additional analytical, business and investment opportunities information,
please contact Global Investment & Business Center, USA
at (703) 370-8082. Fax: (703) 370-8083. E-mail: ibpusa3@gmail.com
Global Business and Investment Info Databank - www.ibpus.com

SBA loan guarantees enable small U.S. exporters to obtain financing through commercial banks, usually short-term (i.e., 12-month) export working-capital loans for single transactions. SBA's international business trade loan program also offers small export-trading and export-management companies long-term financing to compete more effectively and to expand or develop export markets.

The Foreign Agricultural Service of the U.S. Department of Agriculture (USDA) administers the Market Promotion Program to help U.S. producers and other organizations finance promotional activities for U.S. products with funds from USDA's Commodity Credit Corporation. These funds can also be used for market research, consumer promotions, and technical assistance.

PROJECT FINANCING

Project finance is available to U.S. investors from the following U.S. government agencies: OPIC, EXIM, and the Trade and Development Administration (TDA). The World Bank's International Finance Corporation (IFC) and the European Community's local development banks and credit agencies also provide project finance, although loans from the latter generally go to local Palestinian companies or to firms with a connection to European companies.

OPIC operates two major financing programs: direct loans and loan guarantees. American investors planning to share significantly in the equity and management of a venture in WB/G may use OPIC medium-to long-term financing (5-12 years). OPIC financing commitment to a new project cannot exceed 50% of the total project cost. OPIC loans usually range from $100,000 to $4 million. Interest rates vary according to the project's financial and political risk.

The OPIC loan guarantee program is available to all U.S. businesses regardless of size. OPIC issues commercial and political risk guarantees under which funding can be obtained from a variety of U.S. financial institutions. Typically, OPIC loan guarantees range from $1 to $25 million but may reach $50 million. Interest rates are comparable to those of other USG-guaranteed issues of similar maturity.

As noted above, EXIM provides project finance in the form of direct loans, guarantees, or a combination of both through its Project Finance Division, in which outside consultants are contracted to evaluate projects. These services are available to major U.S. suppliers and to project sponsors without access to bank or government guarantees. The equity investor must be both creditworthy and exposed to meaningful financial risk. The direct loan and/or guarantee can cover up to 85% of the contract amount. EXIM is committed to completing its evaluation and issuing a preliminary indication of willingness to finance a project within 45 days from the day all the required documentation is submitted with the application for financing.

The Trade and Development Administration (TDA) promotes economic development in developing countries by funding feasibility studies, consultancies, training programs, and other project-planning services. TDA has financed feasibility studies for a food-processing facility, a West Bank olive oil production facility, and a petroleum refinery in Gaza. TDA also organized and financed orientation visits to the U.S. for power and telecommunications officials from WB/G.

The International Finance Corporation (IFC), the private sector arm of the World Bank, was established to encourage private-sector activities in developing countries. IFC provides loans, equity investments, guarantees, and stand-by financing.

Following the signing of the Declaration of Principles in September 1993, the United States pledged $500 million for assistance to the Palestinians over a five-year period. Of this amount, $375 million was to be administered though U.S. Agency for International Development (USAID) programs and the remaining $125 million through OPIC-provided investment guarantees, as described above. The United States increased its pledge at the November 1998, Donors' Conference in Washington following the signing of the Wye River Memorandum.

USAID funds activities and programs to increase private-sector economic opportunities for Palestinians, encouraging broad-based growth by addressing key problems which hinder economic opportunities: small and micro-enterprise access to financial services, access to markets, productivity and competitiveness of Palestinian firms, and the policy framework for private-sector development. Improving private-sector opportunities to achieve increased employment and incomes will help build support for the peace process and provide a stable foundation for long-term prosperity.

BANKS WITH CORRESPONDENT U.S. BANKING ARRANGEMENTS

The Cairo-Amman Bank and Arab Bank, the largest banks operating in the PA, have correspondence relationships with several U.S. banks. Also two international banks operate in the PA: HSBC and Standard Chartered (formerly known as ANZ Grindlays).

Impact of Current Events on Operations of Commercial Banks

The current situation has impacted the commercial banks operations in two areas: a rise in the number of bounced checks and defaulters on loan repayments. However, the liquidity and general financial standing of banks have not been seriously affected because over the last five years banks have been following a very conservative lending policy.

In December 1999 total bank deposits in the PA were $ 2,875.14 million while total outstanding credit was $ 1,00.547 million and out of that $613.8 million was credit to business. Also in December 1999 the overall lending to deposit ratio stood at 34.9 percent while the longest-term loans had a three-year repayment period.

Currently, for example, L/C's are still being issued but full payment is required up front and loans and overdrafts are not available except for top rated customers who can provide collateral.
Clearing of checks between banks is taking longer periods (up to two weeks) and Israeli businesses often refuse to accept checks drawn out on banks operating in WB/G. Most banks are not hiring new staff and those that leave are not being replaced.

To the best of our knowledge, the information contained in this report is accurate as of the date published. However, the Department of Commerce does not take responsibility for actions readers may take based on the information contained herein. Readers should always conduct their own due diligence before entering into business ventures or other commercial arrangements. The Department of Commerce can assist companies in these endeavors.

For additional analytical, business and investment opportunities information,
please contact Global Investment & Business Center, USA
at (703) 370-8082. Fax: (703) 370-8083. E-mail: ibpusa3@gmail.com
Global Business and Investment Info Databank - www.ibpus.com

TRAVEL TO PALESTINE

GENERAL INFORMATION GENERAL INFORMATION

TRAVEL & INFORMATION IN PALESTINE

TRAVEL & INFORMATION IN PALESTINE

The recently opened Gaza Airport offers scheduled flights to nearby countries. Direct air travel is also available through Lod Airport.

Jordan and Egypt have open borders with palestine.

By sea, Palestine can only be reached through ferries from Haifa, Israel.
There are regular ferries to/from Haifia, Greece, Cyprus, and Egypt

CAR HIRE

Local car hire firms generally offer lower rates than the international companies like Avis, Budget and Hertz. If clients are planning to drive throughout the country, it can be a good idea to use a company that has a few offices in case they need a replacement car.

- Prices vary dramatically and shopping around is recommended. Based on 3 day's rental, you should be looking at around $55 to $75 per day for a Fiat Uno or similar with air conditioning, insurance and unlimited mileage. July and August prices are substantially higher than the rest of the year.
- Note: Most car hire companies require that the driver is over 21 and has a driver's license without record of previous auto accidents..
- It is not permitted to take hired vehicles into Sinai or over the border into Jordan.
- All cars are fully insured.

Palestinian Car Rental Companies:

Holy City - East Jerusalem, behind the U.S. Consulate
Tel: 02 5820223
Fax: 02 5824329

Orabi - Jerusalem Street, Al-Bireh, near Ramallah
Tel: 02 9953521, 9955601
Fax: 02 9953521
Branches also in Bethlehem, Jericho and Nablus

Petra - Main Street, East Jerusalem
Tel: 02 5820716
Fax: 02 5822668

Car Rental companies at Ben Gurion Airport:

Avis
Tel: 03 9711919

Budget
Tel: 03 9711504

Eurodollar
Tel: 03 9731271

Europcar
Tel: 03 9721097

Hertz
Tel: 03 9711165

TAXIS

Taxis are widely available in all Palestinian cities. Fares are negotiable. West Bank blue and green license plates are not permitted to enter Jerusalem. Israeli operated taxis (with yellow plates) may enter the West

Bank and Gaza Strip at the driver's discretion. If the driver declines it is easy to transfer to a Palestinian taxi at the checkpoints.

An inexpensive alternative are Service Taxis. These are usually stretch Mercedes seating up to seven passengers, or little Ford vans, which operate on a fixed route for a fixed price just like the public bus. If uncertain about the fare, just ask fellow passengers. Regular rates are normally about 20% more than the bus. Most of them travel between towns and cities from recognized taxi ranks, departing when they are full. This might involve waiting for six other people but the system is very popular and long delays are rare. The locals also tend not to sit inside and wait, but stand around outside instead. Passengers can get out anywhere along the way, but you pay the same fare regardless. After dropping off a passenger a replacement passenger is picked up where possible.

POST AND TELEPHONES

Letters posted in Palestine take seven to ten days to reach North America and Australia and a little less to Europe. Incoming mail is fairly quick, taking about five to seven days for Europe and around ten days for places further afield.

Israel and Palestine have a state of the art card operated public telephone system and international calls can be made from any phone box. Telecards can be bought from news agents, bookshops and post offices.

MONEY

Currencies used in Palestine include the Jordanian dinar and the U.S. dollars but most popular is the New Israeli Shekel (NIS). The Shekel is divided into 100 agorot. There are 200, 100, 50 and 20 NIS notes; 10, 5, and 1 NIS coins; and 50, 10 and 5 agorot coins. There are no restrictions on the amount of foreign currency one can take in or out of the country, nor is one compelled to change any set amount on arrival. Visitors are advised to take dollars, but any other major European currency can also be freely changed at banks and with money changers.

Major credit cards - Visa, MasterCard, Diners Club and American Express are all accepted. Nearly every establishment takes credit cards. Many bank foyers are equipped with cash dispensing ATMs accepting all of the major international credit cards. Travelers cheques are also accepted and visitors will have no trouble getting them cashed. Bearers of Eurocheques can even exchange them at branches of the post office or go to one of the non commission currency exchange bureaus. At the end of a visit Shekels can be exchanged at the airport or at the port in Haifa. Visitors are allowed to freely convert up to US$500 worth of Shekels but for anything over that a bank receipt must be produced as a proof of the original exchange.

HEALTH

Palestine presents no major health hazards for visitors and no vaccinations are legally required. However, probably the biggest health worries one can expect are over exposure to the sun and possibly an upset stomach caused by the change in diet. To avoid the worst worries of the latter, it is advisable to wash fruits and vegetables and to bring anti diarrhea medication for when these precautions fail. A good barrier suntan lotion is essential for protection against sunburn. Drinking plenty of fluids, keeping up salt intake to avoid dehydration and wearing a hat against the sun are advisable. Mosquitoes can sometimes be a problem during the summer. To avoid getting bitten, take a mosquito repellent with you especially if you intend to sleep or camp near the beach.

For additional analytical, business and investment opportunities information, please contact Global Investment & Business Center, USA at (703) 370-8082. Fax: (703) 370-8083. E-mail: ibpusa3@gmail.com Global Business and Investment Info Databank - www.ibpus.com

Tap water is safe to drink throughout the country. One should always be able to get the locally produced mineral water. It is inadvisable to drink from wells or streams unless they are clearly marked as safe to drink.

BUSINESS HOURS

Standard shopping hours are Monday to Thursday 8am - 1pm and 4pm - 7pm or later. Christian owned businesses concentrated in Jerusalem Old City close on Sunday. As for Muslim areas such as East Jerusalem, Gaza strip and the West Bank towns, they remain open on Saturday but are generally closed all day Friday. On Shabbat, most Israeli shops, offices and places of entertainment close down. Shabbat starts at sunset on Friday and ends at sunset on Saturday.

WEATHER

The climate is clear anytime of the year. In winter, Jericho is a favourite resort and even the Jerusalem sun can be warm during the day. Winter can be cold, rainy with the possibility of snow in some areas. In summer, the only problem is how to cool off. The visitor can be better off heading for the higher and drier places inland. Spring is definitely the best time to visit, the weather is temperate enough making it enjoyable to travel around.

Absolute Maximum Tempreature(Celsius)

	Jan	Feb	Mar	Apr	May	Jun	Jul	Aug	Sep	Oct	Nov	Dec
Jerusalem	20.2	21.8	26.3	34.5	38.0	36.8	35.6	37.3	37.2	37.2	27.2	26.5
Nablus	22.9	28.1	30.4	35.0	38.6	38.0	38.1	38.6	38.8	35.3	30.7	28.0
Jenin(BeitQad)	25.0	26.0	26.8	38.6	40.4	37.6	37.0	35.8	37.0	39.0	29.0	25.4
Tulkarm	20.0	20.7	23.0	31.0	32.0	31.0	36.9	34.0	33.2	32.5	27.7	22.3
Jerico	25.0	27.6	33.8	41.4	46.4	45.0	44.0	45.6	43.4	40.6	34.8	28.8
Hebron	21.4	21.0	23.6	32.6	34.0	33.5	38	33.4	34.6	31.6	31.6	22.0
Al-Far'a	27.0	33.1	36.0	45.1	47.2	49.0	48.0	47.0	43.5	42.0	38.8	32.0
Gaza	31.2	34.4	34.8	41.2	43.5	40.0	36.0	32.8	38.8	37.4	35.4	31.6

Absolute MinimumTempreature(Celsius)

	Jan	Feb	Mar	Apr	May	Jun	Jul	Aug	Sep	Oct	Nov	Dec
Jerusalem	-4.1	-3.4	1.0	0.2	4.6	9.0	13.6	14.4	8.6	8.5	0.2	-1.0
Nablus	-0.6	-2.8	-1.0	0.6	6.9	11.4	12.3	15.9	13.0	9.3	1.4	0.3
Jenin(BeitQad)	2.0	1.0	5.0	3.4	12.8	17.0	21.4	21.0	17.8	11.0	11.0	6.0
Tulkarm	4.2	4.8	7.2	9.6	12.6	16.1	18.5	20.3	18.5	14.9	10.8	7.3
Jerico	0.2	-0.4	2.8	2.4	10.4	15.4	18.0	19.0	13.2	11.4	4.2	2.1
Hebron	-1.0	-3.0	-0.5	1.0	6.5	10.0	13.0	12.0	12.0	9.0	2.0	-0.4

| Al-Far'a | 0.5 | 2.0 | 3.0 | 5.0 | 10.5 | 14.5 | 16.5 | 20.0 | 17.5 | 12.0 | 6.5 | 2.7 |
| Gaza | 2.0 | 2.6 | 3.6 | 7.4 | 11.4 | 14.8 | 18.5 | 19.2 | 16.2 | 12.2 | 7.5 | 3.4 |

Sunshine Duration (hour/day)

	Jan	Feb	Mar	Apr	May	Jun	Jul	Aug	Sep	Oct	Nov	Dec
Jerusalem	5.4	7.1	7.4	9.4	11.4	12.4	12.1	11.8	10.1	7.3	6.5	5.9
Nablus	4.2	4.8	6.4	8.2	8.9	8.4	9.6	10.9	10.2	9.8	7.0	4.5
Jenin(BeitQad)	5.4	5.6	6.8	7.8	9.7	11.3	11.1	10.0	9.1	8.1	6.8	5.4
Jerico	5.5	5.9	7.7	9.3	9.4	11.8	11.7	11.6	10.5	8.7	6.5	5.6
Hebron	4.7	4.8	6.4	8.1	9.0	8.3	9.6	10.9	10.3	9.8	7.0	4.7
Gaza	5.2	5.9	7.3	8.2	8.9	9.7	10.5	10.4	9.3	8.5	6.5	5.1

Rainfall (mm)

	Jan	Feb	Mar	Apr	May	Jun	Jul	Aug	Sep	Oct	Nov	Dec	Total
Jerusalem	143.0	118.0	96.0	27.0	4.0	0.0	0.0	0.0	0.0	18.0	64.0	115.0	585.0
Nablus	149.0	144.0	101.0	32.0	7.0	0.0	0.0	0.0	2.0	18.0	67.0	143.0	663.0
Jenin(BeitQad)	107.0	62.0	66.0	25.0	6.0	0.0	0.0	0.0	0.0	16.0	40.0	93.0	415.0
Methalun	148.0	121.9	87.0	26.9	5.9	0.0	0.0	0.0	0.0	18.4	72.1	138.8	619.7
Tulkarm	153.0	110.0	77.0	25.0	4.0	0.0	0.0	0.0	0.0	27.0	97.0	170.0	663.0
Jerico	36.0	31.0	25.0	10.0	2.0	0.0	0.0	0.0	0.0	7.0	22.0	33.0	166.0
Hebron	145.0	131.0	90.0	37.0	4.0	0.0	0.0	0.0	1.0	14.0	63.0	116.0	601.0
Gaza	105.0	88.0	37.0	9.0	1.0	0.0	0.0	0.0	0.0	36.0	71.0	99.0	446.0

HANDICRAFTS

Cross-stitch embroidery is an ancient art form in Palestine. Using natural homemade materials, women artistically embroider dresses, jackets, vests, cushions, tablecloths, and much more. Jerusalem pottery is another art in Palestine. Ceramic ware decorated with geometric patterns, the stained glass made into crystal wine, and champagne glasses are very popular. Religious ornaments, handmade made from olive wood and mother-of-pearl with a painstaking attention to detail, are especially attractive. Palestine's world-renowned olive wood artifacts are made from the local olive trees. Olive trees in Palestine are not only found in abundance but some date back to the times of Jesus. Exquisite olive wood statues, boxes, crosses, and other artifacts can be found at the numerous souvenir shops in Bethlehem and Jerusalem.

ACCOMMODATION

Most major Palestinian cities and towns offer a variety of conveniently located places to stay, including hotels, hospices and bed & breakfast and Bedoin Villages. Located in Christian convents, hospices offer the same facilities and prices as hotels. B&B is inexpensive and offers the visitor a unique opportunity to become acquainted with Palestinian family life.

For additional analytical, business and investment opportunities information, please contact Global Investment & Business Center, USA at (703) 370-8082. Fax: (703) 370-8083. E-mail: ibpusa3@gmail.com Global Business and Investment Info Databank - www.ibpus.com

LOCAL CUISINE

Palestinian cuisine is very popular among visitors. Diners are offered an appetizing a s s o r t m e n t o f h o r s - d'oeuvres, known as mezze. Humus and baba ghanouj, widely known in Europe and the United States are made to perfection in Palestine. Main courses include a savory collec- tion of meat, poultry, seafood, and vegetable dishes. Palestine is also renowned f o r i t s s u c c u l e n t s w e e t pastries.

CLIMATE

There are four seasons in Palestine. Winter is mildly cold and rainy while summer is usually hot and dry. Autumn is pleasant and spring is beautiful with the wide array of wild flowers and blooming tress. Average temperatures in Palestine range from 9-18 C in winter and 26-30 C in summer. Regardless of the season, visitors are advised to wear modest dress especially when visiting holy sites.

COMMUNICATION

International calls can be made from domestic telephones, including public pay phones. Fax and E-mail services are available.

CURRENCY

In the absence of a Palestinian monetary unit, the New Israeli Shekel remains in use. All major credit cards and travelers cheques are accepted. Foreign currencies can easily be exchanged at any bank or money exchange shop.

ECONOMY

Palestine has a developing economy in tourism and agriculture and this generates the country's main economic income. With seven agroclimatic zones with at least 20 different soils, nearly 60 agricultural crops are grown in Palestine. Industry and trade are still small-scale, largely due to Israeli restrictions.

LANGUAGE

Arabic is the official language in Palestine. English is widely spoken, while Italian, French, Spanish and German are spoken to a lesser extent.

TRANSPORTATION

Car rental companies in major Palestinian cities provide self-driven cars at reasonable prices. Taxis are both comfortable and widely available. However, since taxis don't operate on meters, it is best to agree on the price before setting off. Shared taxis operating on regular lines, called Service, are also widely used.

LOCAL TIME

Palestinian time is GMT +2 hours in winter and GMT +3 hours in summer.

SHOPPING

Shopping in Palestine is an enjoyable experience, with customers and merchants often haggling over prices. The country's main streets and old markets are filled with shops selling local and imported items. Especially appealing to tourists are numerous shops selling exotic hand-made items, aromatic Middle Eastern spices, jewelry, tasty oriental sweets and much more.

TRAVEL

The recently opened Gaza airport offers scheduled flights to nearby countries. Direct air travel is also available through Lod Airport.

WORKING HOURS

Government offices open from 8:00a.m. – 2:30p.m. Banks open from 8:00a.m. – 12:30p.m., with some banks reopening again from 3:00 – 5:00p.m. Most shops open from around 8:00a.m. until around 7:00 p.m.

Muslim-owned shops usually close on Friday while the Christian-owned on Sunday. The official weekend is Friday.

US STATE DEPARTMENT SUGGESTIONS FOR TRAVEL TO ISRAEL, THE WEST BANK AND GAZA

WARNING: The Department of State warns U.S. citizens to defer travel to Israel, the West Bank and Gaza. The U.S. Government has indications that there is a heightened threat of terrorist incidents in Israel, the West Bank and Gaza. In light of several recent terrorist bombings in Israel and continuing violence in Gaza and the West Bank, American citizens should exercise extreme caution and avoid shopping areas, malls, public buses and bus stops as well as crowded areas and demonstrations. U.S. Embassy and Consulate employees and their families have been prohibited from using public buses. American citizens should maintain a low profile and take appropriate steps to reduce their vulnerability.

Violent clashes and confrontations continue to take place throughout the West Bank and Gaza. U.S. Embassy and Consulate employees have been prohibited from traveling to the West Bank, Gaza, commercial districts of East Jerusalem, and the Old City of Jerusalem, except for mission essential business. Private American citizens should avoid travel to these areas at this time and Americans residing in the West Bank and Gaza should consider relocating to a safe location, if they can do so safely.

From time to time, the Embassy or Consulate General will temporarily suspend public services as necessary to review its security posture. In those instances U.S. citizens who require emergency services may telephone the Consulate General in Jerusalem at (972) (2) 622-7230 or the Embassy in Tel Aviv at (972) (3) 519-7355.

COUNTRY DESCRIPTION: The State of Israel is a parliamentary democracy with a modern economy. Tourist facilities are widely available. Israel occupied the West Bank, Gaza Strip, Golan Heights, and East Jerusalem as a result of the 1967 War. Pursuant to negotiations between Israel and the Palestinians, an elected Palestinian Authority now exercises jurisdiction in parts of Gaza and the West Bank. Palestinian Authority police are responsible for keeping order in those areas and the Palestinian Authority exercises a range of civil functions. The division of responsibilities and jurisdiction in the West Bank and Gaza between Israel and the Palestinian Authority is complex. Definitive information on entry, customs requirements, arrests, and other matters in the West Bank and Gaza is subject to change without prior notice or may not be available.

ENTRY REQUIREMENTS: Israel: A valid passport, an onward or return ticket, and proof of sufficient funds are required for entry. A no-charge three-month visa may be issued upon arrival and may be renewed. Travelers carrying official or diplomatic U.S. passports must obtain visas from an Israeli embassy or consulate prior to arrival in Israel. Anyone who has been refused entry or experienced difficulties with his/her visa status during a previous visit, or who has overstayed a visa, should consult the Israeli Embassy or nearest Israeli Consulate before attempting to return to Israel. Anyone seeking returning resident status must obtain permission from Israeli authorities before traveling.

West Bank and Gaza: Except during periods of heightened security restrictions, most U.S. citizens may enter and exit the West Bank and Gaza on a U.S. passport with an Israeli entry stamp. It is not necessary to obtain a visitor's permit from the Palestinian Authority to travel to the West Bank or Gaza. Private vehicles may not cross from Israel into Gaza and may be stopped at checkpoints entering or leaving the West Bank.

The Allenby Bridge crossing from the West Bank into Jordan, and the Rafah crossing from Gaza into Egypt are under the jurisdiction of the Israeli Government, which also controls entry and exit via the Gaza International Airport. This may have special ramifications for Palestinian Americans and other Arab Americans.

Palestinian Americans: American citizens of Palestinian origin who were born on the West Bank or Gaza or resided there for more than three months, may be considered by Israeli authorities to be residents,

- 120 -

especially if they or their parents were issued a Palestinian ID number. Any American citizen whom Israel considers to be a resident is required by Israel to hold a valid Palestinian passport to enter or leave the West Bank or Gaza via Israel, the Gaza International Airport, or the Rafah or Allenby Bridge border crossing. American citizens in this category who arrive without a Palestinian passport will generally be granted permission to travel to the West Bank or Gaza to obtain one, but may only be allowed to depart via Israel on a Palestinian passport rather than on their U.S. passport. The Government of Israel does not require travel on a Palestinian passport for visits of less than 90 days, but may instead require a transit permit for travel to the West Bank or Gaza.

During periods of heightened security restrictions, Palestinian Americans with residency status in the West Bank or Gaza may not be allowed to enter or exit Gaza or the West Bank, even if using their American passports. Specific questions may be addressed to the nearest Israeli Embassy or Consulate.

Israel-Jordan Crossings: International crossing points between Israel and Jordan are the Arava crossing (Wadi al-'Arabah) in the south, near Eilat, and the Jordan River crossing (Sheikh Hussein Bridge) in the north, near Beit Shean. American citizens using these two crossing points to enter either Israel or Jordan need not obtain prior visas, but will have to pay a fee at the bridge. Visas should be obtained in advance for those wanting to cross the Allenby Bridge between Jordan and the occupied West Bank. (Note: The Government of Israel requires that Palestinian Americans with residency status in the West Bank or Gaza only enter Jordan by land by means of the Allenby Bridge.) Procedures for all crossings into Jordan are subject to frequent changes.

For further entry information on Israel, travelers may contact the Embassy of Israel at 3514 International Drive NW, Washington, D.C. 20008, telephone (202) 364-5500, or the Israeli Consulates General in Los Angeles, San Francisco, Miami, Atlanta, Chicago, Boston, New York, Philadelphia, or Houston.

In an effort to prevent international child abduction, many governments have initiated procedures at entry/exit points. These often include requiring documentary evidence of relationship and permission for the child's travel from the parent(s) or legal guardian not present. Having such documentation on hand, even if not required, may facilitate entry/departure.

DUAL NATIONALITY: Israeli citizens naturalized in the United States retain their Israeli citizenship, and their children usually become Israeli citizens. In addition, children born in the United States to Israeli parents usually acquire both U.S. and Israeli nationality at birth. Israeli citizens, including dual nationals, are subject to Israeli laws requiring service in Israel's armed forces. U.S.-Israeli dual nationals of military age who do not wish to serve in the Israeli armed forces should contact the Israeli Embassy in Washington, D.C. to learn more about an exemption or deferment from Israeli military service before going to Israel. Without this document, they may not be able to leave Israel without completing military service or may be subject to criminal penalties for failure to serve. Israeli citizens, including dual nationals, must enter and depart Israel on their Israeli passports.

Palestinian Americans whom the Government of Israel considers residents of the West Bank or Gaza may face certain travel restrictions (see Entry Requirements above). These individuals are subject to restrictions on movement between Israel, the West Bank and Gaza and within the West Bank and Gaza imposed by the Israeli Government on all Palestinians for security reasons. During periods of heightened security concerns these restrictions can be onerous. Palestinian-American residents of Jerusalem are normally required to use laissez-passers (documents issued by the Israeli Government) which contain re-entry permits approved by the Israeli Ministry of Interior.

All U.S. citizens with dual nationality must enter and depart the U.S. on their U.S. passports.

SAFETY AND SECURITY: Israel has strict security measures that may affect visitors. Prolonged questioning and detailed searches may take place at the time of entry and/or departure at all points of entry to Israel, including entry from the West Bank and Gaza. Travelers with Arabic surnames, those who ask that Israeli stamps not be entered into their passports, and unaccompanied female travelers have been delayed and subjected to close scrutiny at points of entry. Security-related delays or obstacles in bringing in or departing with cameras or electronic equipment are not unusual. Laptop computers and other electronic equipment have been confiscated from travelers leaving Israel from Ben Gurion Airport during security checks. While most are returned prior to departure, some equipment has been damaged, destroyed or lost as a result. Americans who have had personal property damaged due to security procedures at Ben Gurion can contact the Commissioner of Complaints at the airport for redress. During searches and questioning, Israeli authorities have denied American citizens access to U.S. consular officers, lawyers, or family members. Palestinian Americans have been arrested on suspicion of security crimes when attempting to enter or leave Israel, the West Bank and Gaza. The Israeli National Police have monitored, arrested and deported members of religious groups who they believed intended to commit violent or disruptive acts in Israel.

TERRORISM: Although they have not been targeted for attack, U.S. citizens have been injured or killed in past terrorist actions in Israel, Jerusalem, the West Bank, and Gaza. Attacks have occurred in highly frequented shopping and pedestrian areas and on public buses. U.S. Embassy and Consulate employees and their families have been prohibited from using public buses. American citizens should exercise extreme caution and avoid shopping areas, pedestrian walkways, malls, public buses and bus stops as well as crowded areas and demonstrations.

American citizens should use caution in the vicinity of military sites, areas frequented by off-duty soldiers, contentious religious sites, and large crowds. Travelers should remain aware of their immediate surroundings, and should not touch any suspicious object.

DEMONSTRATIONS AND CIVIL UNREST: In the West Bank, Gaza and Jerusalem, demonstrations or altercations can occur spontaneously and have the potential to become violent without warning. If such disturbances occur, American visitors should leave the area immediately. In Jerusalem's Old City, where exits are limited, American visitors should seek safe haven inside a shop or restaurant until the incident is over. Demonstrations are particularly dangerous in areas such as checkpoints, settlements, military areas, and major thoroughfares where protesters are likely to encounter Israeli security forces.

Demonstrations by Arab Israelis in northern Israel have occurred on Land Day (March 30) and on Israeli Independence Day (date varies). These demonstrations have generally been peaceful, but on occasion Embassy staff have been told to avoid certain areas on those dates.

AREAS OF INSTABILITY: Jerusalem: In Jerusalem, travelers should exercise caution at religious sites on holy days, Fridays, Saturdays, and Sundays. Dress appropriately when visiting the Old City and ultra-orthodox Jewish neighborhoods. Most roads into ultra-orthodox Jewish neighborhoods are blocked off on Friday nights and Saturdays. Assaults on secular visitors, either for being in cars or for being "immodestly dressed," have occurred in these neighborhoods. Isolated street protests and demonstrations can occur in the commercial districts of East Jerusalem (Salah Eddin Street and Damascus Gate areas) during periods of unrest. U.S. Government employees have been prohibited from traveling to the commercial areas of East Jerusalem, including the Old City, except for mission essential business. Private American citizens should avoid travel to these areas at this time.

West Bank and Gaza: The U.S. Government currently prohibits U.S. Government employees, officials, and dependents from traveling to the West Bank and Gaza, except for mission essential business. Private American citizens should avoid travel to these areas at this time. Embassy staff have also been prohibited from using Rt. 443 (the Modi'in Road) in Israel to travel to Jerusalem.

During periods of unrest, access to the West Bank and Gaza are sometimes closed off by the Israeli government. Travel restrictions may be imposed with little or no warning. Strict measures have frequently been imposed following terrorist actions and the movement of Palestinian Americans with residency status in the West Bank or Gaza and foreign passport holders have been severely impaired

In the Golan Heights, there are live land mines in many areas and visitors should walk only on established roads or trails. Near the northern border of Israel, rocket attacks from Lebanese territory can occur without warning.

CRIME: The crime rate is moderate in Israel, Jerusalem, the West Bank and Gaza. The loss or theft of a U.S. passport abroad should be reported immediately to local police and the nearest U.S. Embassy or Consulate. U.S. citizens may refer to the Department of State's pamphlets, *A Safe Trip Abroad* and *Tips for Travelers to the Middle East and North Africa.* They are available from the Superintendent of Documents, U.S. Government Printing Office, Washington, DC 20402, via the internet at http://www.access.gpo.gov/su_docs, or via the Bureau of Consular Affairs home page at http://travel.state.gov.

MEDICAL FACILITIES: Modern medical care and medicines are available in Israel. Some hospitals in Israel and most hospitals in the West Bank and Gaza, however, fall below U.S. standards. Travelers can find information in English about emergency medical facilities and after-hours pharmacies in the "Jerusalem Post" and English language "Ha'aretz" newspapers.

MEDICAL INSURANCE: The Department of State strongly urges Americans to consult with their medical insurance company prior to traveling abroad to confirm whether their policy applies overseas and whether it will cover emergency expenses such as a medical evacuation. U.S. medical insurance plans seldom cover health costs incurred outside the United States unless supplemental coverage is purchased. Further, U.S. Medicare and Medicaid programs do not provide payment for medical services outside the United States. However, many travel agents and private companies offer insurance plans that will cover health care expenses incurred overseas including emergency services such as medical evacuations.

When making a decision regarding health insurance, Americans should consider that many foreign doctors and hospitals require payment in cash prior to providing service and that a medical evacuation to the U.S. may cost well in excess of $50,000. Uninsured travelers who require medical care overseas often face extreme difficulties, whereas travelers who have purchased overseas medical insurance have, when a medical emergency occurs, found it life-saving. When consulting with your insurer prior to your trip, ascertain whether payment will be made to the overseas healthcare provider or whether you will be reimbursed later for expenses you incur. Some insurance policies also include coverage for psychiatric treatment and for disposition of remains in the event of death.

Useful information on medical emergencies abroad, including overseas insurance programs, is provided in the Department of State's Bureau of Consular Affairs brochure *Medical Information for Americans Traveling Abroad,* available via the Bureau of Consular Affairs home page or autofax: (202) 647-3000.

OTHER HEALTH INFORMATION: Travelers from regions where contagious diseases are prevalent may need to show shot records before entry into Israel. Information on vaccinations and other health precautions may be obtained from the Centers for Disease Control and Prevention's international travelers hotline at 1-877-FYI-TRIP (1-877-394-8747), fax: 1-888-CDC-FAXX (1-888-232-3299), or by visiting the CDC Internet home page at http://www.cdc.gov.

TRAFFIC SAFETY AND ROAD CONDITIONS: While in a foreign country, U.S. citizens may encounter road conditions that differ significantly from those in the United States. The information below is provided for general reference only, and may not be totally accurate in a particular location or circumstance.

Israel:

Safety of Public Transportation: good*
Urban Road Conditions/Maintenance: good
Rural Road Conditions/Maintenance: good
Availability of Roadside Assistance: good

*U.S. Embassy and Consulate employees and their families have been prohibited from using public buses (please review the earlier section entitled "Terrorism.")

Israeli roads and highways tend to be crowded, especially in urban areas. Aggressive driving is a serious problem and few drivers maintain safe following distances. Drivers should use caution, as there is a high rate of fatalities from automobile accidents.

For specific information concerning Israeli driver's permits, vehicle inspection, road tax and mandatory insurance, contact the Israel Ministry of Tourism office in New York via the internet at http://www.goisrael.com.

West Bank and Gaza:

Safety of Public Transportation: poor
Urban Road Conditions/Maintenance: poor
Rural Road Conditions/Maintenance: poor
Availability of Roadside Assistance: poor

Crowded roads and aggressive driving are common in the West Bank and Gaza. During periods of heightened tensions, cars with Israeli license plates have been stoned. Emergency services may be delayed by the need for Palestinian authorities to coordinate with Israeli officials. Seat belt use is required outside of cities, drivers may not drink alcohol, and travel by motorcycle is not allowed. Individuals involved in accidents resulting in death or injury may be detained by police pending an investigation.

For additional information about road safety, see the Department of State, Bureau of Consular Affairs home page road safety overseas feature at http://travel.state.gov/road_safety.html.

AVIATION SAFETY OVERSIGHT: The U.S. Federal Aviation Administration has assessed the Government of Israel's Civil Aviation Authority as Category 1 - in compliance with international aviation safety standards for oversight of Israel's air carrier operations. For further information, travelers may contact the Department of Transportation within the U.S. at 1-800-322-7873, or visit the FAA's website at http://www.faa.gov/avr/iasa/index.html. The U.S. Department of Defense (DOD) separately assesses some foreign air carriers for suitability as official providers of air services. For information regarding the DOD policy on specific carriers, travelers may contact DOD at (618) 229-4801.

CUSTOMS REGULATIONS: Video cameras and other electronic items must be declared upon entry to Israel. Please contact the Embassy of Israel for specific information regarding customs requirements. Definitive information on customs requirements for the Palestinian Authority is not available.

CRIMINAL PENALTIES: While in a foreign country, a U.S. citizen is subject to that country's laws and regulations, which sometimes differ significantly from those in the United States and may not afford the protections available to the individual under U.S. law. Penalties for breaking the law can be more severe than in the United States for similar offenses. Individuals traveling to the West Bank and Gaza through Israel or Israeli-controlled entry points are also subject to Israeli law and jurisdiction. Persons violating Israel's or the Palestinian Authority's laws, even unknowingly, may be expelled, arrested or imprisoned. Penalties for possession, use, or trafficking in illegal drugs in Israel are strict and convicted offenders can expect jail sentences and heavy fines. The Palestinian Authority also has strict penalties for the possession, use, or trafficking in illegal drugs by persons visiting or residing in its jurisdiction.

ARRESTS AND DETENTION: U.S. citizens arrested by the Israeli National Police (INP) in Israel and charged with crimes are entitled to legal representation and consular notification and visitation. Typically the INP notifies the Embassy or Consulate General within two days of arrest, and consular access is normally granted within four days. This procedure may be expedited if the arrested American shows a U.S. passport to the police, or asks the police to contact the U.S. Embassy or Consulate.

U.S. citizens arrested by the Israeli Security Police for security offenses, and U.S. citizens arrested in the West Bank or Gaza for criminal or security offenses may be prevented from communicating with lawyers, family members, or consular officers for lengthy periods. The U.S. Consulate General and the Embassy are often not notified of such arrests, or are not notified in a timely manner. Consular access to the arrested individual is frequently delayed. U.S. citizens have been subject to mistreatment during interrogation and pressured to sign statements in Hebrew which have not been translated. Under local law they may be detained for up to six months at a time without charges. Youths over the age of 14 have been detained and tried as adults. When access to a detained American citizen is denied or delayed, the U.S. government formally protests the lack of consular access to the Israeli government. The U.S. Government also will protest any mistreatment to the relevant authorities as well.

U.S. citizens arrested by the Palestinian Authority (PA) Security Forces in the West Bank or Gaza for crimes are entitled to legal representation and consular notification and access. The PA Security Forces normally notify the Embassy (for Gaza) or Consulate General (for West Bank) within two days of arrest and consular access is normally granted within four days. This procedure may be expedited if the arrested American shows a U.S. passport to the police, or asks the police to contact the U.S. Embassy or Consulate.

U.S. citizens arrested by the PA Security Forces in the West Bank or Gaza for security offenses may be prevented from communicating with lawyers, family members, or consular officers for lengthy periods. In addition, they may be held in custody for protracted periods without formal charges or before being taken in front of a judge for an arrest extension. The U.S. Consulate General is often not notified by the PA of the arrests in a timely manner, and consular access to the arrested is occasionally delayed. The U.S. Government does not have a formal mechanism for protesting these delays in notification or access to the Palestinian Authority; however, our concerns are pursued with local PA officials.

COURT JURISDICTION: Civil courts in Israel actively exercise their authority to bar certain individuals, including nonresidents, from leaving the country until monetary and other legal claims against them can be resolved. Israel's rabbinical courts exercise jurisdiction over all Jewish citizens and residents of Israel in cases of marriage, divorce, child custody and child support. In some cases, Jewish Americans who entered Israel as tourists have become defendants in divorce cases filed by their spouses in Israeli rabbinical courts. These Americans have been detained in Israel for prolonged periods while the Israeli courts consider whether they have sufficient ties to Israel to establish rabbinical court jurisdiction. Jewish American visitors should be aware that they might be subject to involuntary and prolonged stays in Israel if a case is filed against them in a rabbinical court, even if their marriage took place in the U.S. and/or their spouse is not present in Israel.

CHILDREN'S ISSUES: For information on the international adoption of children and international parental child abduction, please refer to our Internet site at http://travel.state.gov/childrens-issues.html or telephone: (202) 736-7000.

REGISTRATION/EMBASSY AND CONSULATE LOCATIONS: The State Department advises American citizens who plan to be in the region for over a month to register at the U.S. Embassy in Tel Aviv or the U.S. Consulate General in Jerusalem. E-mail registration for the U.S. Embassy is possible at amctelaviv@state.gov and for the U.S. Consulate General at jerusalemacs@state.gov. When registering, U.S. citizens can obtain updated information on travel and security in the area.

The U.S. Embassy in Tel Aviv, Israel is located at 71 Hayarkon Street. The U.S. mailing address is PSC 98, Box 0001, APO AE 09830. The telephone number is (972)(3) 519-7575. The number after 4:30 p.m. and before 8:00 a.m. local time is (972)(3) 519-7551. The fax number is (972)(3) 516-4390. The Embassy's e-mail address is amctelaviv@state.gov and its Internet web page is http://consular.usembassy-israel.org.il.

The Consular Section of the U.S. Embassy should be contacted for information and help in the following areas: Israel, the Gaza Strip, the Golan Heights and ports of entry at Ben Gurion Airport, Gaza International Airport, Haifa Port, and the northern (Jordan River) and southern (Arava) border crossings connecting Israel and Jordan.

The Consular Section of the U.S. Consulate General in Jerusalem is located at 27 Nablus Road. The U.S. mailing address is Unit 7228, Box 0039, APO AE 09830. The telephone number is (972)(2) 622-7200. The number after 4:30 p.m. and before 8:00 a.m. local time is (972)(2) 622-7250. The fax number is (972)(2) 627-2233. The Consulate's e-mail address is jerusalemacs@state.gov and its Internet web page is http://www.uscongen-jerusalem.org.

The U.S. Consulate General should be contacted for information and help in the following areas: West and East Jerusalem, the West Bank, and the Allenby Bridge border crossing connecting Jordan with the West Bank.

There is a U.S. Consular Agent in Haifa at 26 Ben Gurion Boulevard, telephone (972)(4) 853-1470, who reports to the Embassy in Tel Aviv. The Consular Agent can provide routine and emergency services in the north.

For additional analytical, business and investment opportunities information, please contact Global Investment & Business Center, USA at (703) 370-8082. Fax: (703) 370-8083. E-mail: ibpusa3@gmail.com Global Business and Investment Info Databank - www.ibpus.com

SUPPLEMENTS

PALESTINIAN MINISTRIES

Ministry	Minister	Tel.	Fax
President's Office		07-824670/1/2	07-822365/6
Ministry of Interior	Ahmad Al-Tamimi	07-829188	07-868809
Ministry of "Wakf" and Religious Affairs	Hassan Tahboub	07-28488607 9987184	07-282085
Ministry of Economy and Trade	Maher Al-Masri	02-5747040	02-574782
Ministry of Industry	Bashir Al-Barghoti	050834593302 9987641/2	
Ministry Of Education	Yasser Amr	02-9985555 07-861409	02-9985559 07-865969
Ministry of Planning and International Cooperation	Nabil Sha'ath	07-829260 02-9574704/5	07-824090 02-5747046
Ministry of Tourism	Ilyas Fraij	02-741581/2/3 02-6470603 07-824856	02-743753 02-6470604 07-824866
AL-Quds "Jerusalem" Affairs	Faisal Husseini	02-627330 6275569	02-6274026
Ministry Of Civil Affairs	Jamil AL- Tarifi	02-9986336/7/8 02-9987452/3	02-9987335 02-9987451
Ministry Of Supply	Abdel Aziz Shahin	07-826420 02-9987894/5	07-826430 02-9987896
Ministry of Information	Yassir Abed Rabbo	02-9986465 02-9954042 9954044 07-866888	02-9954043 07-824926
Ministry of Culture	Yassir Abed Rabbo	02-9986205/6 07-824850/60	02-9986204 07-824870
Ministry of Local Government	Sa'eb Erikat	02-9921260 9986610	02-9921240 02-9951282
Ministry of Labor	Samir Gosheh	Telefax 02-9986496	
Ministry of Transport	Ali Qawasmi	02-9986954	02-9986570
Ministry of Communication	Imad Falouji	07-824200	07-867709
Ministry of Social Affairs	Intisar Al- Wazir	02-9986182/3/4 07-829189	07-863917 02-9955723
Ministry of Health	Dr. Riyad Al- Za'noun	Telefax 07-829173 09-384771	
Ministry of Housing	Abdel Rahman Hamad	07-822233	07-822935

For additional analytical, business and investment opportunities information, please contact Global Investment & Business Center, USA at (703) 370-8082. Fax: (703) 370-8083. E-mail: ibpusa3@gmail.com Global Business and Investment Info Databank - www.ibpus.com

		02-9957744	
Ministry of Finance	Muhammad Nashashibi	02-9985881 Telefax 07-829243	02-9985882
Ministry of Agriculture	Abdel Jawad Saleh	02-9922425 07-829123/4	02-9986502
Ministry of Justice	Fraih Abu-Meddein	07-829118 07-829116	07-867109
Ministry of Youth and Sport	Talal Sider	02-9985981/2 07-822743	02-9985991 07-868045
Ministry of Public Works	Azzam Al-Ahmad	02-9987888 07-856235 050-356422	07-823653
Ministry of Higher Education	Hanan Ashrawi	02-9954495	02-9954490
Palestine Broadeasting Corporation		02-9987580 02-65640163	02-9987581 02-6564029
Palestine Monetary Authority		07-864144 07-825713 02-9986595	07-824817
Palestine Central Bureau of Statistics		02-9986340/3	02-9986343
Palestine National Committee for Education, Culture, and Science		02-9986333 050369183	02-9958325
Palestine Geographic Center		Telefax02-5747111	
Negotiations Affairs Dept.		07-823487	07-821578

SELECTED CONTACTS

CULTURAL CENTERS

BETHLEHEM

Al-Liqa' Centre for Religious & Heritage Studies
Dir: Dr. Geries Khoury - P.O.Box 11328 - Hebron Rd. Bethlehem - Tel: 02-2741639
Research & studies on religious traditions & institutions of the people of the Holy Land & the region; interfaith promotion.

Anat Palestinian Folk and Craft Women's Centre
Mrs.Mary Mousallam Qumsieh - P.O.Box 1003 - Bethlehem - Tel: 02-2772024 & Fax: 02-2772024
Social and cultural activities; income-generating projects / marketing folkloric handicrafts; lectures; training for women.

Bethlehem Folklore Musem - Arab Women's Union - P.O.Box 19 - Tel: 02-2742589

International Centre of Bethlehem - Rev. Dr. Mitri Raheb - P.O.Box 62 - Paul VI St.
Tel: 02-2770047 & Fax: 02-2770048
Depts. For Women studies, Int. Relations, Adult Education, Alternative Tourism, Faith, German-Palestinian culture.

Palestinian Group for Revival of Popular Heritage
Jalil Elias - P.O.Box 282 - Tel: 02-2743249 & Fax: 02-2741449

Palestinian Heritage Centre - Director: Maha Saca - P.O.Box 146 - Manger St.
Tel: 02-2742381 & Fax: 2742642

GAZA

Amal Cultural Centre - Adib Jarada - Gaza City - Tel: 07-864301
Cultural and training programmes

Cultural Centre for Gaza - Mohammed Najja - P.O.Box 1062
Tel: 07-864599/821104 & Tel: 07-868965

Culture and Light Centre - Isam Farah - Rimal - Gaza Est. - Tel: 07-865896
Library; scientific & cultural services.

Gaza Cultural Group - Att: Iyad Al Saraj - P.O.Box 87 - Tel: 07-821242/865978 & Tel: 07-861460

Rashad Shawwa Cultural Centre - Tel: 07-864599/869965

HEBRON

Beit Ula Cultural Centre - Dir: Jamal Talab - Beit Ula
Hebron District Est. 1994
Developing knowledge and creativity; encouraging science, education & literature; cultural activities; vocational training; library.

Organisation for Free Thought & Culture - P.O.Box 616 - Al-Saba Rd.
Tel: 02-9920272
Arts, cultural programs, festivals, theatre & TV for children; leadership training.

JERUSALEM

Al-Kasaba Theatre - George Ibrahim - 2 Abu Obeidah St. - Tel: 02-5894052

Al-Hakawati (Al-Masrah for Pal. Culture & Art)
Jamal Ghosheh - P.O.Box 20462 - Abu Obeida St. - Nuzha Bulding
Tel: 02-6280957/6288189 - Tel: 02-6281218
Promotion of Palestinian culture; Palestinian theatre performances; folklore.

Arab Graduates Club - Dr. Amin Khatib - P.O.Box 19476 - Tel: 02-6272721

Al-Wasiti Art Centre - Jack Persekian - P.O.Box 21873 - Tel: 02-5822859 & 02-5817853
Gallery; arts library, cultural research/education.

Ashtar for Theatre Education & Training
Edward Muallem - P.O.Box 17170 - Tel: 02-5827218 & 02-5827218
Theatre; "Theatre Day at School".

Armenian Museum - Att: Goerge Entilia'n - Tel: 02-6284549

Dar Al-Tifil Museum - Elain Abo Hadid - Tel: 02-6273477
Folklore and Heritage

Ashyaa Puppet Theatre Group - Yavoub Abu Arafeh - P.O.Box 19290 - Tel: 02-6264089

Islamic Museum - Khader Salameh - Old City - Tel: 02-6285708

Greek Orthodox Museum - Tel: 02-284006

P.E.N Centre for Palestinian Writers - Hanan Awad - Tel: 02-5813698 & 02-5894620
Promotion of Palestinian writers & freedom of writing; cultural workshops & seminars

Jerusalem Centre for Arabic Music - Mustafa al-Kurd - P.O.Box 20334
Tel: 02-6274774/6272874

YABOUS - Contact: Jerusalem Hotel - Tel: 02-6283282 & 02-6271356
Production of artistic & musical performances; cultural activities & exchange; organizing summer music & art festival (Jerusalem Festival).

Sabreen Musical Centre - Dir: Daid Murad - P.O.Box 51875
Tel: 02-6273591 & 02-6283282
(famous Palestinian musical ensemble); course in voice, instruments, sound technology & construction of traditional instruments; music library (LPs, CDs. Tapes).

JERICHO

Jericho Culture & Art - Naim Yaghi - P.O.Box 123 - Ein Sultan St.
Tel: 02-9921047

NABLUS

Cultural and Social Sports Club - Rafi'a Abdul Hadi - P.O.Box 751 - Shwaitreh St.
Lectures & workshops; folklore & fashion exhibition; swing; food processing; dormitory for college students; pre-school; weaving; training.

RAMALLAH

In'ash al-Usra Society Centre for Heritage & Folk
Dr. Ahmad Baker - P.O.Box 549 - Behind al-Bireh Municipality - Tel: 02-2828962/2952876
Embroidery; heritage studies; museum.
Publ.: Society and Heritage (quarterly).

Institute of Arts - Kasem Abdul Hadi - P.O.Box 1129 - Tel: 02-2955974
Music and Art courses

Manar Cultural Centre -Mohammad Karajeh - Tel: 02-2957937
Courses in computer, languages, electronic and secretary skills, calligraphy and media.

Ramallah First Sarriyeh - Tel: 02-2952091
Parades, sports, music & folklore centre; art & cultural activities; dabka dancing group.

Khalil al-Sakakini Cultural Centre - P.O.Box 147 - Tel: 02-2987374
Arts exhibitions, concerts, literature and arts awareness projects.
E.mail: sakakini@mail.palnet.com

RIWAQ - Dr. Souad Amri - P.O.Box 212 - Nablus Road, Sharafeh
Tel: 02-2958187 & Tel: 02-2958186
E-mail: riwaq@baraka.org
Archaeological & heritage surveys & research.

For additional analytical, business and investment opportunities information,
please contact Global Investment & Business Center, USA
at (703) 370-8082. Fax: (703) 370-8083. E-mail: ibpusa3@gmail.com
Global Business and Investment Info Databank - www.ibpus.com

As-Siraj for Culture, Arts & Theatre - P.O.Box 237 - Al-Jimal St.
Tel: 02-2957037
arts; theatre; folklore; dancing; library; cultural activities for children.

AL-BIREH

Popular Art Centre - Suheil Khoury - P.O.Box 3627 - Nablus Rd.,
Tel: 02-2953891 & 02-2952851
Library/videos on arts, music & dancing; dancing/music groups & classes; exhibitions; music festivals.

Gallery "79" - Isam Bader - Nahda Street - Tel: 02-2951462/9955859

MAIN HOTELS

BETHLEHEM

Alexander Hotel (42 rooms; bf; mr; res) Tel: 02-2770780 Fax: 02-2770782

AndalusGuesthouse Tel: 02-2741348 Fax: 02-2742280

Beit Al-Baraka Youth Hostel (19 rooms) Tel: 02-2229288 Fax: 02-2229288

Bethlehem Hotel (180 rooms; bf; cf; mr; res) Tel: 02-2770702 Fax: 02-2770706
e-mail: bhotel@p-ol.com

Bethlehem Inn (36 rooms; bf; mr; res) Tel: 02-2742423 Fax: 02-2742424

Bethlehem Palace Hotel (25 rooms; bf; res) Tel: 02-2742798 Fax: 02-2741562

Bethlehem Star Hotel (72 rooms; cf; bf; res) Tel: 02-2743249/2770285 Fax: 02-2741494
e-mail: hstar@hally.net

Grand Hotel (50 rooms; bf; cf; mr; res) Tel: 02-2741602/2741440 Fax: 02-2741604
e-mail: bandak@p-ol.com

Nativity Hotel (89 rooms; bf; cf; mr; res) Tel: 02-2770650 Fax: 02-2744083
e-mail: nativity@nativity- hotel.com http://www.nativity-hotel.com

Palace Hotel (25 rooms; bf; mr; res) Tel: 02-2742798 Fax: 02-2741562

Paradise Hotel (129 rooms; cf; bf; mr; res) Tel: 02-2744542/2744543 Fax: 02-2744544
e-mail: paradise@p-ol.com

Saint Antonio Hotel (26 rooms; mr; res) Tel: 02-2744308 Fax: 02-2770524

Shepherd Hotel Tel: 02-2740656 Fax: 02-2744888

St. Nicholas Hotel (25 rooms; res; mr) Tel: 02-2743040/1/2 Fax: 02-2743043

Al-Zaytouna Guest House (7 rooms; bf; res; mr) Telfax: 02-2742016 (Beit Jala)

GAZA

Adam Hotel (76 rooms; bf; cf; mr; res) Tel: 07-2823519 Fax: 07-2866976

For additional analytical, business and investment opportunities information,
please contact Global Investment & Business Center, USA
at (703) 370-8082. Fax: (703) 370-8083. E-mail: ibpusa3@gmail.com
Global Business and Investment Info Databank - www.ibpus.com

Al-Amal Hotel Tel: 07-2841317 Fax: 07-2861832

Beach Hotel (25 rooms; bf; mr; res) Tel: 07-2828800 Fax: 07-2828604

Cliff Hotel (24 rooms; bf; mr; res) Tel: 07-2823450 Fax: 07-2820742

Al-Hilal Al-Ahmar Tel:07-2054261 Fax:07-2054621

EAST JERUSALEM

Addar Suite Hotel (21 Suites; bf; mr; res) Tel: 02-6263111 Fax: 02-6260791

Alcazar Hotel (38 rooms; bf; mr; res) Tel: 02-6281111 Fax: 02-6287360
e-mail: admin@jrscazar.com   http://www.jrscazar.com

Ambassador Hotel (122 rooms; bf; cf; mr; res) Tel: 02-5828515 Fax: 02-5828202

American Colony Hotel (84 rooms; bf; cf; mr; res) Tel: 02-6279777 Fax: 02-6279779
e-mail: reserv@amcol.co.il   http://www.americancolony.com

Capitol Hotel (54 rooms; bf; mr; res) Tel: 02-6282561/6282562 Fax: 02-6264352

Capitolina Hotel (ex. YMCA) (55 rooms; bf; cf; mr; res) Tel: 02-6286888 Fax: 02-6276301

City Hotel (25 rooms; bf; res) Tel: 02-5328212 Fax: 02-5328092

Christmas Hotel (37 rooms; bf; mr; res) Tel: 02-6282588 Fax: 02-6264417

Commodore Hotel (45 rooms; cf; mr; res) Tel: 02-6271414 Fax: 02-6284701

Gloria Hotel (72 rooms; mr; res) Tel: 02-6282431 Fax: 02-6282401

Golden Walls (formerly Pilgrim's Palace Hotel) (90 rooms; bf; mr; res) Tel: 02-6272416 Fax: 02-6264658
e-mail: admin@pilgrimpal.com

Holy Land Hotel (105 rooms; bf; cf; mr; res) Tel: 02-6272888/6284841 Fax: 02-6280265

Jerusalem Claridge Hotel (30 rooms; bf; mr; res) Tel: 02-2347137 Fax: 02-2347139

Jerusalem Hotel (14 rooms; bf; mr; res; live music) Tel: 02-6283282 Fax: 02-6283282
http://www.jrshotel.com

Jerusalem Meridian Hotel (74 rooms; bf; mr; res) Tel: 02-6285212/6285213 Fax: 02-6285214
http://www.jerusalem- meridian.com

Jerusalem Panaroma Hotel (74 rooms; bf; mr; res) Tel: 02-6272277 Fax: 02-6273699
email: panaroma@trendline.com.il

Lawrence Hotel (30 rooms; business facilites; res) Tel: 02-6264208 Fax: 02-6271285
e-mail: karine@actcom.co.il

For additional analytical, business and investment opportunities information,
please contact Global Investment & Business Center, USA
at (703) 370-8082. Fax: (703) 370-8083. E-mail: ibpusa3@gmail.com
Global Business and Investment Info Databank - www.ibpus.com

Mount of Olives (61 rooms; bf; mr; res) Tel: 02-6284877 Fax: 02-6264427
e-mail: info@mtolives.coml http://www.mtolives.com

Mount Scopus Hotel (65 rooms; bf; mr; res) Tel: 02-5828891 Fax: 02-5828825
e-mail: mtscopus@netvision.net.il

National Palace Hotel (110 rooms; bf; cf; mr; res) Tel: 02-6273273 Fax: 02-6282139

New Imperial Hotel (45 rooms) Tel: 02-6272000 Fax: 02-6271530

New Metropole Hotel (25 rooms; mr; res) Tel: 02-6283846 Fax:02-6277485

New Regent Hotel (24 rooms; bf; mr; res) Tel: 02-6284540 Fax: 02-6264023
e-mail: atictour@palnet.com

Notre Dame Hotel Tel: 02-6279111 Fax:02-6271995

Palace Hotel (68 rooms; mr) Tel: 02-6271126 Fax: 02-6271649

Petra Hostel and Hotel Tel: 02-6282356

Pilgrims Inn Hotel (16 rooms; bf; mr; res) Tel: 02-6284883 Fax: 02-6264658

Ritz Hotel (102 rooms; bf; mr; res) Tel: 02-6273233 Fax: 02-6286768

Rivoli Hotel Tel: 02-6284871 Fax: 02-6274879

Seven Arches Hotel (197 rooms; bf; mr; res) Tel: 02-6267777 Fax: 02-6271319
e-mail: svnarch@trendline.co.il

St. George Hotel (144 rooms; bf; cf; mr; res) Tel: 02-6277232/6277323 Fax: 02-6282575

St. George's Pilgrim Guest House (25 rooms; bf; res) Tel: 02-6283302 Fax: 02-6282253
e-mail: sghostel@netvision.net.il

Strand Hotel (88 rooms; mr; res) Tel: 02-6280279 Fax: 02-6284826

Victoria Hotel (50 rooms; bf; res) Tel: 02-6273858/6274466 Fax: 02-6274171

YMCA Hotel (55 rooms; bf; cf; mr;res) Tel: 02-6286888 Fax: 02-6276301
e-mail: capitol@cast-jerusalem- ymca.org

YWCA Hotel (30 rooms; bf; mr) Tel: 02-6282593 Fax: 02-6284654
e-mail: ywca@pl.org

Al-Zahra Hotel (25 rooms; res) Tel: 02-6282447/6283960 Fax: 02-6282415

NABLUS

Al-Qaser Hotel (38 rooms; bf; cf; mr; res) Tel: 09-2385444/2392385 Fax: 09-2395944
e-mail: alqasr@netvision.net.il

Al-Yasmeen Motel & Souq (30 rooms; cf; mr; res) Tel: 09-374060 Fax: 09-384033
e-mail: alyasmeen@palgate.com http://www.alyasmeen.com

Al-Bireh Tourist Hotel (50 rooms; cf; res) Telefax: 02-2400803

Best Eastern Hotel (91 rooms; cf; res) Tel: 02-2960450 Fax: 02-2958452
e-mail: besteastern@jrol.com

City Inn Hotel (89 rooms; bf; cf; res) Tel: 02-2959191 Fax: 02-2959189
e-mail: cityinn@p-ol.com http://www.cityinn-hotel.com

Grand Park Hotel & Resorts (38 rooms; bf; cf; mr; res) Tel: 02-2986194 Fax: 02-2956950
http:// www. ramallahgrandpark.com

Al-Hajal Hotel (22 rooms; bf) Telefax: 02-2987858

Merryland (25 rooms) Tel: 02-2987074 Telefax: 02-2987176

Al-Murouj Pension (Jifna village) (8 rooms; res) Telefax: 02-2957881

Pension Miami (12 rooms) Telefax: 02-2956808

PlazaPension Telefax: 02-2982020

Ramallah Hotel (28 rooms; bf; mr; res) Tel: 02-2952559 Fax: 02-2955029

Al-WihdehPension Tel: 02-2956452 Fax: 02-2980412

Deir Hijleh Monastery Tel: 02-9943038 050-348892

Jericho Resort Village (60 rooms; 46 studios; bf; cf; mr; res) Tel: 02-2321255 Fax: 02-2322189
e-mail:marketing@jericho- resort.com http://www.jericho-resort.com

Jerusalem Hotel (22 rooms) Tel: 02-2322444 Fax: 02-9923109

RESTAURANTS

Al-Amir Tel: 02-2742783
Al-Garden Tel: 02-2777177
Abu Shanab Tel: 02-1742985
Al-Atlal Tel: 02-2741104
Andalos Tel: 02-2743519
Ararat Tel: 02-2772410
BarbaraTel: 02-2744578
Bahamas Tel: 02-2745450
Central Tel: 02-2741378
DalilahTel: 02-2743634
Diwan Tel: 02-2770333; 02-2770329
Dolphin Tel: 02-2743432

For additional analytical, business and investment opportunities information,
please contact Global Investment & Business Center, USA
at (703) 370-8082. Fax: (703) 370-8083. E-mail: ibpusa3@gmail.com
Global Business and Investment Info Databank - www.ibpus.com

Golden Roof Tel: 02-2743224
Al-Karawan Tel: 02-2747439
Mariachi (Grand Hotel) Tel: 02-2741440
Piano Tel: 050-356160
Tachi Chinese Tel: 02-2744382
Saint George Tel 02-2743780
Dalilah Tel: 02-2743634
Sababa Tel: 02-2744006
Nissan Tel: 02-2741248

GAZA

Abu Nuwas Tel: 07-2845211
Al-Andalus Tel: 07-2821272
Al-Baidar Tel: 07-2861321
Broaster Chicken Tel: 07-2842855
Al-Diwanea Tourist Tel: 07-2825062
Alladin Tel: 07-2823355
An-Nawras Tourist Resort Tel: 07- 2833033
Cyber Internet Café Tel: 07-2844704
Deleice Tel: 07-2822569
Fisher Tourist Tel: 07-2834779
Granada Tel: 07-2822165
Haifa Tel: 07-2534655
Al-Marsa Tel: 07-2863599
Al-Molouke Tel: 07-2868397
Mika Cafeteria Tel: 07-2866040
Matouq Tel: 07-2826245
La Mirage Tel: 07-2865128
Lido Tel: 07-2864198
Lotus Tel: 07-2842431
Love Boat Tel: 07-2861353
Palm Beach Tel: 07-2860142
Pizza Inn Tel: 07-2840415
Regency 050-520190
Sea Breeze Cafeteria Tel: 07-28426
Summer land Village Tel: 07-2453441
Al-Salam Tel: 07-2822705
Al-Sammak Tel: 07-2864385
As-Sayad Tel: 07-2834779
Salam Beach Tel: 07-2844964
White Tent Tel: 07-2860380

JERUSALEM

Antonio's (Ambassador Hotel) Tel: 02-5828515
Arabesque, Poolside & Patio Restaurants (American Colony Hotel) Tel: 02-6279777
Armenian Tavern Tel: 02-6273854
Askidinya Tel: 02-5324590
Café Europe Tel: 02-6284313
Kan Zaman (Jerusalem Hotel) Tel: 02-6271356
Nafoura Tel: 02-6260034
National Palace Hotel Tel: 02-6273273
Notre Dame Hotel Tel: 02-6271995
Papa Andreas Tel: 02-6284433
Pasha's Tel: 02-5825162
Petra Tel: 02-6283655
Philadelphia Tel: 02-6289770
Pizza,House Tel: 02-6273970
Popular Arab Tel: 02-5833226
Al-Shuleh Grill Tel: 02-6273768
Az-Zahra Tel: 02-6282447

JERICHO

Al-Khaiam Tel: 02-322477

Al-Gandul Tel: 02-322585
Maxim Tel: 02-322410
Al-Nauura Tel: 02-323300
Ar-Rabia Tel: 02-2323500
Al-Rawda Tel: 02-2322555
Al-Amara Tel: 052-975768
Green Valley Park Tel: 02-2322349
Jabal Quruntul Tel: 02-2322614; 02-2322593
Old Jericho Tent Tel: 02-2323820
Papaya Park Tel: 050-286067
Samhouri Tel: 02-2323252
Spanish Park Tel: 050-515518
Seven Trees Tel: 02-2322781
Shallal Tel: 050-520932
Tahhan Tel: 02-2322600

NABLUS

Saleem Afandi 09-2371332
Kan Zaman Tel: 050-240584
Grand Frost 050-521680
AlaaEldean Tel: 09-2332203
Holy Land Son Tel: 050-580808
Tal Al Marah Tel: 050-399303
Al-Mankal Tel: 09-2675362
Rozana Tel: 09-2385676

RAMALLAH

Ajami Tel: 02-2980605
Al-Aseel Tel: 02-2955751
Al-Bardauni's Tel: 02-2951410
Angelo's Tel: 02-2956408
Al-Bahri Tel: 02-2954004
Aramesque Tel: 050-523643
Al-Bayt Al-Falastini Tel: 02-2987188
Café Olé Tel: 02-2984135
Café Mocha Rena Tel: 02-2981460
Casablanca Tel: 02-2987658
Caesar's (Grand Park Hotel) Tel: 02-2986194
Chez Vatche's Café (Grand Park Hotel) Tel: 02-2986194
Fattoush Tel: 02-2955834
Fawanees Tel: 02-2987046
Flamingo's Tel: 02-2985813
Kanbata Zaman Tel: 02-2956146
K5M-Internet Café Tel: 02-2956813
Layali As-Sultan Roof Tel: 02-2980275
Magic Tel: 02-2956057
Muntaza Restaurant & Garden Tel: 02-2956835
Plaza Restaurant & Park Tel: 02-2956020
Pronto Resto-Café Tel: 02-2987312
Red Valley Restaurant & Garden (Jifna village) Tel: 050-567550
Garage Café Tel: 052-675879
Urjuwan Tel: 02-2958434
Rukab's Ice Cream Tel: 02-2956467
Rumours Tel: 02-2953770
Uncle Sam's Tel: 02-2958075
At-Taboun Tel: 02-2980505
Top Burger Tel: 02-2956057
Fino Tel: 02-2980456
Zarour Bar BQ Tel: 02-2981869

For additional analytical, business and investment opportunities information,
please contact Global Investment & Business Center, USA
at (703) 370-8082. Fax: (703) 370-8083. E-mail: ibpusa3@gmail.com
Global Business and Investment Info Databank - www.ibpus.com

SOUVENIR STORES

BETHLEHEM

The Three Arches Co. Ltd - Owner: Nicolar Canavati & Co. - Manger St.
P.O.Box 214 - Tel: 02-2741261

The Nativity Store - Owner: Victor Tabash - Manger Square - P.O.Box 192
Tel: 02-2742678

The Holy Land Hand Craft Cop. - Owner: Administrative Board for 1996
Shepherd's Field - P.O.Box 20 - Tel: 02-2773088 & Fax: 02-2775245

Bethlehem Gift Store - Owner: Edward John Tabash - Milk Grotto St.
P.O.Box 144 - Tel: 02-2742736 & Fax: 02-2744710

La Grotto Store - Owner: Saliba Mikhael Al-Sous - Milk Grotto St.
P.O.Box30 - Tel: 02-2743461

Diek Souvenir Store - Owner: Anton Said Diek - Milk Grotto St.
P.O.Box 434 - Tel: 02-27443663 & Fax: 02-2742665

Diek Souvenir Store - Owner: Anton Said Diek - Milk Grotto St.
P.O.Box 434 - Tel: 02-27443663 & Fax: 02-2742665

Holy Land Art Museum - Owner: Issa, Jeries, Ange, Yousif Giacaman - Manger Square
P.O.Box 80 - Tel: 02-2742835

Jeries Elias Freij & Sons - Owner: Jeries Elias Freij & Sons - Manger Square
P.O.Box 707 - Tel: 02-2742888

Issa Abu Aita & Fils - Owner: George Issa Abu Aita - Manger Square
P.O.Box 55 - Tel: 02-2742911

Bethlehem Star Store - Owner: George Nicola Baboul - Milk Grotto St.
P.O.Box 292 - Tel: 02-2773297

Lama Bros. - Owner: Michael, Edward, Tawfic, Charli Lama - Manger St.
P.O.Box 377 - Tel: 02-2742649

The Oriental Souvenir Shop - Owner: Saliba & George Canavati - Milk Grotto St.
P.O.Box 37 - Tel: 02-2742328

Bethlehem Oriental Store - Owner: Saleh, Salem & Jacob Miguel - Milk Grotto St.
P.O.Box 32 - Tel: 02-2742812

Good Shepherds Store - Owner: Tanas, Sami, Naji Abu Aita - Manger St.
P.O.Box 96 - Tel: 02-2742249/743769 & Fax: 02-2744544

Souvenir Oriental Dress Store - Owner: Atta Shaban Amin Amer Inheritance
Najajreh St. - Tel: 02-2747393

King David Store - Owner: Raji Michael Kumsieh - Manger Square
P.O.Box 196 - Tel: 02-274247

For additional analytical, business and investment opportunities information,
please contact Global Investment & Business Center, USA
at (703) 370-8082. Fax: (703) 370-8083. E-mail: ibpusa3@gmail.com
Global Business and Investment Info Databank - www.ibpus.com

Tresure Gate - Owner: Ziyad Hanna Yousif Al Bandak - Milk Grotto St.
P.O.Box 609 - Tel: 02-2770234

Presents House - Owner: Michel Najeeb Awad - Milk Grotto St.
Tel: 02-2743021

Milk Grotto Art Store - Owner: Assad Abdallah Giacaman - Milk Grotto St.

San George Gift Store - Owner: Emil Miguel - Milk Grotto St
P.O.Box 284 - Tel: 02-2745217

Holy Land Arts Museum - Owner: Issa, Jeries, Angel, Yousif Giacaman - Milk Grotto St.
Tel: 02-2744819

Holy Land Souvenirs - Owner Anton Yousif Tabash - Milk Grotto St.
P.O.Box 476 - Tel: 02-2743386

San George Gift Store - Owner: Issa Manoly - Milk Grotto St.
P.O.Box 237 - Tel: 02-2742565

Herodion Store - Owner: Costandi Mikhael Canavati - Manger St.
P.O.Box 306 - Tel: 02-2742881 & Fax: 02-2741565

Halaseh Souvenir Store - Owner: Hassan Mohammad Halaseh - Manger St.
Tel: 02-2743592

Bethlehem New Store - Owner: Afram & George Nisan - Manger St.
P.O.Box 220 - Tel: 02-2743589 & Fax: 02-2743985

The Caravan Souvenir Store - Owner: Hanna Inrahim Sabat - Manger St.
P.O.Box 43 - Tel: 02-2742839

Barakat Souvenir Store - Owner: Daidy Ahmad Fayad Barakat - Manger St.
Tel: 02-2743737

United Stores Co. Ltd - Owner: Issa, Anwar, Samir, Victor Saca - Manger St.
P.O.Box 184 - Tel: 02-2741313/743886 & Fax: 02-2741355

El Badawi Souvenir Store - Owner: Atta Shaban Amin Amer Inheritance - Manger St.

Manger Square Souvenir Store - Owner: George Shukri Mitri - Manger Sqaure - Star St.
Tel: 02-2743729

Bethlehem International Store - Owner: Anton & Louis Miguel - Milk Grotto St.
P.O.Box 32 - Tel: 02-2742812

The Canavati Store - Owner: Saleh & George Canavati - Near Rachel's Tomb
P.O.Box 400 - Tel: 02-2741511/741844 & Fax: 02-2741855

Fatima Store - Owner: Issa Spiro Facouseh - Manger St.
P.O.Box 394 - Tel: 02-2742695

For additional analytical, business and investment opportunities information,
please contact Global Investment & Business Center, USA
at (703) 370-8082. Fax: (703) 370-8083. E-mail: ibpusa3@gmail.com
Global Business and Investment Info Databank - www.ibpus.com

Holy Manger Store - Owner: Adnan Mahmoud Safi Nashash - Manger St.
P.O.Box 367 - Tel: 02-2742288

Elbambino Arts & Sculpture - Owner: Salem, Ibrahim, Miguel, Amal Giacaman - Manger Square
P.O.Box 238 - Tel: 02-2743937 & Fax: 02-2743937

Johny's Souvenir Shop - Owner: Johny Shukri Aboud Canavati - Manger St.
P.O.Box 37 - Tel: 02-2744008

Palestinian Heritage Center - Owner: Maha Jeries Al Saca - New Rd.
Tel: 02-2742381 & Fax: 02-2742642

Gallery Magus - Owner: Jamal Issa Salameh - Rachel Tomb
Tel: 02-2770417 & Fax: 02-2770417

Angels Souvenir Store - Owner: George Salman Malky - Kirkafa Street
Tel: 050-289529

Alexander Gift - Owner: Yvonne Canavati - Alexander Hotel
Tel: 02-2770780/1 & Fax: 02-2770782

Boaz Field Souvenir Store - Owner: Michel Odeh Bannourah - Shepherd's Field
Tel: 02-2743605

HEBRON

Holy Land Ceramics & Glass Co. Ltd - Owner: Fayes & Radwan Abu Omar
Halhul - P.O.Box 66 - Tel: 02-9929767 & Fax: 02-9929677

JERICHO

Jericho Oriental Gifts - Owner: Ibrahim Jalil Mitri - Jerusalem St.
Tel: 02-9922215

Oasis Souvenir Store - Owner: Nadia Othman Abdel Fatah Zaideh - Ein Al-Sultan St.
Tel: 02-9922432

Temptation Souvenir Store - Owner: Khalid Ikab Abdel Razak - Tel El-Sultan -P.O.Box 11 Tel: 02-9922614 & Fax: 02-9922659

NABLUS

Mosleh Antiquities Store - Owner: Adli Mahmud Muhammad Mosleh - Sebastia
P.O.Box 438 - Tel: 09-386162

Rajab Store Souvenir & Antiquities - Owner: Omar Hafez Kayed - Sabastia
Tel: 09-379420

Dukan Al-Qaser Souvenir Oriental - Owner: Naser Abdel Hadi - Al-Qaser Hotel
P.O.Box 166 - Tel: 09-385444

RAMALLAH

Abdeen Souvenir Store - Owner: Taisier Abdel Majed Abdeen - Al Biereh Market
Tel: 02-9955154

For additional analytical, business and investment opportunities information,
please contact Global Investment & Business Center, USA
at (703) 370-8082. Fax: (703) 370-8083. E-mail: ibpusa3@gmail.com
Global Business and Investment Info Databank - www.ibpus.com

Owner: El Rami Exhibition Oriental Souvenir - Shihada Mousa, Abdel Jabbar
Near The Police Station

TOUR OPERATORS

BETHLEHEM

Bethlehem Tourist Agency Tel: 02-2770833 Fax: 02-2770833
e-mail: oshtls@jrol.com

Crown Tours & Travel Co. Ltd. P.O.Box 847 Tel: 02-2740911/12 Fax: 02-2740910
e-mail: crowntt@p-ol.com http://www.crown-tours.com

Golden Gate Tours & Travel 02-2766044 Fax 02-2766045 e-mail:ggtours@palnet.com

Gloria Tours & Travel Tel: 02-2740835 Fax: 02-2743021
e-mail: gloria@p-ol.com

King David Tourist & Travel Agency Tel: 02-2770054 Fax: 02-2770054
e-mail: kdtravel@p-ol.com

Lama Tours International Inc. Tel: 02-2743717/274.2847 Fax: 02-2743747
e-mail: litco@p-ol.com

Mousallam International Tours. Tel & Fax: 02-2770054 e-mail: mitours@palnet.com

Petra Tours Tel: 02-2745996-7

Alternative Tourism Group Study Center (Beit Sahour) Tel: 02-2772151 Fax: 02-2772211
e-mail: atg@p-ol.com http://www.patg.com

Kokali Tours & Travel Tel: 02-2772024 Fax: 02-2773047

GAZA

Al-Ahli Company Ltd. Tel: 07-2828534/286.4009/ 2827296 Fax: 07-2822350
e-mail: ahliuda@yahoo.com

Al-Naser Tours & International Aviation (Halabi Tours) Tel: 07-2823704/2860562 Fax: 07-2866075

El-Muntaza Tours & Travel Agency Tel: 07-2827919 Fax: 07-2824923

Trust Travel & Tourism Co. Ltd. Tel: 07-2842313/303 Fax: 07-2842323
e-mail: trustravel@hotmail.com

Universal Tourist Agency Tel: 07-2828202 Fax: 07-2828202

Zaatarah & Co.Tourist & Travel Agency Tel: 07-2825170/2821530/ 2825180/2863194 Fax: 07-2821872

HEBRON

Al-Nisr Al-Arabi Co. Tel: 02-2220527

Al-Kiram Tours and Travel Tel: 02-2256501/2/3 Fax: 02-2256504
e-mail: Alkiram@bitl.net

Peace Travel &Tours Co. Tel: 02-2226747 Fax: 02-2226747

JERUSALEM

Albina Tours, Ltd. Tel: 02-6283397/6271967 Fax: 02-6281215
e-mail: albina@netvision.net.il

Arab Tourist Agency Tel: 02-6277442 Fax: 02-6284366

Atic Tours & Travel, Ltd. Tel: 02-6286159/6271223 Fax: 02-6264023
e-mail: atictour@palnet.com http://www.atictour.com

Awad & Co. Tourist Tel: 02-6284021 Fax: 02-6287990
e-mail: admin@awad-tours.com http://www.awad-tours.com

Aweidah Bros. & Co. Tel: 02-6282365 Fax: 02-6282366
e-mail: aweidah@netvision.net.il http://www.aweidah.com

Ayoub Caravan Tours Tel: 02-6284361/6288563 Fax: 02-6285804
e-mail: caravan@palnet.com

Bible Land Tours Tel: 02-6271169/6283903 Fax: 02-6272218
e-mail: links@palnet.com

Blessed Land Tours Tel: 02-6282525/7 Fax: 02-628526
e-mail: blt@blessedland.com

Dakkak Tourist Agency Tel: 02-6286592/3 Fax: 02-628 5812
e-mail: dakkak@netmedia.net.il

George Garabedian Co. Ltd. Tel: 02-6283398 Fax: 02-6287896
e-mail: garo@netvision.net.il

Guiding Star Ltd. Tel: 02-6273150 Fax: 02-6273147
e-mail: guidingstar@GuidingstarLtd.com

J. Sylvia Tours Tel: 02-6281146/6288277 Fax: 02-6288277
e-mail: sylviatours@yahoo.com

Jordan Tourist Agency Tel: 02-6284052/6284590 Fax: 02-6287621
e-mail: Jordanta@netvision.net.il

Kim's Tourist & Travel Agency Ltd. Tel: 02-6283861/6279725 Fax: 02-6274626/6279726
e-mail: kim@shabaka.net

Lawrence Tours & Travel Co. Tel: 02-6284867/628.1283/ 6271274 Fax: 02-6271285
e-mail: info@lawrence-tours.com

Mount of Olives Tours Ltd. Tel: 02-6271122 Fax: 02-6285551
e-mail: moot@netvision.net.il http://www.olivetours.com

Nativity Tours Ltd. Tel: 02-6262312 Fax: 02-6277512
e-mail: nativity@palnet.com

Nawas Tourist Agency Tel: 02-6282491 Fax: 02-6285755

Near East Tourist Agency (NET) Tel: 02-6282515 Fax: 02-6282415
e-mail: info@netours.com

New Holy Land Tours Ltd. Tel: 02-6264422 Fax: 02-626 4421
e-mail: holyland@palnet.com

O. S. Hotel Services Tel: 02-6289260/6273687 Fax: 02-6264979
e-mail: oshtls@jrol.com

Overseas Travel Bureau Tel: 02-6287090 Fax: 02-6284442
e-mail: otb@netvision.net.il

Safieh Tours & Travel Agency Tel: 02-6264447 Fax: 02-6284430

Samara Tourist & Travel Agency Tel: 02-6276133/6271956 Fax: 02-6271956
e-mail: samto@palnet.com

"Shepherds" Tours & Travel Co. Ltd. Tel: 02-6284121/6287859/ 6276965/6276967 Fax: 02-6280251
e-mail: shepherd@baraka.org

Siniora Star Tours Tel: 02-6286257 Fax: 02-6289078

Tony Tours Tel: 02-6288844 Fax: 02-6288013

United Travel Ltd. Tel: 02-6271247 Fax: 02-6283753
e-mail: unidas@palnet.com http://www.accessone.com/unitedtravel

Universal Tourist Agency Tel: 02-6284383/6287339 Fax: 02-6264448
e-mail: uta@palnet.com http://www.universal-jer.com

Zaatarah Tourist & Travel Agency Tel: 02-6262101/2, 02-6272725 Fax: 02-6289873
e-mail: zaatarah@jrol.com

JERICHO

Four M Travel - Mai Mahmoud Abu Lafi - 050-359138

NABLUS

Elwan Travel Agency Tel: 09-2386312 Fax: 09-2386313

Un Limited Tourism Co. Sufian Street Tel: 09-2385949 Fax: 09-2385949
e-mail: ult@Zaytona.com http://www.home.Zaytona. com/ult/ult.html

Yaish International Tours Tel: 09-2372111 Fax: 09-2381411
e-mail: yaishtvl@palnet.com

Jarrar Tours (Jenin) Tel: 06-2436335/2503359 Fax: 06-2501122
e-mail: Jarra@hally.com   http://www.rannet.com/Jarrar

Assia Tours (Jenin) 06-2438056

For additional analytical, business and investment opportunities information,
please contact Global Investment & Business Center, USA
at (703) 370-8082. Fax: (703) 370-8083. E-mail: ibpusa3@gmail.com
Global Business and Investment Info Databank - www.ibpus.com

Al-Taneeb Co for Travel & Transportation (Tulkarem)Tel: 09-2672971

Dama Travel & Tourism (Tulkarem)Tel: 09-2676272

Al-Dawliah for travel & Tourism(Tulkarem) Tel: 09-2677660

RAMALLAH

Ameptco Ltd. for Tourism Tel: 02-2898123

Raha for Travel & Tourism 02-2961780

Alasmar Travel Agency Tel: 02-2954140 Fax: 02-2954140

Amani Tours Tel: 02-2987013 Fax: 02-2987013
e-mail: amanitr@p-ol.com

Arab Office for Travel & Tourism Tel: 02-2956640 Fax: 02-2951331

Atlas Tours & Travel Tel: 02-2952180/2986395 Fax: 02-2961841
e-mail: atlas@palnet.com

Aweidah Tours & Travel Tel: 02-2987060/1/2, 02-2961610 Sita Line: 02-2986285 Fax: 02-2986286

Darwish Tourist & Travel Agency Tel: 02-2956221/2953777 Fax: 02-2957940
e-mail: darwish@palnet.com, kodarwish@hotmail.com

Issis & Co. Travel & Tourist Bureau Tel: 02-2956250/2956975 Fax: 02-2954305
e-mail: iissis@p-ol.com

Jordan River Travel Tourist Agency Tel: 02-2985023 Fax: 02-2955442

Kashou Travel Agency Tel: 02-2955229 Fax: 02-2953107
e-mail: mkashou@palnet.com

Ramallah Travel Agency Tel: 02-2953692 Fax: 02-2955029
e-mail: kaoud@bigfoot.com

Shbat & Abdelnur Tel: 02-2956267 Fax: 02-2957246

Trust Travel & Toursim Tel: 02-2404894/5/6 Fax: 02-2404897
e-mail: trustwb@palnet.com

Zaatarah & Co. Travel and Tours Tel: 02-2986949/2986950 Fax: 02-2986949

BASIC TITLES ON PALESTINE TERRITORIES

For additional analytical, business and investment opportunities information,
please contact Global Investment & Business Center, USA
at (703) 370-8082. Fax: (703) 370-8083. E-mail: ibpusa3@gmail.com
Global Business and Investment Info Databank - www.ibpus.com

Title
Palestine (West Bank & Gaza) Business and Investment Opportunities Yearbook Volume 1 Strategic Information and Opportunities
Palestine (West Bank & Gaza) Business Law Handbook - Strategic Information and Basic Laws
Palestine (West Bank & Gaza) Business Law Handbook - Strategic Information and Basic Laws
Palestine (West Bank & Gaza) Country Study Guide Volume 1 Strategic Information and Developments
Palestine (West Bank & Gaza) Investment and Business Guide - Strategic and Practical Information
Palestine (West Bank & Gaza) Investment and Business Guide - Strategic and Practical Information
Palestine A "Spy" Guide - Strategic Information and Developments
Palestine A Spy" Guide"
Palestine Business and Investment Opportunities Yearbook
Palestine Business and Investment Opportunities Yearbook

For additional analytical, business and investment opportunities information,
please contact Global Investment & Business Center, USA
at (703) 370-8082. Fax: (703) 370-8083. E-mail: ibpusa3@gmail.com
Global Business and Investment Info Databank - www.ibpus.com

Title
Palestine Business Intelligence Report - Practical Information, Opportunities, Contacts
Palestine Business Intelligence Report - Practical Information, Opportunities, Contacts
Palestine Business Law Handbook - Strategic Information and Basic Laws
Palestine Business Law Handbook - Strategic Information and Basic Laws
Palestine Clothing & Textile Industry Handbook
Palestine Clothing & Textile Industry Handbook
Palestine Country Study Guide - Strategic Information and Developments
Palestine Diplomatic Handbook - Strategic Information and Developments
Palestine Diplomatic Handbook - Strategic Information and Developments
Palestine Ecology & Nature Protection Handbook
Palestine Ecology & Nature Protection Handbook
Palestine Ecology & Nature Protection Laws and Regulation Handbook
Palestine Economic & Development Strategy Handbook
Palestine Economic & Development Strategy Handbook
Palestine Education System and Policy Handbook
Palestine Energy Policy, Laws and Regulation Handbook
Palestine Government and Business Contacts Handbook
Palestine Government and Business Contacts Handbook
Palestine Government and Foreign Policy Guide
Palestine Government and Foreign Policy Guide
Palestine Investment and Business Guide - Strategic and Practical Information
Palestine Investment and Business Guide - Strategic and Practical Information
Palestine Justice System and National Police Handbook
Palestine Justice System and National Police Handbook
Palestine Medical & Pharmaceutical Industry Handbook
Palestine Medical & Pharmaceutical Industry Handbook
Palestine President Handbook
Palestine President Handbook
Palestine Recent Economic and Political Developments Yearbook
Palestine Recent Economic and Political Developments Yearbook
Palestine Recent Economic and Political Developments Yearbook
Palestine Research & Development Policy Handbook
Palestine Research & Development Policy Handbook
Palestine Research & Development Policy Handbook
Palestine Taxation Laws and Regulations Handbook
Palestine: How to Invest, Start and Run Profitable Business in Palestine Guide - Practical Information, Opportunities, Contacts

For additional analytical, business and investment opportunities information,
please contact Global Investment & Business Center, USA
at (703) 370-8082. Fax: (703) 370-8083. E-mail: ibpusa3@gmail.com
Global Business and Investment Info Databank - www.ibpus.com

INTERNATIONAL BUSINESS PUBLICATIONS, USA

ibpusa@comcast.net. http://www.ibpus.com

WORLD ISLAMIC BUSINESS LIBRARY
Price: $149.95 Each

Islamic Banking and Financial Law Handbook
Islamic Banking Law Handbook
Islamic Business Organization Law Handbook
Islamic Commerce and Trade Law Handbook
Islamic Company Law Handbook
Islamic Constitutional and Administrative Law Handbook
Islamic Copyright Law Handbook
Islamic Customs Law and Regulations Handbook
Islamic Design Law Handbook
Islamic Development Bank Group Handbook
Islamic Economic & Business Laws and Regulations Handbook
Islamic Environmental Law Handbook
Islamic Financial and Banking System Handbook vol 1
Islamic Financial and Banking System Handbook Vol. 2
Islamic Financial Institutions (Banks and Financial Companies) Handbook
Islamic Foreign Investment and Privatization Law Handbook
Islamic Free Trade & Economic Zones Law and Regulations Handbook
Islamic International Law and Jihad (War(Law Handbook
Islamic Labor Law Handbook
Islamic Legal System (Sharia) Handbook Vol. 1 Basic Laws and Regulations
Islamic Legal System (Sharia) Handbook Vol. 2 Laws and Regulations in
Selected Countries
Islamic Mining Law Handbook
Islamic Patent & Trademark Law Handbook
Islamic Taxation Law Handbook
Islamic Trade & Export-Import Laws and Regulations Handbook

For additional analytical, business and investment opportunities information,
please contact Global Investment & Business Center, USA
at (202) 546-2103. Fax: (202) 546-3275. E-mail: rusric@erols.com

FISHING AND AQUACULTURE
INDUSTRY HANDBOOK LIBRARY
(PRICE $99.95)

**Ultimate handbooks Fishing and Aquaculture
Industry laws and regulation in selected countries**

TITLE
Albania Fishing and Aquaculture Industry Handbook - Strategic Information, Regulations, Opportunities
Algeria Fishing and Aquaculture Industry Handbook - Strategic Information, Regulations, Opportunities
Angola Fishing and Aquaculture Industry Handbook - Strategic Information, Regulations, Opportunities
Antigua and Barbuda Fishing and Aquaculture Industry Handbook - Strategic Information, Regulations, Opportunities
Argentina Fishing and Aquaculture Industry Handbook - Strategic Information, Regulations, Opportunities
Armenia Fishing and Aquaculture Industry Handbook - Strategic Information, Regulations, Opportunities
Australia Fishing and Aquaculture Industry Handbook - Strategic Information, Regulations, Opportunities
Bahamas Fishing and Aquaculture Industry Handbook - Strategic Information, Regulations, Opportunities
Bahrain Fishing and Aquaculture Industry Handbook - Strategic Information, Regulations, Opportunities
Bangladesh Fishing and Aquaculture Industry Handbook - Strategic Information, Regulations, Opportunities
Barbados Fishing and Aquaculture Industry Handbook - Strategic Information, Regulations, Opportunities
Belarus Fishing and Aquaculture Industry Handbook - Strategic Information, Regulations, Opportunities
Belgium Fishing and Aquaculture Industry Handbook - Strategic Information, Regulations, Opportunities
Belize Fishing and Aquaculture Industry Handbook - Strategic Information, Regulations, Opportunities
Benin Fishing and Aquaculture Industry Handbook - Strategic Information, Regulations, Opportunities
Bolivia Fishing and Aquaculture Industry Handbook - Strategic Information, Regulations, Opportunities
Botswana Fishing and Aquaculture Industry Handbook - Strategic Information, Regulations, Opportunities
Brazil Fishing and Aquaculture Industry Handbook - Strategic Information, Regulations, Opportunities
Bulgaria Fishing and Aquaculture Industry Handbook - Strategic Information, Regulations, Opportunities
Burkina Faso Fishing and Aquaculture Industry Handbook - Strategic Information, Regulations, Opportunities
Burundi Fishing and Aquaculture Industry Handbook - Strategic Information, Regulations, Opportunities
Cabo Verde Fishing and Aquaculture Industry Handbook - Strategic Information, Regulations, Opportunities
Cambodia Fishing and Aquaculture Industry Handbook - Strategic Information, Regulations, Opportunities
Cameroon Fishing and Aquaculture Industry Handbook - Strategic Information, Regulations, Opportunities
Canada Fishing and Aquaculture Industry Handbook - Strategic Information, Regulations, Opportunities
Central African Republic Fishing and Aquaculture Industry Handbook - Strategic Information, Regulations, Opportunities
Chad Fishing and Aquaculture Industry Handbook - Strategic Information, Regulations, Opportunities
Chile Fishing and Aquaculture Industry Handbook - Strategic Information, Regulations, Opportunities
China Fishing and Aquaculture Industry Handbook - Strategic Information, Regulations, Opportunities
Colombia Fishing and Aquaculture Industry Handbook - Strategic Information, Regulations, Opportunities
Comoros Fishing and Aquaculture Industry Handbook - Strategic Information, Regulations, Opportunities
Congo Fishing and Aquaculture Industry Handbook - Strategic Information, Regulations, Opportunities

**For additional analytical, business and investment opportunities information,
please contact Global Investment & Business Center, USA
at (202) 546-2103. Fax: (202) 546-3275. E-mail: ibpusa3@gmail.com**

TITLE
Congo, Dem. Rep. of the Fishing and Aquaculture Industry Handbook - Strategic Information, Regulations, Opportunities
Cook Islands Fishing and Aquaculture Industry Handbook - Strategic Information, Regulations, Opportunities
Costa Rica Fishing and Aquaculture Industry Handbook - Strategic Information, Regulations, Opportunities
Croatia Fishing and Aquaculture Industry Handbook - Strategic Information, Regulations, Opportunities
Cuba Fishing and Aquaculture Industry Handbook - Strategic Information, Regulations, Opportunities
Cyprus Fishing and Aquaculture Industry Handbook - Strategic Information, Regulations, Opportunities
Czech Republic Fishing and Aquaculture Industry Handbook - Strategic Information, Regulations, Opportunities
Côte d'Ivoire Fishing and Aquaculture Industry Handbook - Strategic Information, Regulations, Opportunities
Denmark Fishing and Aquaculture Industry Handbook - Strategic Information, Regulations, Opportunities
Djibouti Fishing and Aquaculture Industry Handbook - Strategic Information, Regulations, Opportunities
Dominica Fishing and Aquaculture Industry Handbook - Strategic Information, Regulations, Opportunities
Dominican Republic Fishing and Aquaculture Industry Handbook - Strategic Information, Regulations, Opportunities
Ecuador Fishing and Aquaculture Industry Handbook - Strategic Information, Regulations, Opportunities
Egypt Fishing and Aquaculture Industry Handbook - Strategic Information, Regulations, Opportunities
El Salvador Fishing and Aquaculture Industry Handbook - Strategic Information, Regulations, Opportunities
Equatorial Guinea Fishing and Aquaculture Industry Handbook - Strategic Information, Regulations, Opportunities
Eritrea Fishing and Aquaculture Industry Handbook - Strategic Information, Regulations, Opportunities
Estonia Fishing and Aquaculture Industry Handbook - Strategic Information, Regulations, Opportunities
Ethiopia Fishing and Aquaculture Industry Handbook - Strategic Information, Regulations, Opportunities
Fiji Fishing and Aquaculture Industry Handbook - Strategic Information, Regulations, Opportunities
Finland Fishing and Aquaculture Industry Handbook - Strategic Information, Regulations, Opportunities
France Fishing and Aquaculture Industry Handbook - Strategic Information, Regulations, Opportunities
Gabon Fishing and Aquaculture Industry Handbook - Strategic Information, Regulations, Opportunities
Gambia Fishing and Aquaculture Industry Handbook - Strategic Information, Regulations, Opportunities
Georgia Fishing and Aquaculture Industry Handbook - Strategic Information, Regulations, Opportunities
Germany Fishing and Aquaculture Industry Handbook - Strategic Information, Regulations, Opportunities
Ghana Fishing and Aquaculture Industry Handbook - Strategic Information, Regulations, Opportunities
Greece Fishing and Aquaculture Industry Handbook - Strategic Information, Regulations, Opportunities
Greenland Fishing and Aquaculture Industry Handbook - Strategic Information, Regulations, Opportunities
Grenada Fishing and Aquaculture Industry Handbook - Strategic Information, Regulations, Opportunities
Guatemala Fishing and Aquaculture Industry Handbook - Strategic Information, Regulations, Opportunities
Guinea Fishing and Aquaculture Industry Handbook - Strategic Information, Regulations, Opportunities
Guinea-Bissau Fishing and Aquaculture Industry Handbook - Strategic Information, Regulations, Opportunities
Guyana Fishing and Aquaculture Industry Handbook - Strategic Information, Regulations, Opportunities
Haiti Fishing and Aquaculture Industry Handbook - Strategic Information, Regulations, Opportunities
Honduras Fishing and Aquaculture Industry Handbook - Strategic Information, Regulations, Opportunities
Iceland Fishing and Aquaculture Industry Handbook - Strategic Information, Regulations, Opportunities
India Fishing and Aquaculture Industry Handbook - Strategic Information, Regulations, Opportunities
Indonesia Fishing and Aquaculture Industry Handbook - Strategic Information, Regulations, Opportunities
Iran Fishing and Aquaculture Industry Handbook - Strategic Information, Regulations, Opportunities
Iraq Fishing and Aquaculture Industry Handbook - Strategic Information, Regulations, Opportunities
Ireland Fishing and Aquaculture Industry Handbook - Strategic Information, Regulations, Opportunities
Israel Fishing and Aquaculture Industry Handbook - Strategic Information, Regulations, Opportunities
Italy Fishing and Aquaculture Industry Handbook - Strategic Information, Regulations, Opportunities
Jamaica Fishing and Aquaculture Industry Handbook - Strategic Information, Regulations, Opportunities

For additional analytical, business and investment opportunities information,
please contact Global Investment & Business Center, USA
at (202) 546-2103. Fax: (202) 546-3275. E-mail: ibpusa3@gmail.com

TITLE
Japan Fishing and Aquaculture Industry Handbook - Strategic Information, Regulations, Opportunities
Jordan Fishing and Aquaculture Industry Handbook - Strategic Information, Regulations, Opportunities
Kazakhstan Fishing and Aquaculture Industry Handbook - Strategic Information, Regulations, Opportunities
Kenya Fishing and Aquaculture Industry Handbook - Strategic Information, Regulations, Opportunities
Kiribati Fishing and Aquaculture Industry Handbook - Strategic Information, Regulations, Opportunities
Korea Republic Fishing and Aquaculture Industry Handbook - Strategic Information, Regulations, Opportunities
Kuwait Fishing and Aquaculture Industry Handbook - Strategic Information, Regulations, Opportunities
Kyrgyzstan Fishing and Aquaculture Industry Handbook - Strategic Information, Regulations, Opportunities
Lao People's Dem. Rep. Fishing and Aquaculture Industry Handbook - Strategic Information, Regulations, Opportunities
Latvia Fishing and Aquaculture Industry Handbook - Strategic Information, Regulations, Opportunities
Lesotho Fishing and Aquaculture Industry Handbook - Strategic Information, Regulations, Opportunities
Liberia Fishing and Aquaculture Industry Handbook - Strategic Information, Regulations, Opportunities
Libya Fishing and Aquaculture Industry Handbook - Strategic Information, Regulations, Opportunities
Lithuania Fishing and Aquaculture Industry Handbook - Strategic Information, Regulations, Opportunities
Macedonia Fishing and Aquaculture Industry Handbook - Strategic Information, Regulations, Opportunities
Madagascar Fishing and Aquaculture Industry Handbook - Strategic Information, Regulations, Opportunities
Malawi Fishing and Aquaculture Industry Handbook - Strategic Information, Regulations, Opportunities
Malaysia Fishing and Aquaculture Industry Handbook - Strategic Information, Regulations, Opportunities
Maldives Fishing and Aquaculture Industry Handbook - Strategic Information, Regulations, Opportunities
Mali Fishing and Aquaculture Industry Handbook - Strategic Information, Regulations, Opportunities
Malta Fishing and Aquaculture Industry Handbook - Strategic Information, Regulations, Opportunities
Marshall Islands Fishing and Aquaculture Industry Handbook - Strategic Information, Regulations, Opportunities
Mauritania Fishing and Aquaculture Industry Handbook - Strategic Information, Regulations, Opportunities
Mauritius Fishing and Aquaculture Industry Handbook - Strategic Information, Regulations, Opportunities
Mexico Fishing and Aquaculture Industry Handbook - Strategic Information, Regulations, Opportunities
Micronesia Fishing and Aquaculture Industry Handbook - Strategic Information, Regulations, Opportunities
Moldova Fishing and Aquaculture Industry Handbook - Strategic Information, Regulations, Opportunities
Morocco Fishing and Aquaculture Industry Handbook - Strategic Information, Regulations, Opportunities
Mozambique Fishing and Aquaculture Industry Handbook - Strategic Information, Regulations, Opportunities
Myanmar Fishing and Aquaculture Industry Handbook - Strategic Information, Regulations, Opportunities
Namibia Fishing and Aquaculture Industry Handbook - Strategic Information, Regulations, Opportunities
Nauru Fishing and Aquaculture Industry Handbook - Strategic Information, Regulations, Opportunities
Nepal Fishing and Aquaculture Industry Handbook - Strategic Information, Regulations, Opportunities
Netherlands Fishing and Aquaculture Industry Handbook - Strategic Information, Regulations, Opportunities
New Zealand Fishing and Aquaculture Industry Handbook - Strategic Information, Regulations, Opportunities
Nicaragua Fishing and Aquaculture Industry Handbook - Strategic Information, Regulations, Opportunities
Niger Fishing and Aquaculture Industry Handbook - Strategic Information, Regulations, Opportunities
Nigeria Fishing and Aquaculture Industry Handbook - Strategic Information, Regulations, Opportunities
Norway Fishing and Aquaculture Industry Handbook - Strategic Information, Regulations, Opportunities
Oman Fishing and Aquaculture Industry Handbook - Strategic Information, Regulations, Opportunities
Pakistan Fishing and Aquaculture Industry Handbook - Strategic Information, Regulations, Opportunities
Palau Fishing and Aquaculture Industry Handbook - Strategic Information, Regulations, Opportunities
Panama Fishing and Aquaculture Industry Handbook - Strategic Information, Regulations, Opportunities
Papua New Guinea Fishing and Aquaculture Industry Handbook - Strategic Information, Regulations, Opportunities
Paraguay Fishing and Aquaculture Industry Handbook - Strategic Information, Regulations, Opportunities
Peru Fishing and Aquaculture Industry Handbook - Strategic Information, Regulations, Opportunities

TITLE
Philippines Fishing and Aquaculture Industry Handbook - Strategic Information, Regulations, Opportunities
Poland Fishing and Aquaculture Industry Handbook - Strategic Information, Regulations, Opportunities
Portugal Fishing and Aquaculture Industry Handbook - Strategic Information, Regulations, Opportunities
Qatar Fishing and Aquaculture Industry Handbook - Strategic Information, Regulations, Opportunities
Romania	Fishing and Aquaculture Industry Handbook - Strategic Information, Regulations, Opportunities
Russian Federation Fishing and Aquaculture Industry Handbook - Strategic Information, Regulations, Opportunities
Rwanda Fishing and Aquaculture Industry Handbook - Strategic Information, Regulations, Opportunities
Saint Kitts and Nevis Fishing and Aquaculture Industry Handbook - Strategic Information, Regulations, Opportunities
Saint Lucia Fishing and Aquaculture Industry Handbook - Strategic Information, Regulations, Opportunities
Saint Vincent/Grenadines Fishing and Aquaculture Industry Handbook - Strategic Information, Regulations, Opportunities
Samoa Fishing and Aquaculture Industry Handbook - Strategic Information, Regulations, Opportunities
Sao Tome and Principe Fishing and Aquaculture Industry Handbook - Strategic Information, Regulations, Opportunities
Saudi Arabia Fishing and Aquaculture Industry Handbook - Strategic Information, Regulations, Opportunities
Senegal Fishing and Aquaculture Industry Handbook - Strategic Information, Regulations, Opportunities
Seychelles Fishing and Aquaculture Industry Handbook - Strategic Information, Regulations, Opportunities
Sierra Leone Fishing and Aquaculture Industry Handbook - Strategic Information, Regulations, Opportunities
Slovakia Fishing and Aquaculture Industry Handbook - Strategic Information, Regulations, Opportunities
Solomon Islands Fishing and Aquaculture Industry Handbook - Strategic Information, Regulations, Opportunities
South Africa Fishing and Aquaculture Industry Handbook - Strategic Information, Regulations, Opportunities
South Sudan Fishing and Aquaculture Industry Handbook - Strategic Information, Regulations, Opportunities
Spain Fishing and Aquaculture Industry Handbook - Strategic Information, Regulations, Opportunities
Sri Lanka Fishing and Aquaculture Industry Handbook - Strategic Information, Regulations, Opportunities
Sudan Fishing and Aquaculture Industry Handbook - Strategic Information, Regulations, Opportunities
Suriname Fishing and Aquaculture Industry Handbook - Strategic Information, Regulations, Opportunities
Swaziland Fishing and Aquaculture Industry Handbook - Strategic Information, Regulations, Opportunities
Sweden Fishing and Aquaculture Industry Handbook - Strategic Information, Regulations, Opportunities
Syrian Arab Republic Fishing and Aquaculture Industry Handbook - Strategic Information, Regulations, Opportunities
Tanzania, United Rep. of Fishing and Aquaculture Industry Handbook - Strategic Information, Regulations, Opportunities
Thailand Fishing and Aquaculture Industry Handbook - Strategic Information, Regulations, Opportunities
Timor-Leste Fishing and Aquaculture Industry Handbook - Strategic Information, Regulations, Opportunities
Togo Fishing and Aquaculture Industry Handbook - Strategic Information, Regulations, Opportunities
Tonga Fishing and Aquaculture Industry Handbook - Strategic Information, Regulations, Opportunities
Trinidad and Tobago Fishing and Aquaculture Industry Handbook - Strategic Information, Regulations, Opportunities
Tunisia Fishing and Aquaculture Industry Handbook - Strategic Information, Regulations, Opportunities
Turkey Fishing and Aquaculture Industry Handbook - Strategic Information, Regulations, Opportunities
Turkmenistan Fishing and Aquaculture Industry Handbook - Strategic Information, Regulations, Opportunities
Tuvalu Fishing and Aquaculture Industry Handbook - Strategic Information, Regulations, Opportunities
Uganda Fishing and Aquaculture Industry Handbook - Strategic Information, Regulations, Opportunities
Ukraine Fishing and Aquaculture Industry Handbook - Strategic Information, Regulations, Opportunities
United Arab Emirates Fishing and Aquaculture Industry Handbook - Strategic Information, Regulations, Opportunities
United Kingdom Fishing and Aquaculture Industry Handbook - Strategic Information, Regulations,

TITLE
Opportunities
United States of America Fishing and Aquaculture Industry Handbook - Strategic Information, Regulations, Opportunities
Uruguay Fishing and Aquaculture Industry Handbook - Strategic Information, Regulations, Opportunities
Uzbekistan Fishing and Aquaculture Industry Handbook - Strategic Information, Regulations, Opportunities
Vanuatu Fishing and Aquaculture Industry Handbook - Strategic Information, Regulations, Opportunities
Venezuela Fishing and Aquaculture Industry Handbook - Strategic Information, Regulations, Opportunities
Vietnam Fishing and Aquaculture Industry Handbook - Strategic Information, Regulations, Opportunities
Yemen Fishing and Aquaculture Industry Handbook - Strategic Information, Regulations, Opportunities
Zambia Fishing and Aquaculture Industry Handbook - Strategic Information, Regulations, Opportunities
Zimbabwe Fishing and Aquaculture Industry Handbook - Strategic Information, Regulations, Opportunities

For additional analytical, business and investment opportunities information,
please contact Global Investment & Business Center, USA
at (202) 546-2103. Fax: (202) 546-3275. E-mail: ibpusa3@gmail.com

WORLD BUSINESS AND INVESTMENT OPPORTUNITIES YEARBOOK LIBRARY

World Business Information Catalog, USA: http://www.ibpus.com
Email: ibpusa3@gmail.com

Price: $99.95 Each

TITLE
Abkhazia (Republic of Abkhazia) Business and Investment Opportunities Yearbook Volume 1 Strategic, Practical Information and Opportunities
Afghanistan Business and Investment Opportunities Yearbook Volume 1 Strategic, Practical Information and Opportunities
Aland Business and Investment Opportunities Yearbook Volume 1 Strategic, Practical Information and Opportunities
Albania Business and Investment Opportunities Yearbook Volume 1 Strategic, Practical Information and Opportunities
Algeria Business and Investment Opportunities Yearbook Volume 1 Strategic, Practical Information and Opportunities
Andorra Business and Investment Opportunities Yearbook Volume 1 Strategic, Practical Information and Opportunities
Angola Business and Investment Opportunities Yearbook Volume 1 Strategic, Practical Information and Opportunities
Anguilla Business and Investment Opportunities Yearbook Volume 1 Strategic, Practical Information and Opportunities
Antigua and Barbuda Business and Investment Opportunities Yearbook Volume 1 Strategic, Practical Information and Opportunities
Antilles (Netherlands) Business and Investment Opportunities Yearbook Volume 1 Strategic, Practical Information and Opportunities
Argentina Business and Investment Opportunities Yearbook Volume 1 Strategic, Practical Information and Opportunities
Armenia Business and Investment Opportunities Yearbook Volume 1 Strategic, Practical Information and Opportunities
Aruba Business and Investment Opportunities Yearbook Volume 1 Strategic, Practical Information and Opportunities
Australia Business and Investment Opportunities Yearbook Volume 1 Strategic, Practical Information and Opportunities
Austria Business and Investment Opportunities Yearbook Volume 1 Strategic, Practical Information and Opportunities
Azerbaijan Business and Investment Opportunities Yearbook Volume 1 Strategic, Practical Information and Opportunities
Bahamas Business and Investment Opportunities Yearbook Volume 1 Strategic, Practical Information and Opportunities
Bahrain Business and Investment Opportunities Yearbook Volume 1 Strategic, Practical Information and Opportunities
Bangladesh Business and Investment Opportunities Yearbook Volume 1 Strategic, Practical Information and Opportunities
Barbados Business and Investment Opportunities Yearbook Volume 1 Strategic, Practical Information and Opportunities
Belarus Business and Investment Opportunities Yearbook Volume 1 Strategic, Practical Information and Opportunities

For additional analytical, business and investment opportunities information,
Please contact Global Investment & Business Center, USA
at (202) 546-2103. Fax: (202) 546-3275. E-mail: ibpusa3@gmail.com

TITLE
Belgium Business and Investment Opportunities Yearbook Volume 1 Strategic, Practical Information and Opportunities
Belize Business and Investment Opportunities Yearbook Volume 1 Strategic, Practical Information and Opportunities
Benin Business and Investment Opportunities Yearbook Volume 1 Strategic, Practical Information and Opportunities
Bermuda Business and Investment Opportunities Yearbook Volume 1 Strategic, Practical Information and Opportunities
Bhutan Business and Investment Opportunities Yearbook Volume 1 Strategic, Practical Information and Opportunities
Bolivia Business and Investment Opportunities Yearbook Volume 1 Strategic, Practical Information and Opportunities
Bosnia and Herzegovina Business and Investment Opportunities Yearbook Volume 1 Strategic, Practical Information and Opportunities
Botswana Business and Investment Opportunities Yearbook Volume 1 Strategic, Practical Information and Opportunities
Brazil Business and Investment Opportunities Yearbook Volume 1 Strategic, Practical Information and Opportunities
Brunei Business and Investment Opportunities Yearbook Volume 1 Strategic, Practical Information and Opportunities
Bulgaria Business and Investment Opportunities Yearbook Volume 1 Strategic, Practical Information and Opportunities
Burkina Faso Business and Investment Opportunities Yearbook Volume 1 Strategic, Practical Information and Opportunities
Burundi Business and Investment Opportunities Yearbook Volume 1 Strategic, Practical Information and Opportunities
Cambodia Business and Investment Opportunities Yearbook Volume 1 Strategic, Practical Information and Opportunities
Cameroon Business and Investment Opportunities Yearbook Volume 1 Strategic, Practical Information and Opportunities
Canada Business and Investment Opportunities Yearbook Volume 1 Strategic, Practical Information and Opportunities
Cape Verde Business and Investment Opportunities Yearbook Volume 1 Strategic, Practical Information and Opportunities
Cayman Islands Business and Investment Opportunities Yearbook Volume 1 Strategic, Practical Information and Opportunities
Central African Republic Business and Investment Opportunities Yearbook Volume 1 Strategic, Practical Information and Opportunities
Chad Business and Investment Opportunities Yearbook Volume 1 Strategic, Practical Information and Opportunities
Chile Business and Investment Opportunities Yearbook Volume 1 Strategic, Practical Information and Opportunities
China Business and Investment Opportunities Yearbook Volume 1 Strategic, Practical Information and Opportunities
Colombia Business and Investment Opportunities Yearbook Volume 1 Strategic, Practical Information and Opportunities
Comoros Business and Investment Opportunities Yearbook Volume 1 Strategic, Practical Information and Opportunities
Congo Business and Investment Opportunities Yearbook Volume 1 Strategic, Practical Information and Opportunities
Congo, Democratic Republic Business and Investment Opportunities Yearbook Volume 1 Strategic, Practical Information and Opportunities
Cook Islands Business and Investment Opportunities Yearbook Volume 1 Strategic, Practical Information and Opportunities
Costa Rica Business and Investment Opportunities Yearbook Volume 1 Strategic, Practical Information and Opportunities

For additional analytical, business and investment opportunities information,
Please contact Global Investment & Business Center, USA
at (202) 546-2103. Fax: (202) 546-3275. E-mail: ibpusa3@gmail.com

TITLE
Cote d'Ivoire Business and Investment Opportunities Yearbook Volume 1 Strategic, Practical Information and Opportunities
Croatia Business and Investment Opportunities Yearbook Volume 1 Strategic, Practical Information and Opportunities
Cuba Business and Investment Opportunities Yearbook Volume 1 Strategic, Practical Information and Opportunities
Cyprus Business and Investment Opportunities Yearbook Volume 1 Strategic, Practical Information and Opportunities
Czech Republic Business and Investment Opportunities Yearbook Volume 1 Strategic, Practical Information and Opportunities
Denmark Business and Investment Opportunities Yearbook Volume 1 Strategic, Practical Information and Opportunities
Djibouti Business and Investment Opportunities Yearbook Volume 1 Strategic, Practical Information and Opportunities
Dominica Business and Investment Opportunities Yearbook Volume 1 Strategic, Practical Information and Opportunities
Dominican Republic Business and Investment Opportunities Yearbook Volume 1 Strategic, Practical Information and Opportunities
Ecuador Business and Investment Opportunities Yearbook Volume 1 Strategic, Practical Information and Opportunities
Egypt Business and Investment Opportunities Yearbook Volume 1 Strategic, Practical Information and Opportunities
El Salvador Business and Investment Opportunities Yearbook Volume 1 Strategic, Practical Information and Opportunities
Equatorial Guinea Business and Investment Opportunities Yearbook Volume 1 Strategic, Practical Information and Opportunities
Eritrea Business and Investment Opportunities Yearbook Volume 1 Strategic, Practical Information and Opportunities
Estonia Business and Investment Opportunities Yearbook Volume 1 Strategic, Practical Information and Opportunities
Ethiopia Business and Investment Opportunities Yearbook Volume 1 Strategic, Practical Information and Opportunities
Falkland Islands Business and Investment Opportunities Yearbook Volume 1 Strategic, Practical Information and Opportunities
Faroes Islands Business and Investment Opportunities Yearbook Volume 1 Strategic, Practical Information and Opportunities
Fiji Business and Investment Opportunities Yearbook Volume 1 Strategic, Practical Information and Opportunities
Finland Business and Investment Opportunities Yearbook Volume 1 Strategic, Practical Information and Opportunities
France Business and Investment Opportunities Yearbook Volume 1 Strategic, Practical Information and Opportunities
Gabon Business and Investment Opportunities Yearbook Volume 1 Strategic, Practical Information and Opportunities
Gambia Business and Investment Opportunities Yearbook Volume 1 Strategic, Practical Information and Opportunities
Georgia Business and Investment Opportunities Yearbook Volume 1 Strategic, Practical Information and Opportunities
Germany Business and Investment Opportunities Yearbook Volume 1 Strategic, Practical Information and Opportunities
Ghana Business and Investment Opportunities Yearbook Volume 1 Strategic, Practical Information and Opportunities
Gibraltar Business and Investment Opportunities Yearbook Volume 1 Strategic, Practical Information and Opportunities
Greece Business and Investment Opportunities Yearbook Volume 1 Strategic, Practical Information and Opportunities

For additional analytical, business and investment opportunities information,
Please contact Global Investment & Business Center, USA
at (202) 546-2103. Fax: (202) 546-3275. E-mail: ibpusa3@gmail.com

TITLE
Greenland Business and Investment Opportunities Yearbook Volume 1 Strategic, Practical Information and Opportunities
Grenada Business and Investment Opportunities Yearbook Volume 1 Strategic, Practical Information and Opportunities
Guam Business and Investment Opportunities Yearbook Volume 1 Strategic, Practical Information and Opportunities
Guatemala Business and Investment Opportunities Yearbook Volume 1 Strategic, Practical Information and Opportunities
Guernsey Business and Investment Opportunities Yearbook Volume 1 Strategic, Practical Information and Opportunities
Guinea Business and Investment Opportunities Yearbook Volume 1 Strategic, Practical Information and Opportunities
Guinea-Bissau Business and Investment Opportunities Yearbook Volume 1 Strategic, Practical Information and Opportunities
Guyana Business and Investment Opportunities Yearbook Volume 1 Strategic, Practical Information and Opportunities
Haiti Business and Investment Opportunities Yearbook Volume 1 Strategic, Practical Information and Opportunities
Honduras Business and Investment Opportunities Yearbook Volume 1 Strategic, Practical Information and Opportunities
Hungary Business and Investment Opportunities Yearbook Volume 1 Strategic, Practical Information and Opportunities
Iceland Business and Investment Opportunities Yearbook Volume 1 Strategic, Practical Information and Opportunities
India Business and Investment Opportunities Yearbook Volume 1 Strategic, Practical Information and Opportunities
Indonesia Business and Investment Opportunities Yearbook Volume 1 Strategic, Practical Information and Opportunities
Iran Business and Investment Opportunities Yearbook Volume 1 Strategic, Practical Information and Opportunities
Iraq Business and Investment Opportunities Yearbook Volume 1 Strategic, Practical Information and Opportunities
Ireland Business and Investment Opportunities Yearbook Volume 1 Strategic, Practical Information and Opportunities
Israel Business and Investment Opportunities Yearbook Volume 1 Strategic, Practical Information and Opportunities
Italy Business and Investment Opportunities Yearbook Volume 1 Strategic, Practical Information and Opportunities
Jamaica Business and Investment Opportunities Yearbook Volume 1 Strategic, Practical Information and Opportunities
Japan Business and Investment Opportunities Yearbook Volume 1 Strategic, Practical Information and Opportunities
Jersey Business and Investment Opportunities Yearbook Volume 1 Strategic, Practical Information and Opportunities
Jordan Business and Investment Opportunities Yearbook Volume 1 Strategic, Practical Information and Opportunities
Kazakhstan Business and Investment Opportunities Yearbook Volume 1 Strategic, Practical Information and Opportunities
Kenya Business and Investment Opportunities Yearbook Volume 1 Strategic, Practical Information and Opportunities
Kiribati Business and Investment Opportunities Yearbook Volume 1 Strategic, Practical Information and Opportunities
Korea, North Business and Investment Opportunities Yearbook Volume 1 Strategic, Practical Information and Opportunities
Korea, South Business and Investment Opportunities Yearbook Volume 1 Strategic, Practical Information and Opportunities

For additional analytical, business and investment opportunities information,
Please contact Global Investment & Business Center, USA
at (202) 546-2103. Fax: (202) 546-3275. E-mail: ibpusa3@gmail.com

TITLE
Kosovo Business and Investment Opportunities Yearbook Volume 1 Strategic, Practical Information and Opportunities
Kurdistan Business and Investment Opportunities Yearbook Volume 1 Strategic, Practical Information and Opportunities
Kuwait Business and Investment Opportunities Yearbook Volume 1 Strategic, Practical Information and Opportunities
Kyrgyzstan Business and Investment Opportunities Yearbook Volume 1 Strategic, Practical Information and Opportunities
Laos Business and Investment Opportunities Yearbook Volume 1 Strategic, Practical Information and Opportunities
Latvia Business and Investment Opportunities Yearbook Volume 1 Strategic, Practical Information and Opportunities
Lebanon Business and Investment Opportunities Yearbook Volume 1 Strategic, Practical Information and Opportunities
Lesotho Business and Investment Opportunities Yearbook Volume 1 Strategic, Practical Information and Opportunities
Liberia Business and Investment Opportunities Yearbook Volume 1 Strategic, Practical Information and Opportunities
Libya Business and Investment Opportunities Yearbook Volume 1 Strategic, Practical Information and Opportunities
Liechtenstein Business and Investment Opportunities Yearbook Volume 1 Strategic, Practical Information and Opportunities
Lithuania Business and Investment Opportunities Yearbook Volume 1 Strategic, Practical Information and Opportunities
Luxembourg Business and Investment Opportunities Yearbook Volume 1 Strategic, Practical Information and Opportunities
Macao Business and Investment Opportunities Yearbook Volume 1 Strategic, Practical Information and Opportunities
Macedonia Business and Investment Opportunities Yearbook Volume 1 Strategic, Practical Information and Opportunities
Madagascar Business and Investment Opportunities Yearbook Volume 1 Strategic, Practical Information and Opportunities
Madeira Business and Investment Opportunities Yearbook Volume 1 Strategic, Practical Information and Opportunities
Malawi Business and Investment Opportunities Yearbook Volume 1 Strategic, Practical Information and Opportunities
Malaysia Business and Investment Opportunities Yearbook Volume 1 Strategic, Practical Information and Opportunities
Maldives Business and Investment Opportunities Yearbook Volume 1 Strategic, Practical Information and Opportunities
Mali Business and Investment Opportunities Yearbook Volume 1 Strategic, Practical Information and Opportunities
Malta Business and Investment Opportunities Yearbook Volume 1 Strategic, Practical Information and Opportunities
Man Business and Investment Opportunities Yearbook Volume 1 Strategic, Practical Information and Opportunities
Marshall Islands Business and Investment Opportunities Yearbook Volume 1 Strategic, Practical Information and Opportunities
Mauritania Business and Investment Opportunities Yearbook Volume 1 Strategic, Practical Information and Opportunities
Mauritius Business and Investment Opportunities Yearbook Volume 1 Strategic, Practical Information and Opportunities
Mayotte Business and Investment Opportunities Yearbook Volume 1 Strategic, Practical Information and Opportunities
Mexico Business and Investment Opportunities Yearbook Volume 1 Strategic, Practical Information and Opportunities

For additional analytical, business and investment opportunities information,
Please contact Global Investment & Business Center, USA
at (202) 546-2103. Fax: (202) 546-3275. E-mail: ibpusa3@gmail.com

TITLE
Micronesia Business and Investment Opportunities Yearbook Volume 1 Strategic, Practical Information and Opportunities
Moldova Business and Investment Opportunities Yearbook Volume 1 Strategic, Practical Information and Opportunities
Monaco Business and Investment Opportunities Yearbook Volume 1 Strategic, Practical Information and Opportunities
Mongolia Business and Investment Opportunities Yearbook Volume 1 Strategic, Practical Information and Opportunities
Montserrat Business and Investment Opportunities Yearbook Volume 1 Strategic, Practical Information and Opportunities
Montenegro Business and Investment Opportunities Yearbook Volume 1 Strategic, Practical Information and Opportunities
Morocco Business and Investment Opportunities Yearbook Volume 1 Strategic, Practical Information and Opportunities
Mozambique Business and Investment Opportunities Yearbook Volume 1 Strategic, Practical Information and Opportunities
Myanmar Business and Investment Opportunities Yearbook Volume 1 Strategic, Practical Information and Opportunities
Nagorno-Karabakh Republic Business and Investment Opportunities Yearbook Volume 1 Strategic, Practical Information and Opportunities
Namibia Business and Investment Opportunities Yearbook Volume 1 Strategic, Practical Information and Opportunities
Nauru Business and Investment Opportunities Yearbook Volume 1 Strategic, Practical Information and Opportunities
Nepal Business and Investment Opportunities Yearbook Volume 1 Strategic, Practical Information and Opportunities
Netherlands Business and Investment Opportunities Yearbook Volume 1 Strategic, Practical Information and Opportunities
New Caledonia Business and Investment Opportunities Yearbook Volume 1 Strategic, Practical Information and Opportunities
New Zealand Business and Investment Opportunities Yearbook Volume 1 Strategic, Practical Information and Opportunities
Nicaragua Business and Investment Opportunities Yearbook Volume 1 Strategic, Practical Information and Opportunities
Niger Business and Investment Opportunities Yearbook Volume 1 Strategic, Practical Information and Opportunities
Nigeria Business and Investment Opportunities Yearbook Volume 1 Strategic, Practical Information and Opportunities
Niue Business and Investment Opportunities Yearbook Volume 1 Strategic, Practical Information and Opportunities
Northern Cyprus (Turkish Republic of Northern Cyprus) Business and Investment Opportunities Yearbook Volume 1 Strategic, Practical Information and Opportunities
Northern Mariana Islands Business and Investment Opportunities Yearbook Volume 1 Strategic, Practical Information and Opportunities
Norway Business and Investment Opportunities Yearbook Volume 1 Strategic, Practical Information and Opportunities
Oman Business and Investment Opportunities Yearbook Volume 1 Strategic, Practical Information and Opportunities
Pakistan Business and Investment Opportunities Yearbook Volume 1 Strategic, Practical Information and Opportunities
Palau Business and Investment Opportunities Yearbook Volume 1 Strategic, Practical Information and Opportunities
Palestine (West Bank & Gaza) Business and Investment Opportunities Yearbook Volume 1 Strategic, Practical Information and Opportunities
Panama Business and Investment Opportunities Yearbook Volume 1 Strategic, Practical Information and Opportunities

For additional analytical, business and investment opportunities information,
Please contact Global Investment & Business Center, USA
at (202) 546-2103. Fax: (202) 546-3275. E-mail: ibpusa3@gmail.com

TITLE
Papua New Guinea Business and Investment Opportunities Yearbook Volume 1 Strategic, Practical Information and Opportunities
Paraguay Business and Investment Opportunities Yearbook Volume 1 Strategic, Practical Information and Opportunities
Peru Business and Investment Opportunities Yearbook Volume 1 Strategic, Practical Information and Opportunities
Philippines Business and Investment Opportunities Yearbook Volume 1 Strategic, Practical Information and Opportunities
Pitcairn Islands Business and Investment Opportunities Yearbook Volume 1 Strategic, Practical Information and Opportunities
Poland Business and Investment Opportunities Yearbook Volume 1 Strategic, Practical Information and Opportunities
Polynesia French Business and Investment Opportunities Yearbook Volume 1 Strategic, Practical Information and Opportunities
Portugal Business and Investment Opportunities Yearbook Volume 1 Strategic, Practical Information and Opportunities
Qatar Business and Investment Opportunities Yearbook Volume 1 Strategic, Practical Information and Opportunities
Romania Business and Investment Opportunities Yearbook Volume 1 Strategic, Practical Information and Opportunities
Russia Business and Investment Opportunities Yearbook Volume 1 Strategic, Practical Information and Opportunities
Rwanda Business and Investment Opportunities Yearbook Volume 1 Strategic, Practical Information and Opportunities
Sahrawi Arab Democratic Republic Volume 1 Strategic Information and Developments
Saint Kitts and Nevis Business and Investment Opportunities Yearbook Volume 1 Strategic, Practical Information and Opportunities
Saint Lucia Business and Investment Opportunities Yearbook Volume 1 Strategic, Practical Information and Opportunities
Saint Vincent and The Grenadines Business and Investment Opportunities Yearbook Volume 1 Strategic, Practical Information and Opportunities
Samoa (American) A Business and Investment Opportunities Yearbook Volume 1 Strategic, Practical Information and Opportunities
Samoa (Western) Business and Investment Opportunities Yearbook Volume 1 Strategic, Practical Information and Opportunities
San Marino Business and Investment Opportunities Yearbook Volume 1 Strategic, Practical Information and Opportunities
Sao Tome and Principe Business and Investment Opportunities Yearbook Volume 1 Strategic, Practical Information and Opportunities
Saudi Arabia Business and Investment Opportunities Yearbook Volume 1 Strategic, Practical Information and Opportunities
Scotland Business and Investment Opportunities Yearbook Volume 1 Strategic, Practical Information and Opportunities
Senegal Business and Investment Opportunities Yearbook Volume 1 Strategic, Practical Information and Opportunities
Serbia Business and Investment Opportunities Yearbook Volume 1 Strategic, Practical Information and Opportunities
Seychelles Business and Investment Opportunities Yearbook Volume 1 Strategic, Practical Information and Opportunities
Sierra Leone Business and Investment Opportunities Yearbook Volume 1 Strategic, Practical Information and Opportunities
Singapore Business and Investment Opportunities Yearbook Volume 1 Strategic, Practical Information and Opportunities
Slovakia Business and Investment Opportunities Yearbook Volume 1 Strategic, Practical Information and Opportunities

For additional analytical, business and investment opportunities information,
Please contact Global Investment & Business Center, USA
at (202) 546-2103. Fax: (202) 546-3275. E-mail: ibpusa3@gmail.com

TITLE
Slovenia Business and Investment Opportunities Yearbook Volume 1 Strategic, Practical Information and Opportunities
Solomon Islands Business and Investment Opportunities Yearbook Volume 1 Strategic, Practical Information and Opportunities
Somalia Business and Investment Opportunities Yearbook Volume 1 Strategic, Practical Information and Opportunities
South Africa Business and Investment Opportunities Yearbook Volume 1 Strategic, Practical Information and Opportunities
Spain Business and Investment Opportunities Yearbook Volume 1 Strategic, Practical Information and Opportunities
Sri Lanka Business and Investment Opportunities Yearbook Volume 1 Strategic, Practical Information and Opportunities
St. Helena Business and Investment Opportunities Yearbook Volume 1 Strategic, Practical Information and Opportunities
St. Pierre & Miquelon Business and Investment Opportunities Yearbook Volume 1 Strategic, Practical Information and Opportunities
Sudan (Republic of the Sudan) Business and Investment Opportunities Yearbook Volume 1 Strategic, Practical Information and Opportunities
Sudan South Business and Investment Opportunities Yearbook Volume 1 Strategic, Practical Information and Opportunities
Suriname Business and Investment Opportunities Yearbook Volume 1 Strategic, Practical Information and Opportunities
Swaziland Business and Investment Opportunities Yearbook Volume 1 Strategic, Practical Information and Opportunities
Sweden Business and Investment Opportunities Yearbook Volume 1 Strategic, Practical Information and Opportunities
Switzerland Business and Investment Opportunities Yearbook Volume 1 Strategic, Practical Information and Opportunities
Syria Business and Investment Opportunities Yearbook Volume 1 Strategic, Practical Information and Opportunities
Taiwan Business and Investment Opportunities Yearbook Volume 1 Strategic, Practical Information and Opportunities
Tajikistan Business and Investment Opportunities Yearbook Volume 1 Strategic, Practical Information and Opportunities
Tanzania Business and Investment Opportunities Yearbook Volume 1 Strategic, Practical Information and Opportunities
Thailand Business and Investment Opportunities Yearbook Volume 1 Strategic, Practical Information and Opportunities
Timor Leste (Democratic Republic of Timor-Leste) Business and Investment Opportunities Yearbook Volume 1 Strategic, Practical Information and Opportunities
Togo Business and Investment Opportunities Yearbook Volume 1 Strategic, Practical Information and Opportunities
Tonga Business and Investment Opportunities Yearbook Volume 1 Strategic, Practical Information and Opportunities
Trinidad and Tobago Business and Investment Opportunities Yearbook Volume 1 Strategic, Practical Information and Opportunities
Tunisia Business and Investment Opportunities Yearbook Volume 1 Strategic, Practical Information and Opportunities
Turkey Business and Investment Opportunities Yearbook Volume 1 Strategic, Practical Information and Opportunities
Turkmenistan Business and Investment Opportunities Yearbook Volume 1 Strategic, Practical Information and Opportunities
Turks & Caicos Business and Investment Opportunities Yearbook Volume 1 Strategic, Practical Information and Opportunities
Tuvalu Business and Investment Opportunities Yearbook Volume 1 Strategic, Practical Information and Opportunities

**For additional analytical, business and investment opportunities information,
Please contact Global Investment & Business Center, USA
at (202) 546-2103. Fax: (202) 546-3275. E-mail: ibpusa3@gmail.com**

TITLE
Uganda Business and Investment Opportunities Yearbook Volume 1 Strategic, Practical Information and Opportunities
Ukraine Business and Investment Opportunities Yearbook Volume 1 Strategic, Practical Information and Opportunities
United Arab Emirates Business and Investment Opportunities Yearbook Volume 1 Strategic, Practical Information and Opportunities
United Kingdom Business and Investment Opportunities Yearbook Volume 1 Strategic, Practical Information and Opportunities
United States Business and Investment Opportunities Yearbook Volume 1 Strategic, Practical Information and Opportunities
Uruguay Business and Investment Opportunities Yearbook Volume 1 Strategic, Practical Information and Opportunities
Uzbekistan Business and Investment Opportunities Yearbook Volume 1 Strategic, Practical Information and Opportunities
Vanuatu Business and Investment Opportunities Yearbook Volume 1 Strategic, Practical Information and Opportunities
Vatican City (Holy See) Business and Investment Opportunities Yearbook Volume 1 Strategic, Practical Information and Opportunities
Venezuela Business and Investment Opportunities Yearbook Volume 1 Strategic, Practical Information and Opportunities
Vietnam Business and Investment Opportunities Yearbook Volume 1 Strategic, Practical Information and Opportunities
Virgin Islands, British Business and Investment Opportunities Yearbook Volume 1 Strategic, Practical Information and Opportunities
Wake Atoll Business and Investment Opportunities Yearbook Volume 1 Strategic, Practical Information and Opportunities
Wallis & Futuna Business and Investment Opportunities Yearbook Volume 1 Strategic, Practical Information and Opportunities
Western Sahara Business and Investment Opportunities Yearbook Volume 1 Strategic, Practical Information and Opportunities
Yemen Business and Investment Opportunities Yearbook Volume 1 Strategic, Practical Information and Opportunities
Zambia Business and Investment Opportunities Yearbook Volume 1 Strategic, Practical Information and Opportunities
Zimbabwe Business and Investment Opportunities Yearbook Volume 1 Strategic, Practical Information and Opportunities

For additional analytical, business and investment opportunities information,
Please contact Global Investment & Business Center, USA
at (202) 546-2103. Fax: (202) 546-3275. E-mail: ibpusa3@gmail.com